Canadian Political Structure and Public Administration

FIFTH EDITION

Geoffrey J. Booth

Laura E. Booth

Andrew J. Rowley

 ▪ Toronto, Canada ▪ 2018

Emond Montgomery Publications Limited
1 Eglinton E., Suite 600
Toronto ON M4P 3A1
http://www.emond.ca/highered

Printed in Canada.
Reprinted April 2019.

We acknowledge the financial support of the Government of Canada.   **Canadä**

Emond Montgomery Publications has no responsibility for the persistence or accuracy of URLs for external or third-party Internet websites referred to in this publication, and does not guarantee that any content on such websites is, or will remain, accurate or appropriate.

Vice president, publishing: Anthony Rezek
Publisher: Mike Thompson
Director, development and production: Kelly Dickson
Developmental editor: Daphne Scriabin
Production supervisor: Laura Bast
Copy editor: Karen Kligman
Permissions editor: Alison Lloyd-Baker
Typesetter: S4Carlisle Publishing Services
Text designer: Tara Agnerian
Proofreader: Dancy Mason
Indexer: S4Carlisle Publishing Services
Cover image: riekephotos/Shutterstock

Library and Archives Canada Cataloguing in Publication

Booth, Geoffrey J., 1962- author
    Canadian political structure and public administration / Geoffrey J. Booth, PhD ,
    Laura E. Booth, Andrew J. Rowley. -- Fifth edition.

Includes index.
ISBN 978-1-77255-275-1 (softcover)

    1. Canada--Politics and government--Textbooks.   I. Booth, Laura E., author   II. Rowley, Andrew J.,
author   III. Title.

JL75.B66 2018   320.971   C2017-907415-6

In memory of Gordon and Geraldine Booth

Brief Table of Contents

Table of Contents

PART I

INTRODUCTORY CONCEPTS

1 Introduction to Politics and Public Administration

PART II

POLITICAL STRUCTURE

2 Unity Through Diversity: Canada Becomes a Nation

3 The Constitution and the Canadian Charter of Rights and Freedoms

4 Welcome to the Machine: Canadian Political Structure and Its Operation

Preface

> "Politics is the art of the possible."
>
> —*Otto von Bismarck*

This is, no doubt, a familiar quotation to any student of politics, and yet, given the current state of our world, it remains as relevant an observation today as it was when first made by the German statesman Otto von Bismarck back in 1867. With this statement in mind, we present the fifth edition of *Canadian Political Structure and Public Administration*. The text has been thoughtfully revised to incorporate current political realities while remaining true to the book's original aim of making the subject accessible and interesting for college-level study. While the basic structure will be familiar to readers of the fourth edition, the new offering not only brings an entirely new set of "Get Real!" segments but also adds a brand new chapter that examines Canada in an international context.

Chapters 1 through 5 provide a foundation for those new to Canadian politics, acquainting students with basic political concepts. It also explores some of the significant historical events and documents that helped shape Canadian democracy, from pre-Confederation to the present day. Chapters 6 to 10 apply this knowledge to help explain the complex bureaucracy that characterizes the justice system in Canada, including a totally revised chapter detailing the numerous departments, ministries, and agencies that make up the justice system. Chapter 11 offers useful information to help readers understand the important role we can all play as citizens of Canada, while the newly added Chapter 12 provides readers with a solid grasp of Canada's role in the world today and the many challenges that our political leaders face as they interact with those of other nations, friend and foe alike.

This journey has been both challenging and rewarding and we look forward to sharing it with you.

Acknowledgments

Revising academic texts such as this one requires the input, support, and encouragement of many individuals over a considerable period of time. The authors wish to thank them all. In particular, we are indebted to the team at Emond Publishing, particularly Paul Emond and Mike Thompson, who undertook to make the fifth edition of this book a reality. Thanks as well to Laura Bast for production supervision, and to Holly Penick for her diligence in marketing what we've created. Special thanks to Daphne Scriabin and Karen Kligman for their masterful developmental editing and copy editing. It is only through their polite but persistent efforts that this project remained on schedule.

We also wish to recognize those who provided the scholarly expertise and research so necessary to a work of this nature. First, thank you to our initial reviewers, whose insights helped get us started on the right track: Laurèl Craib, Algonquin College; Howard Doughty, Seneca College; Lynn Fournier-Ruggles, Seneca College; and Christine Ter-Steege, Sheridan College. We would also like to thank the dedicated staff at Statistics Canada, Rama Police

Chief John Domm, correctional investigator Howard Sapers, and Mount Allison University professor Erin Steuter for their input. We are indebted and truly grateful to them for their expertise and advice.

Lastly, to our friends and family, whose patience and encouragement kept us going, we say a heartfelt thank you.

Additional Resources

For information on the teaching resources available to instructors who have chosen this book for their courses, visit the For Instructors tab on the book's website, **emond.ca/ CPSPA5**. Contact your Emond Publishing sales representative for more details.

About the Authors

Geoffrey J. Booth has taught at Georgian College since 1998, in the areas of Human Services and Community Safety, as well as in the University Partnership Centre. He has designed several courses related to politics and history during that time, and has participated in numerous program launches and course renewals. Geoffrey holds a PhD in the history of education from the Ontario Institute for Studies in Education at the University of Toronto, where he also completed an undergraduate, a Master's, and a teaching degree. He also holds a diploma in print journalism from Centennial College. He has been an author with Emond Publishing since 2001.

Laura E. Booth is a journalist who has reported for daily newspapers across the country. Laura has a Master's degree in political science from York University, and an advanced diploma in journalism from Humber College.

Andrew J. Rowley is a consultant and writer. He served as the National Communications Director for the Mounted Police Association of Ontario (MPAO) throughout their successful fight to secure association rights for the RCMP. He holds an MA in history from Trent University, where his thesis examined national media trends.

PART I

Introductory Concepts

CHAPTER 1 Introduction to Politics and Public Administration

Introduction to Politics and Public Administration

1

LEARNING OUTCOMES

After completing this chapter, you should be able to

- describe basic tenets of political theory such as power, compliance, and the rule of law;

- define politics and the various ways that it affects Canadian citizens;

- explain the evolution of government as a social institution and how we as citizens determine the extent of a government's authority and legitimacy;

- describe the relationship between politics and public administration from a practical, as well as a theoretical, standpoint;

- understand, in general, the purpose and content of this text; and

- discuss some of the ways in which social media are transforming political discourse and the manner in which citizens and their political representatives understand and interact with one another.

What Is Politics?

To many people, the terms "politics" and "public administration" are both mysterious and intimidating. This disconnection is reinforced daily by media reports of dishonesty, corruption, and ineptitude, which seem increasingly frequent. It may surprise you that anyone pays attention to what goes on in government, let alone becomes involved in public life. However, thousands of people continue to play a part in governing Canada, and without them we would, in fact, have no country. The evolution of our system of government reveals much about our history and our values as Canadians. And, despite the seemingly endless barrage of criticism hurled at it, Canada's governmental foundation remains one of the best models of problem solving through political compromise and dialogue in the world today.

How did our political structure come to be respected globally? What are the essential components of Canadian political structure, and how do they interact with one another? What is the historical context for this intricate and ever-changing dance among political partners? And, finally, how does all of this express itself in the realms of law enforcement and public safety? These are but a few of the many topics covered in the chapters that follow. To begin, some terms necessary for a clear understanding of politics and public administration in Canada are defined.

Politics is about relationships. Folksinger Pete Seeger once noted that putting two human beings together in a room is all that is required to begin a political dialogue. Because we have competing opinions and ideas about what is desirable, our relationships with one another imply power. In other words, the capacity to make others comply with your wishes means that you have power over them. The study of politics concerns itself with the distribution of power and how it is used in a particular social context. This study ranges from individuals' interaction to the international level, where nation-states coexist and compete with one another. Wherever and whenever we come into contact with others, there is politics.

politics
the social system that decides who has power and how it is to be used in governing the society's affairs

At its root, **politics** is fundamentally about power and who decides how this power is to be used. We can think of power as the capacity of one person or group to impose decisions on another person or group. In other words, politics is about getting your own way. Likewise, "compliance" refers to the obedience that an individual or group demonstrates in response to the wishes of those who have power.

There are many ways to achieve power. Charisma, compromise, influence, negotiation, persuasion, and even brute force are only some of them. Perhaps without knowing it, you have already experienced examples of this in your own life. Growing up, you may have had to share a television with other members of your family. How did you decide who got to watch what program at what time of day? What if something you wanted to watch was in someone else's time slot? What about programs that exceeded your time allotment? Did your age, attitude, or status have any influence on whether you got to watch what you wanted? What role did your parents play in determining what was acceptable viewing for your family? All of these questions help to illustrate the power relations between you and members of your family. Now consider what it would be like to come to a decision about virtually anything in a country of 36 million people. This happens every day as government officials engage in the shared task of running Canada. We elect politicians at the federal, provincial, and municipal levels of government to represent our individual and collective interests and bring them to the attention of the state.

His charisma and ability to connect directly with voters helped Justin Trudeau return the federal Liberal Party to power in the 2015 election.

What Is Power?

Before proceeding, it is useful to establish some fundamental elements of political theory so that, as we move to examine Canada's political structure, you will be able to make useful connections between politics as an academic discipline and politics as it is practised in reality. In political theory, power is often subdivided into three main categories: force, persuasion, and legitimate authority. Force, or coercion as it is sometimes called, refers to the threat or actual use of violence (death, injury) or social sanctions (imprisonment, fines) to enforce compliance. Persuasion refers to debate, discussion, compromise, and any other non-violent means of achieving one's will. While force and persuasion embody external submission on the part of an individual, legitimate authority refers to an internal recognition by an individual that others have the power to impose their will by virtue of their position or the institution they represent. In other words, we respect their decision because we respect the source of their power and agree to obey its representatives.

Governments use all three types of power to impose decisions on citizens, but it is legitimate authority that justifies political power in a modern democracy such as Canada. We agree to abide by the laws of our country as they are passed down from our political establishment because those who create them (politicians) are ultimately answerable to us through the electoral process. In other words, political accountability ensures that political power is used in a fair, reasoned, and justifiable manner.

What Is Government?

"Why can't we all just get along?" This might be considered a standard observation of a newcomer to the study of politics. After all, if politics is about power, then let's just agree not to bother one another and everything should be fine, right? This formula for social harmony appears enticing (particularly to those of us old enough to remember the 1960s); however, it presupposes an almost intuitive sensitivity and saint-like deference. People will eventually disagree about something, and some mutually acceptable process is needed to resolve these disputes. We achieve this to varying degrees through the exercise of government. A brief story might help to clarify some of these concepts for you.

Life in Hobbes Hall

It's your first day at college and you are ecstatic. You were lucky enough to land a room in Hobbes Hall, the new campus residence. Funds for its creation were donated by a group of political science instructors, in recognition of Thomas Hobbes, a 17th-century British political philosopher.[1] The opportunity to stay at Hobbes Hall appealed to you because there is only one rule: "There are no rules." Because the place is new, the donors have decided to allow students total freedom to create, in effect, a society as they might wish it to be. All summer long you anticipated the possibilities of living away from your parents, free of obligations and responsibilities to anyone but yourself. The first couple of weeks at

---

1 This story reflects many of the so-called truths illustrated by Hobbes in *Leviathan* (1985, Chapters XIII, XVII). Written in 1651, this seminal work of political theory demonstrated the absolute necessity of sovereign government by describing a world in which there were no rules at all. The inevitable result, according to Hobbes, would be a "war of every man against every man" because people would have no legitimate authority through which to resolve conflicts, nor would they trust one another to be fair and impartial. Thus the dictums contained within *Leviathan* underscore the importance of public respect for the rule of law and the agents of public law enforcement who uphold it.

Hobbes Hall are great, if a little noisy. Everyone you meet is happy, and it appears as if the semester will be a positive experience. Soon, however, differences in lifestyle begin to create rifts in the residential population. Some people play loud music at all hours; others leave dirty dishes in the communal kitchen sink for days on end; and still others have friends over who show no concern for the litter they leave behind. This is a never-ending source of irritation for you, but others on your floor don't seem to mind. "Take it easy," they tell you, reminding you that there are neither rules nor enforcement protocols and that the minor annoyances are not worth getting upset over.

By November, the residence has taken on the look of a trash heap. Nobody has assumed any social obligation to keep common areas clean. It seems that individuals have resorted to looking after only what is directly under their control, and some have not even bothered to do that. One weekend, several rooms are broken into and valuables stolen. This causes a furor among residents, and some blame neighbours for the incidents. A couple of weeks later, it happens again. This time, accusations result in some pushing and shoving. It is clear to you that things are getting out of hand. Leaving the situation alone is bound to have disastrous consequences as students trade recriminations and threaten one another with revenge for alleged acts and suspected wrongdoings. Order and security presuppose collective responsibility, but this in turn necessitates rules, thus limiting individual freedom. You discuss this with other concerned students, and, collectively, you draw up an agenda to discuss the situation. Your first challenge is to convince everyone living at the residence that these issues must be addressed. In other words, all individuals affected by these decisions must recognize and respect their validity and agree to abide by the principles they represent. They must accept that these rules are objective and are applied fairly to all. There are some other fundamental issues to be addressed:

1. What is an acceptable balance between individual freedom and the "collective good"?
2. Who will draft the rules and oversee the interests of Hobbes Hall?
3. How will the rules be enforced?
4. How will disputes be mediated in a manner that all parties will find acceptable?
5. What if a complaint is made against a residence action, rule, or decision?

Although fictitious, this scenario illustrates the absolute necessity of government in human affairs. Because we are social by nature, we need to organize ourselves in a way that protects us all from external and internal threats, yet allows us to preserve and nourish our individual differences. The questions posed above address some of the fundamental challenges that face modern democracies such as Canada. They also touch on the importance of public respect and acceptance of government's authority over its citizens. For example, you cannot simply draft your own rules for Hobbes Hall and expect others to abide by them. You lack any legitimate authority to do so. Being selected by your peers to represent their interests through a residence election may grant this power to you. However, you maintain this position only so long as you maintain their respect and support. The power that we grant our politicians, although much broader in scope, is no different. They must be prepared to justify their decisions during their term in office and make every effort to demonstrate to the public that they are acting in the best interests of constituents.

Now that you are familiar with the need for government as a concept, it will be easier to understand how and why government functions the way it does in a country such as Canada and, more importantly, how it relates to justice and law enforcement. All countries rely on power to survive. One of the basic tests of state recognition is the state's ability to control a fixed population and geographic territory. As indicated earlier, the power required to acquire such prerequisites can be coercive or persuasive or granted by citizens through legitimate authority. Although non-democratic countries tend to resort to the more brutal elements of power, democracies rely on authority for their continued legitimacy. This requires democratic forms of government to be accountable to citizens. Furthermore, this must be evident at all stages in the political process; otherwise, citizens may lose faith in the legitimacy of the system and thus imperil its credibility. Because this text is concerned with Canadian political institutions, it focuses primarily on how we, as Canadians, facilitate and manage political power at the federal, provincial, and municipal levels of government while preserving public respect for it.

Answering the question "What is government?" is complicated. **Government** is a formal system within which political power is exercised. Still, this doesn't capture the incredible complexity of government, both as a concept and as a practice. Government is present in so many aspects of our lives that many of its activities go unnoticed.

Government has a long history dating back as far as the beginning of human civilization itself, and many people have written about its form and function. **Authority** refers to government's ability to make decisions that are binding on its citizens. As long as the general population accepts that some groups or individuals in society have power to issue and enforce these commands, they will obey these commands. If citizens respect where the decisions come from, they will accept these decisions, whether they agree with them or not. **Legitimacy** refers to the moral obligation citizens feel to obey the laws and pronouncements issued by those in authority.

Taken together, these concepts explain why we, as Canadians, abide by the laws that our governments make for us. Even if we disagree with a particular law, we still recognize that our politicians have the right to pass laws for the greater good of society. If each Canadian decided instead to disobey laws whenever he or she chose, the system of law and its enforcement would simply break down. Imagine the implications that this scenario could have in the area of transportation. The absence of a general acceptance of rules, enforced by police and other authorities, would quickly lead to misunderstandings over road use, disputes arising from accidents, arbitrary vehicle speeds, and ultimately unsafe conditions for everyone. As members of a society that recognizes the wisdom of authority and legitimacy in its political system, we assume that our governments will act for the greater good of society, even if this means that our personal freedom is limited by these decisions.

In a democracy, the concepts of authority and legitimacy are tied directly to what is known as the **rule of law**.[2] The rule of law ensures that all citizens, regardless of social rank, are subject to the laws, courts, and other legal institutions of the nation. For example, a prime minister who is found guilty of a crime cannot pass a law to make his or her infraction legitimate. The rule of law also demands that *all* government actions be legal—that is, they must be approved and accepted by a justice system that is free from state interference. This guards against the possibility that government officials might resort to illegal actions to accomplish a task. This is also why police forces take such care to ensure that officers respect the law in the course of carrying out their duties. Violating the rights of an accused or collecting evidence illegally damages the credibility of an investigation, almost always results in charges being dropped, and may result in legal action being taken by the defendant. The rule of law ensures fair and equitable treatment for all by a government and, as outlined later, it forms an integral part of Canada's system of justice and public safety.

government
a formal system within which political power is exercised

authority
government's ability to make decisions that are binding on its citizens

legitimacy
the moral obligation citizens feel to obey the laws and pronouncements issued by those in authority

rule of law
the concept that all citizens, regardless of social rank, are subject to the laws, courts, and other legal institutions of the nation

---

2 For further reading on the legislative history and social construction of the rule of law, see the late British judge and jurist Bingham (2011).

How Law Enforcement Fits In

Policing is fundamental to Canada's public justice system and is therefore essential in preserving the rule of law. If people lose faith in their government, there is a danger that they will also lose faith in the rule of law. This is why, as a society, we go to such lengths not only to "do justice"—for example, protect the rights of accused individuals and ensure that police follow proper legal procedures—but also to demonstrate to all Canadians that justice is seen to be done.

As part of the network of government agencies involved in law enforcement, police services represent an essential component of Canada's justice system by helping to maintain respect for the rule of law.

How and Why We Accept the Rule of Law

The process of demonstrating that justice has been carried out belongs in large part to the media, which cover both the successes and the failures of the justice system in this regard. For example, it is common practice for the media to publish the details of a court case. This practice is consistent with the public's right to know the workings of the justice system. In some rare situations, however, this right is suspended in order to ensure an accused person's right to a fair trial. Public trust in the legal system can never be taken for granted in any society. We must be reminded through the words and deeds of public officials that every effort is being made to ensure that justice is done so that when problems occur they can be remedied efficiently and effectively.

An important reason Canadians live within the framework of laws, regulations, and political decisions is that they can hold their political representatives accountable through the process of elections. Elections are a way to ensure continued citizen support for the authority and legitimacy of their governments, and they force elected politicians to be accountable for what they have done (or not done) during their term as elected representatives. However, not all eligible voters turn out to vote on election

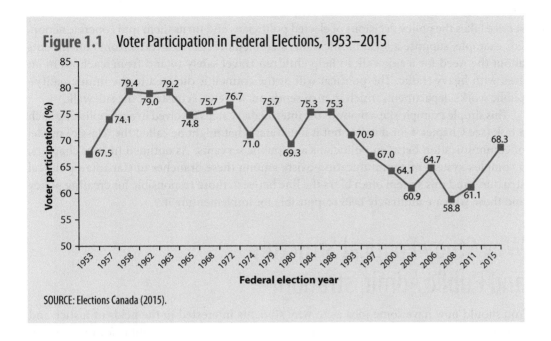

Figure 1.1   Voter Participation in Federal Elections, 1953–2015

SOURCE: Elections Canada (2015).

day. Participation at the federal level, for example, has generally declined since the 1990s (see Figure 1.1), and this often raises questions about the health of our democracy and the legitimacy of a particular government.

As explained in later chapters, Canadian political tradition, the process of choosing candidates, party affiliation, and other socio-economic issues play a large part in determining how the public's judgment manifests itself in the political scene.

The Art of Government: Politics and Public Administration

The aim of this textbook is to give you a practical overview of Canada's political structure and the bureaucracy through which much of its operation is carried out. Politics and public administration, which share a common purpose of furthering the public good, often go about doing so in different ways. The nature of this relationship can be complementary or competitive, resulting in new approaches to government policy.

For the purposes of this text, the term "politics" will be used to refer to the work of politicians at the federal, provincial, and municipal levels of government who are elected by the people they represent. We treat the subject of politics separately from that of public administration because, although one can argue that all aspects of government involve both political and administrative elements, it is politicians who must ultimately answer to us for what their particular level of government has done from one election to the next.

Public administration is more challenging to define because, as you will discover later in this text, it can be understood to include every non-elected person who is employed by government. Often referred to as the **civil service** or **public service**, this branch of Canadian political structure hypothetically includes anyone employed in a publicly funded activity, such as policing, firefighting, and teaching. However, convention normally limits public administration to people who are directly tied to the administrative function of a particular level of government, such as policy implementation and evaluation. The public

public administration
the branch of the political structure, consisting of public employees, that turns the policy decisions of elected politicians into action

civil service
people who are directly tied to the administrative function of a particular level of government; see also *public administration*

public service
civil service or public administration

service takes the policy decisions of elected politicians and turns them into concrete action. For example, suppose a local municipality's councillors hear concerns from constituents about the need for a sidewalk to help children travel safely to and from a school in an area with heavy traffic. The political will of the council is dictated to the municipality's public works department, which in turn sends out a crew to construct the sidewalk.

This simple example skips many of the intermediary steps involved in accomplishing such a task (see Chapter 4 for details), but it illustrates what might be called the "classic" model of communication between politicians and public servants. As outlined in later chapters, a complex system of communication exists among these branches of Canadian political structure, and this system often blurs the line between those responsible for creating policy and those who are ultimately held responsible for implementing it.

Why Study Political Structure and Public Administration?

You should now have some idea as to why students interested in the fields of justice and public safety must understand Canadian political structure and public administration. As an agent of law enforcement, it is essential that you understand your legal rights and obligations. This knowledge extends beyond the rules and regulations of your employer to encompass where and how the legitimate authority of the state is delegated to public agencies, such as police services, whose sworn duty it is to uphold laws passed by the state and to maintain respect for the rule of law. In this sense, you represent the public good and therefore have a responsibility to know how government works—that is, the origin and implementation of public policy through government legislation. This knowledge enables you to understand and appreciate more fully your role in the overall administration of justice and to understand the roles of other key players in developing, interpreting, and administering the law.

This text, and the course it represents, also provides you with an understanding of your rights and responsibilities as a Canadian citizen. This, too, should help to better acquaint you with the structure and day-to-day practice of government at the federal, provincial, and municipal levels and with their relationship to justice and public safety. Your familiarity with Canadian political structure and public administration will give you an advantage as you prepare to meet the challenges and changes currently facing our country.

Structure of This Book

Following is a brief overview of some of the topics you will encounter as you read through the sections of this book. Keep in mind that while each chapter attempts to focus on a particular area of interest, all of the topics are interrelated because issues and decisions in one sector of government and public administration often have an impact on other sectors.

Chapter 2 presents a brief history of the events that led to Confederation in 1867 and how Canada's political structure was established at that time. The chapter explains the origin of the three levels of government in the context of the Canadian Constitution and provides some historical background that will help you better understand the political issues that face Canadians today.

Chapter 3 focuses on the Constitution from its inception as the *British North America Act* through its patriation in 1982, including attempts at constitutional reform. Attention is given to the *Canadian Charter of Rights and Freedoms* (1982), its impact on Canadians' individual and collective rights, and its effects on law enforcement and the role of the courts in the political and constitutional process.

Chapter 4 begins with an explanation of representative and responsible government and then explores the electoral process and the role of candidates. It goes on to examine the structure and roles of the three levels of government—federal, provincial, and municipal—and defines their executive, legislative, and judicial functions. The process of making laws at each level of government is also explained. The chapter introduces the interrelationships among the three levels of government, a topic that will be explored in more detail in later chapters. Chapter 4 also presents a brief history of the relationship between Indigenous and non-native government.

Chapter 5 describes the evolution of government services in Canada in general and law enforcement in particular. The chapter then encourages you to look at the big picture by using what you learned in the previous chapters to discuss some current issues in Canadian politics as they relate to policing and the justice system. Particular attention is paid to influences on the political process at all levels of government and how these have direct and indirect effects on law enforcement. Chapter 5 concludes with a discussion of police responses to changing social realities.

With this political context in place, the focus shifts to an emphasis on public administration. Chapters 6 and 7 explore the meaning of public administration, with a view to helping you recognize its relevance and relation to the political process. In particular, you will discover how political and public administration entities rely on each other for mutual benefit and, ultimately, survival. It will become evident that tension also characterizes this relationship as political and administrative forces attempt to achieve specific goals. These chapters also briefly summarize theories of bureaucracy to see how they have influenced the evolution of a modern public service in Canada. You will then have an opportunity to explore the similarities and differences between private and public administration. Particular attention is given to recent trends toward government privatization of public facilities, such as prisons.

Chapter 8 focuses on the "glue" that binds politics and administration—public policy. Using examples, the chapter illustrates the many complex—and often unpredictable—stages that take place while policy is being created, implemented, and evaluated. The chapter ends by examining how creating public policy can be a difficult balancing act, especially when policy-makers strive to protect the Charter rights of all Canadians while, at the same time, attempting to keep government spending (and thus taxes) at a satisfactory minimum.

Chapters 9 and 10 complete our exploration of the complex world of public administration by examining the structure and organization of the civil service in Canada today, with particular emphasis on those components that play a role in the system of justice and law enforcement. These chapters describe the many ministries, agencies, and Crown corporations that constitute the public service. You will discover how public policy is transformed into administrative law and become aware of the differences between this type of legislation and others, such as constitutional law. As well, you will see how politicians and public servants work together to meet the challenges that arise in government. By analyzing examples, such as the role of Ontario's Special Investigations Unit (SIU) in overseeing police activity, you will also discover that disagreement and conflict are an ongoing part of the relationship between government and the public service.

Chapter 11 focuses on your part as a constituent in our government system. The chapter presents some of the benefits of getting involved in politics, especially at the municipal level, as well as some suggestions on how to do so. As you prepare for a career in law enforcement, it is our hope that at this point you will understand and feel confident about your role in Canadian society, both as a representative of law enforcement and as a private citizen.

Chapter 12 examines Canada's role in the world more broadly. It leans on core concepts from the previous chapters to explore how Canada contributes to global initiatives and order; leads, diverges from, and trails its closest trading partners and allies; and contributes to global development and innovation. It is our hope that you pair your new-found confidence as a Canadian citizen with a global perspective, are inspired to defend proud and essential institutions of government, and are committed to grow and improve.

Get Real!

Fake News

"News," whether obtained through newspapers, social media, television, radio, or podcasts, is the generally accepted term we use to describe information about what's going on in the world around us. Think of the last news story you read. What did you learn from it, and how did you feel afterward? We form opinions based on the stories we read, and those opinions can influence our actions.

So what is fake news and why is it problematic? "It's news that's not true and mostly it's intentional," says Erin Steuter (personal communication, May 19, 2017), a Mount Allison University professor who has been a media analyst and researcher for 25 years. "Sometimes it's for satire or a bit of mischief making but more commonly it's to mislead and to create misinformation for political reasons, sometimes economic reasons, sometimes for ideological reasons." It's estimated that 49 percent of Canadians have read a fake news story, and 26 percent have had their opinion wrongly informed because of fake news, according to a 2017 poll by Abacus Data (Anderson & Coletto, 2017).[3]

Have you read a fake news story lately? Maybe you didn't even know it. In identifying fake news, it's important to note that legitimate news organizations do not create fake news, although journalists aren't immune from making unintentional mistakes. "Sometimes people get things wrong," says Steuter, adding that fake news is created purposefully.

It was the 2016 American election campaign between Democrat Hillary Clinton and Republican Donald Trump that threw modern-day fake news into the spotlight. According to Steuter, "there were people who wanted to give an edge to one of the candidates in particular," noting that much of the fake news supported the Trump campaign. For example, in July 2016, a fake news story was published online by a website called WTOE 5 News that claimed Pope Francis had endorsed Trump (Snopes, 2016). "You need to kind of think a little bit . . . does that seem plausible that the Pope would endorse Donald Trump?" she says, adding that not all fake news is as easy to spot.

Steuter also points out that the problem has become significant enough that some social media are attempting to curb the spread of fake news on their social media platforms. Facebook, for example, is intensifying the screening process for those who purchase advertisements on its site. The company is also changing newsfeed settings to limit low quality web links from appearing. "We've found that a lot of fake news is financially motivated," Facebook's Adam Mosseri (2017) has observed. "These spammers make money by masquerading as legitimate news publishers and posting hoaxes that get people to visit their sites, which are often mostly ads."

---

3   The survey was conducted online between April 21 and 24, 2017 with 1,500 Canadian participants 18 years of age and older. Also, a random sample of panelists was invited to complete the survey from a panel of more than 500,000 Canadians. The margin of error for a random sample of 1,500 is about 2.6 percent.

But Steuter points out that fake news isn't necessarily a new phenomenon, although it has more recently been making headlines. Late 19th-century New York newspaper owners Joseph Pulitzer and William Randolph Hearst were able to dramatically increase the circulation of their papers by publishing sensational and sometimes fabricated stories in their "penny papers" (Forde & Foss, 2012, p. 132). Termed "yellow journalism," these stories sometimes twisted the truth to entertain the reader and boost newspaper sales, which both owners did.

To combat fake news in the present day, we as consumers also have a part to play in making sure the information we read on the Internet is legitimate. "You have to educate yourself about things you don't know," says Steuter. "If you don't know whether it's true or not, you have to go do some digging." Cross-referencing questionable assertions by consulting a variety of trusted news sources is one quick way to do this. You can also visit websites such as Snopes, which specializes in exposing false content.

Where do you turn to for your news? Do you know fake news when you read it? Recognizing the difference between legitimate and phoney content is an essential part of staying properly informed about issues that are important to you and other citizens.

CHAPTER SUMMARY

We can understand politics both as an abstract concept and as a concrete practice. At its root, politics is about power and who gets to decide how it is used. Power is the ability of one person or group to impose decisions on another person or group. The degree to which the latter person or group obeys the former determines the degree of compliance. Power can be exercised through external means, such as coercion and persuasion, or through citizen respect for legitimate authority. In concrete terms, politics, government, and public administration are different, but interrelated, components of the Canadian political structure. Politics is about power and who decides how it is to be used in the management of a country's affairs. Government is a system of organizing a society so that disputes can be resolved or prevented. Public administration, as the term is used in this book, refers to the process of administering the functions of government and to the people who perform those functions (often called the civil service).

The concepts of authority and legitimacy, which are closely linked to the rule of law, help to explain why Canadians are willing to allow governments and their representatives to make laws and policy decisions and are willing to abide by those laws and decisions.

The remainder of this book discusses these topics and the interrelationships among them in more detail, with a view to placing the role of law enforcement in a larger political context.

KEY TERMS

WEBSITES

Canadian Civil Liberties Association: https://ccla.org

The Council of Canadians: https://canadians.org

Federation of Canadian Municipalities: https://fcm.ca/home.htm

Government of Canada: https://www.canada.ca/home.html

Government of Ontario: https://www.ontario.ca/page/government

History of the Magna Carta: http://www.history.com/topics/british-history/magna-carta

House of Commons Procedure and Practice: http://www.ourcommons.ca/MarleauMontpetit/DocumentViewer.aspx?DocId=1001&Language=E&Sec=Ch01&Seq=2

How Social Media Can Make History: https://www.ted.com/talks/clay_shirky_how_cellphones_twitter_facebook_can_make_history

The Internet in Society: https://www.youtube.com/watch?v=Uk8x3V-sUgU&playnext=1&list=PL72E201FF8C97750D&feature=results_main

Parliament of Canada: http://www.parl.ca/?Language=E

REFERENCE LIST

Anderson, B., & Coletto, D. (2017, April 29). Canadian news media and "fake news" under a microscope. Retrieved from http://abacusdata.ca/canadian-news-media-and-fake-news-under-a-microscope/#sthash.AWqCm6pU.dpuf

Bingham, T. (2011). *The rule of law*. London: Penguin.

Canadian Charter of Rights and Freedoms, Part I of the *Constitution Act, 1982*, being Schedule B to the *Canada Act 1982* (UK), 1982, c 11 [Charter]

Elections Canada. (2015). Forty-second general election official voting results. Retrieved from http://elections.ca/res/rep/off/ovr2015app/41/table4E.html

Forde, K.R., & Foss, K.A. (2012). The facts—the color!—the facts: The Idea of a report in American print culture. *Book History, 15,* 132.

Hobbes, T. (1985). Chapters XIII, XVII. *Leviathan*: Book I. London: Penguin.

Mosseri, A. (2017, April 6). Working to stop misinformation and false news. Retrieved from https://newsroom.fb.com/news/2017/04/working-to-stop-misinformation-and-false-news/

Snopes. (2016, July 24). Nope Francis. Retrieved from http://www.snopes.com/pope-francis-donald-trump-endorsement/

EXERCISES

True or False?

_____ **1.** Government has existed for as long as human civilization.

_____ **2.** In political terms, "compliance" refers to the obedience of a person or group to the wishes of a person or group with power.

_____ **3.** Police services are the only government agencies responsible for preserving public faith in the rule of law.

_____ **4.** One of the fundamental challenges of politics is balancing individual freedom with the public good.

_____ **5.** In Canada, the prime minister has the right to pass a law to avoid being charged with a crime he or she has committed.

Multiple Choice

1. The rule of law ensures that

  a. all citizens are subject to the laws of the nation

  b. even top-ranking politicians cannot override the law

  c. government treats all citizens fairly and equitably

  d. all government actions are legal

  e. all of the above

2. "Politics" can be defined as

  a. the loss of authority

  b. power, decision-making, and who has control

  c. budgets and tax cuts

  d. the conflict between two formal political parties

3. In modern democracies such as Canada, public support of government rests on the concept(s) of

  a. legitimate authority

  b. zero-tolerance law enforcement

  c. supremacy of unelected authority, such as the police

  d. benevolent dictatorship

4. High-profile court cases require substantial amounts of time and money to prosecute due to

  a. the rule of law

  b. statements made by government ministers

  c. special exemptions under the Constitution

  d. the public's demand for justice

5. The fundamental role of public administration is to

  a. formulate public policy

  b. make laws for Canadians

  c. govern Canadian society

  d. make decisions that are binding on citizens

  e. turn policy decisions of politicians into concrete action

Short Answer

1. Define "politics" and explain the various ways that it affects Canadian citizens.

2. How do we, as citizens, determine the extent of a government's authority and legitimacy?

3. What is the relationship between politics and public administration from a practical, as well as a theoretical, standpoint?

PART II

Political Structure

Unity Through Diversity: Canada Becomes a Nation

2

LEARNING OUTCOMES

After completing this chapter, you should be able to

- understand the historical development of Canada and its federalist system of government;

- explain the British and Canadian roots of Canada's original Constitution;

- identify the origins of the three levels of government in Canada;

- describe the division of powers between the federal and provincial governments; and

- discuss the decline of sovereignty in Quebec following the federal election of 2011, as represented by the rise of the New Democratic Party (NDP) in that province in that election.

Introduction

This chapter provides a brief summary of Canada's historical evolution and how these events influenced our founding political document—the *British North America Act*. You might be wondering why students studying politics would benefit from such a discussion. The answer is pretty straightforward.

Understanding Canadian politics requires a working knowledge of Canadian history. Therefore, this chapter briefly summarizes some of the major events and factors that have contributed to the current shape and evolving character of our country and its justice system. In addition, this background will assist you in better comprehending Canada's position in international affairs, a topic explored in Chapter 12.

The British North American and British officials who laid the political foundations for what became the nation of Canada might have some difficulty recognizing this country today. Canada has undergone many changes, particularly over the past 200 years, that have had a profound impact on the way Canadians understand themselves and their country.

Pre-Confederation

Canada became a country on July 1, 1867, marking the culmination of centuries of social, political, and economic development. Although estimates vary widely, the general consensus among scientists is that the first humans arrived on the continent approximately 60,000 years ago.[1] They gradually migrated along the Pacific Coast and then into the interior as glaciers receded. Eventually, they populated all regions of North and South America. Indigenous societies were many and diverse by the time Europeans first made contact with this part of the world. These societies had a collective population estimated at 100 million, 10 million of whom lived north of Mexico (Francis, Jones, & Smith, 2002, pp. 7–8). European contact with Indigenous peoples can be traced to the year 1000; however, it was not until the French began a colony along the St. Lawrence River in the early 1600s that Europeans began to settle permanently in northern North America.

Know Your History, Know Your Politics

Origins of Canada and Its System of Justice

When we think of Canada as it is today, many of us take for granted that we have always been a nation composed of ten provinces stretching from the Atlantic to the Pacific oceans and three northern territories. It is easy to forget that today's Canada has undergone many changes. In fact, our country has a shared native–non-native heritage involving politics, geography, and social structure that dates back some 400 years. Jacques Cartier's tentative voyages during the 1530s and Samuel de Champlain's establishment of Quebec in 1608 are generally considered the benchmarks for European settlement in Canada. In what became known as New France, settlement grew along the St. Lawrence River valley, while French explorers and traders eventually made their way through the Great Lakes region and down

---

1 Conservative estimates place this migration as recently as 10,000 years ago, although more liberal approximations date the movement as far back as 100,000 years. The estimates vary widely, depending on which evidence is cited. Confirmed archaeological finds in British Columbia, Alberta, and Nova Scotia prove that human settlement existed at least 10,000 years ago, but general consensus that a land bridge between Asia and Alaska existed up to 70,000 years ago has pushed estimates back (Dickason, 2002, pp. 4–11; Francis, Jones, & Smith, 2002, pp. 1–5).

the Mississippi River to the Gulf of Mexico. Many Indigenous groups participated in this trade alliance. However, as the Dutch and then the British increasingly challenged the French for dominance in this area, pressure mounted on Indigenous peoples living there to take sides in the dispute and to surrender land for settlement.

Although a basic system of justice existed in New France in its early development, it was not until King Louis XIV elevated the colony to a royal province of France in 1663 that a formal bureaucracy took shape. In accordance with this designation, New France was headed by a governor, who wielded ultimate power over the entire colony. Directly below him was the intendant, who was responsible for justice, public order, and financial matters. As such, the intendant managed the colony's military and administrative budget, headed its police, and oversaw municipal fortifications. He also came to preside over the Sovereign Council (Superior Council after 1703), which made laws and supervised the lower courts. Court cases and other administrative details were the responsibility of the attorney general. Together, these officials administered legislation passed by the council. Petty disputes were often decided by the seigneur (landowner) of the community or the local priest.[2]

Frontier conditions created unique problems for justice officials in New France. Laws could be enacted, but enforcement was often difficult since settlement was scattered and officials were few in number. As one historian has observed, inhabitants "obeyed when it was convenient, and ignored the law when it suited them" (Carrigan, 1991, pp. 21–22). However, as the colony grew, this improved over time.[3]

The Atlantic colonies of Nova Scotia, New Brunswick, Prince Edward Island, and Newfoundland developed justice systems in keeping with English criminal and civil customs. However, a lack of qualified people and the requisite government institutions resulted in a somewhat uneven evolution. Thus each settlement adopted the necessary infrastructure to fulfill justice-related obligations according to local needs. For example, Halifax already boasted a jail by 1758, only nine years after the city was established. Conversely, in spite of being one of Britain's oldest colonial outposts, Newfoundland lacked a legal system until 1719 and was not granted a legislature until 1824.[4] The fact that the legal system relied heavily on citizen volunteers further discouraged an embrace of fundamental principles of justice. As one author has noted:

> Policing was carried out by volunteer and usually reluctant citizens. Magistrates were appointed from the ranks of the general population, had little or no knowledge of the law or judicial procedures, and some could barely read or write. They were the subjects of constant complaints and ridicule. (Carrigan, 1991, p. 307)

With the cession of New France to the British in 1763, English criminal and civil law were applied there. However, political realities soon forced the British to acknowledge the widespread acceptance of the *French Civil Code*, which had been brought from France in the 1660s and had been in effect until the conquest. Officially recognized in the *Quebec Act of 1774*, this system of laws remained in effect until 1857, when major reforms were undertaken, culminating in the *Civil Code of Lower Canada*, proclaimed in 1866. It was updated again in 1994 and is now known as the *Quebec Civil Code*. Thus, while all other

---

2 Seigneurs had limited judicial authority over the habitants living on their lands, but they seldom exercised it. Priests enjoyed no such official powers, relying on moral influence to settle matters (Carrigan, 1991, p. 299).

3 The overall crime rate in New France fell slightly, from 1 in 139 in the 17th century to 1 in 150 in the 18th century (Carrigan, 1991, pp. 21–22).

4 The delay was due in part to the transient nature of the fishery and British reluctance to ensure the administrative costs of a permanent settlement on the island (Matthews, 1988, pp. 131–150).

jurisdictions in Canada apply English common law to civil matters, Quebec's long tradition of using the *Civil Code* continues.[5] Although distinct from English common law, the *Civil Code* proved no more successful than its counterpart. For many similar reasons, "justice in Lower Canada was, at best, dispensed very unevenly and in a most inequitable manner" (Carrigan, 1991, p. 301).[6] However, matters gradually improved as officials and citizens came to appreciate the importance of professional qualifications in the justice system.

The *Constitution Act of 1791* divided Quebec into Upper and Lower Canada (later Ontario and Quebec, respectively). In 1792, the Upper Canadian legislature adopted the principles of British law as the basis for its system of justice. In spite of pressure from some legal professionals to substitute English with American precedents in arguing civil cases, senior court officials insisted on the preservation of the former, in deference to what they thought to be "superior" British legal decisions and traditions. Locally, a justice of the peace and district sheriff administered the law. The former presided over court sessions held four times yearly in each area. The Courts of Quarter Session merged with the civil district courts in 1795, laying the foundation of local justice until 1841. As in the British legal system, more serious crimes were heard in the assize courts. These courts convened periodically in the colonies and were presided over by judges, who travelled from district to district to hear cases.

As had been the case in New France a century earlier, justice as it was practised in the British North American colonies often fell short of the standards to which it aspired. As one historian put it, "[I]n a day when police forces were non-existent, investigation methods were primitive, and crimes went unreported, many offenders must have escaped detection" (Carrigan, 1991, p. 30).

As the 19th century progressed and Enlightenment attitudes took hold, more attention was paid to justice issues in each of the colonies. Through acceptance of ideas such as equality and freedom, the public came increasingly to appreciate the importance of establishing and maintaining a fair and equitable legal system, complete with courts and professional legal officials. Thus, on the eve of **Confederation**, Canada embraced two legal systems, each of which had distinct origins and had adapted to a particular set of circumstances.

Confederation
the union of former British colonies that resulted in the formation of Canada on July 1, 1867

Considering Confederation

On a more general level, the British North American colonies confronted several political, social, and economic challenges during the middle decades of the 19th century.

Earlier attempts at political union had failed. However, by the 1860s a number of factors coaxed the Province of Canada (in 1841, Britain united Upper and Lower Canada into the Province of Canada, giving each—now called Canada West and Canada East—equal political representation in a United Assembly), New Brunswick, and Nova Scotia into considering the creation of one central government while retaining their respective rights to govern themselves provincially.

The populations of the British North American colonies in the 1860s were, for the most part, small and rural. They were also largely isolated from one another by geography, the sheer size of the land they occupied, and a limited transportation system. The four founding members of Confederation had little in common. The largest by population,

---

5   For a brief overview of the evolution of both English common law and the *Civil Code*, and the implications of each for Canadian law, see Sworden (2014, pp. 1–24).

6   During the years 1802 and 1825, people were hanged for crimes ranging in severity from shoplifting to murder.

Canada West, contained mostly English, Scottish, and Irish immigrants. Canada East's French-speaking population was mainly native-born with a shared history going back to the 1600s; the Catholic Church had a strong influence in this colony, where local governments reflected the local church parishes. The much smaller populations of the Atlantic colonies were also mainly native-born and English-speaking (Conrad, Finkel, & Jaenen, 1993, p. 487).

A proposed political union of the British North American colonies in 1841 failed to resolve many of the political problems that had led to rebellions in 1837 and 1838 in Upper Canada and Lower Canada. The reasons for these rebellions had been building for years and were the result of social and economic inequality, ethnic tensions in Lower Canada between francophones and anglophones, and frustration over the lack of democratic representation in the colonial governments, which were dominated by members of a wealthy elite.

Although Lower Canada's population had historically been larger than that of Upper Canada, this was not the case by the 1860s. Due to large waves of immigration, Upper Canada grew very quickly after the War of 1812, quadrupling from 100,000 to 400,000 inhabitants between the years 1815 and 1840. By 1851, the population of Canada West surpassed that of Canada East for the first time (Francis, Jones, & Smith, 2002, pp. 245, 256, 353). At Confederation, there were approximately 1.5 million people living in Ontario and about 1 million in Quebec. Canada at this time had a total population of 3.5 million.[7]

The new assembly of 1840 passed laws for both colonies, but its members continued to reflect the interests of their respective territories, reproducing the split between French and English Canadians. Thus the government remained deadlocked. Another form of government was sought and, by the early 1860s, calls to unite the British North American colonies began to be heard. The Atlantic colonies sought a maritime federation as well to strengthen their economies.

The Desire for Union

One factor that contributed to interest in a new union was the growing desire to build an intercolonial railway to connect all of British North America. The railway would facilitate trade and help bring more settlers into the region. At the time, most transportation was by water. Canals helped to connect the many lakes and rivers to otherwise landlocked areas, but they were of little use in the winter. Railways were a logical alternative. The only problem was their cost—building and maintaining them was extremely expensive, a fact that put railways out of the reach of any one colony. Working together, however, such a venture was feasible.

Confederation also promised trade advantages. Until 1849, the colonies had enjoyed preferential treatment in their trade with Britain. Colonial exports were guaranteed a share of the British market, even if these goods could be obtained more cheaply elsewhere. Britain abandoned this policy after 1849, however, opting for free trade—an economic system based on buying goods at the lowest possible price. The British North American colonies now had to compete among themselves and with bigger, established American competitors who benefited from a much larger population base. It made economic sense for the colonies to unite to create a strong market capable of competing in trade.

---

7   For deeper analysis regarding the broader implications of this dramatic increase in population and its effect on the political relationship between Upper and Lower Canada, see Curtis (2001).

Finally, concerns about defence made Confederation seem increasingly attractive. Since its inception, the United States had clashed repeatedly with British interests and had attempted outright invasion of the British North American colonies during the American Revolution and the War of 1812. The US Civil War (1861–1865) had now produced for its victorious northern leaders a powerful military force, which some argued should be used to invade British North America. This premise stemmed from a popular idea held by many Americans called "Manifest Destiny"—the idea that the United States was destined to acquire all of North America. Tacit British support for the defeated Confederate side during the Civil War had further fanned support for this movement. The time seemed right to band together in the interest of self-preservation.

Confederation

In September 1864, representatives of three of the Atlantic colonies—New Brunswick, Nova Scotia, and Prince Edward Island—met in Charlottetown to discuss the possibility of a maritime union. Representatives from the Province of Canada joined the Charlottetown Conference to try to persuade the Atlantic colonies of the benefits of a larger union. The Atlantic delegates weren't convinced but agreed to meet with the Canada West and Canada East representatives in Quebec in October to discuss the idea further.

Debates over Confederation and the form of government of the new union continued at the Quebec Conference and in the colonies. Newfoundland took part in these negotiations, as did Prince Edward Island, but these two colonies eventually decided against joining the new union.

On July 1, 1867, the Dominion of Canada, containing the four new provinces of Ontario, Quebec, New Brunswick, and Nova Scotia, came into existence when the British Parliament passed the *British North America Act* (BNA Act).[8] Canada's form of government was unique in the world: our country was part of the British Empire (later the Commonwealth); its head of state was the British monarch; and its Constitution—embodied in the BNA Act—was a British statute. Today, Canada is an independent nation, but the decisions made at Confederation continue to affect and inform Canadian government and politics.

The New Government

Canada was born out of a compromise among its four founding provinces. Because of the strong local traditions and allegiances that existed at the time of this political union, the would-be provinces of the new country were reluctant to transfer all of their political power to the newly formed national government. What resulted was a **federal system** whereby political powers were split between a strong central, or federal, government and the governments of the original four provinces. Each level of government was granted certain powers over specific areas, as stated in the BNA Act. Although the federal government was allotted most of the political power initially, the later growth in importance of areas of provincial jurisdiction, such as health and education, increasingly challenged the position of the federal government to decide many political matters.

A country as geographically vast and culturally diverse as Canada needed a system of government based on equality in a context of diversity. The federal system means that

federal system
Canada's government structure, which divides political power between the federal government and the provincial governments, with greater power resting in the federal government

---

8   Later renamed the *Constitution Act, 1867*. This is discussed in detail in Chapter 3. For a complete text of the BNA Act, see http://www.justice.gc.ca/eng/rp-pr/csj-sjc/constitution/lawreg-loireg/p1t11.html.

political power is shared between the federal government based in Ottawa and the provincial governments. It is doubtful that Canada would or could have been created in any other way. Today, the federal government serves all Canadians, including the ten provinces and three territories, while each provincial government serves only the people living within that province (the territories, although they have more independence today than in the past, are still financially dependent on the federal government and do not have the same constitutional powers as the provinces).

Confederation was seen by its supporters as a solution for many of the difficulties discussed earlier. It was thought that a union would brace the scattered provinces against possible US aggression and make it easier to defend their navigational rights on the St. Lawrence River and their fishing rights at sea. Confederation was further designed to foster a national economy in which there would be improved transportation facilities, including winter access to the sea. It was hoped that the resources and industries of the provinces would complement one another, thus increasing the prosperity and self-sufficiency of the whole. The Fathers of Confederation—those who met to discuss the union of British North America—also looked toward the future, when the united country would help to speed up the development and settlement of the Canadian Northwest and ultimately include a Pacific province.

There was significant pressure for political union, but also equally strong counterpressures calling for local cultures, traditions, and interests to be preserved. These counterpressures were particularly strong in French-speaking Canada and the Maritimes. Although a compromise on a federal system was worked out and embodied in the BNA Act, the actual terms of the Act were not universally supported by all the people who were affected, including Indigenous peoples, who were placed under the control of the federal government. This helps to explain the struggle that continues to this day for Indigenous recognition and the right of self-determination, which are discussed in chapters 4 and 5 of this book.

Post-Confederation

Wooing the West Coast: British Columbia

The most densely populated area of pre-European North America, the northwest coast of the continent, was first visited by Spaniards in about 1590. Russian fishing fleets frequented the coastline in search of sea otter and other wildlife; however, Britain soon became dominant in the area. In 1849, Britain asked the Hudson's Bay Company to establish and look after a settlement on Vancouver Island. That same year, Victoria became its capital. The new colony of British Columbia was established in 1858 to protect British sovereignty against the thousands of Americans who flocked north to the Fraser River Gold Rush. The two colonies—Vancouver Island and British Columbia—merged in 1866 but decided not to accept an offer to join Confederation. However, following the American purchase of Alaska in 1867, many people in the colony feared that it might be annexed by the United States. With Britain seeking to reduce its colonial possessions, the only realistic solution was to join the new country of Canada. The federal government of John A. Macdonald promised to assume the colony's debts and dangled the prospect of a rail link that would ultimately connect Canada from the Atlantic to the Pacific. Macdonald's offer did the trick, and British Columbia joined Confederation in 1871. The 25,000 Indigenous people that represented more than 75 percent of British Columbia's population were never consulted.

The last spike of the Canadian Pacific Railway (CPR) being driven at Craigellachie, BC in 1885. The CPR was instrumental in bringing the West into Confederation, but in British Columbia, the majority Indigenous population was never consulted about joining Canada.

The Way Out West: Rupert's Land

Named in honour of a cousin of Britain's King Charles II, this vast area of land included parts of modern-day Quebec, northern Ontario, all of Manitoba, and parts of Saskatchewan, Alberta, and the Arctic. Rupert's Land had been granted to the newly formed Hudson's Bay Company in 1670 as a means of establishing an English presence in the North American fur trade, at that time dominated by New France. Following Confederation, the federal government moved quickly to acquire the land and, thanks to British pressure, purchased it in 1869 for $1.5 million, quite a bargain considering that the United States had paid Russia $7.2 million for Alaska just two years earlier. The province of Manitoba was created in 1870, following skillful negotiations between Métis leader Louis Riel and the federal government. The province's initially limited geographic area was eventually extended north to include the southern part of the District of Keewatin in 1912.

The completion of the Canadian Pacific Railway in 1885 opened up areas of settlement farther west, resulting in the eventual creation of the provinces of Saskatchewan and Alberta in 1905. The Yukon Gold Rush of 1896 prompted the federal government to create a separate district, called Yukon Territory, to protect and reinforce Canadian jurisdiction in an area flooded by 40,000 people in just four years.[9]

Maritime Holdouts: Prince Edward Island and Newfoundland

Representatives of both Prince Edward Island and Newfoundland attended pre-Confederation conferences. The initial meeting had even taken place in Charlottetown in September 1864. Prince Edward Island already had more than 100 years of British colonial history behind it by the 1860s. Proud of local tradition, many Islanders did not like the terms of Confederation, and some even preferred annexation to the United States. In the end, overwhelming debt incurred through an overambitious railway project forced Prince Edward Island to approach the federal government in 1873 for financial assistance. Rather than see their taxes increase dramatically, Islanders decided to join the Dominion that same year.

---

9 For more information, see Conrad, Finkel, & Jaenen (1998).

Initially, Newfoundland seemed much more amenable to the prospect of Confederation. But its strong tradition and historical affinity for a British, rather than a Canadian, connection made joining the mainland a hard sell. Confederation with Canada became the main issue in the colony's 1869 election. With 19 of 27 seats in the House of Assembly taken by anti-Confederate supporters, the issue fell off the political agenda. Eventually, however, economic depression and British pressure brought Newfoundland into Confederation, albeit 82 years later, in 1949 (Francis, Jones, & Smith, 2000, pp. 42–43).

The Constitution

British Roots

As mentioned above, the BNA Act was the piece of British legislation that united the four founding provinces of the new country and gave Canada its **Constitution**—a document that outlines the basic principles of government of a country and the fundamental rights and freedoms enjoyed by its citizens. The Act also allowed for future provinces to join the federation.

Both the written and the implied parts of the Act bore the unmistakable imprint of Britain, although the federal structure was an important exception. Formally, the Act provided that the British monarch (whose representative in Canada is the governor general) was to be the chief executive officer and head of the new country. There was also to be a **bicameral legislature**—two Houses of Parliament—consisting of the House of Commons and the Senate (explained in more detail in Chapter 4), which correspond to the British House of Commons and House of Lords. Each House was to have an equal voice in Canadian legislation, except that, as in the British Parliament, financial measures were to be initiated in the House of Commons. This practice still exists: no government financial bills may initiate in the Senate. Canada also inherited from Britain

- the political party tradition;
- the principle under which executive authority resides in the prime minister and Cabinet and only nominally in the Queen and governor general (discussed in more detail in Chapter 4);
- the principle of responsible government (also discussed in Chapter 4), which was hard won by the provinces at Confederation, requiring that the executive must at all times be responsible to and retain the support (or confidence) of a majority of the popularly elected House of Commons; and
- the theory of the supremacy of Parliament and of the provincial legislatures, within their respective powers, as determined ultimately by the courts.

Canadian Contributions

In addition to those parts of the Constitution inherited from British tradition, a large number of conventions and practices of constitutional significance have gradually been developed and established within Canada.

An outstanding exception to the general rule of British influence on the Canadian Constitution was Canada's departure from the unitary state. The United Kingdom, then as now, was a unitary state in which the local authorities were established and governed by legislation passed by the British Parliament. At first, in the pre-Confederation conferences, the representatives of what was to become Ontario favoured the creation of a **legislative union**, as the unitary state was then usually called, with power concentrated entirely in the central Parliament and government. It became clear, however, that the French-speaking

Constitution
a document that outlines the basic principles of government of a country and the fundamental rights and freedoms enjoyed by its citizens

bicameral legislature
a government structure that consists of two Houses of Parliament—in Canada, the House of Commons and the Senate

legislative union
a structure of government in which power is concentrated in a central Parliament

and maritime colonies would not agree to surrender complete legislative jurisdiction to any central authority and that a federal system that gave the provinces the right to make and administer laws relating to mainly local matters was the only practical solution.

Division of Powers

division of powers
jurisdiction over major
policy areas, as divided
between the federal and
the provincial governments

jurisdiction
sphere of influence
or power

The strong regional differences that led each province to insist on retaining certain powers and responsibilities resulted in the **division of powers** between the federal and provincial governments. The powers and responsibilities—or **jurisdiction**—of each level of government are set out in sections 91–93 of the BNA Act. Section 91 lists the powers of the federal government, while sections 92–93 list those of the provinces. Section 95 gives the federal and provincial governments shared powers over immigration and agriculture. Table 2.1 summarizes the division of powers.

Section 92(8) gives the provinces the power to form municipalities and municipal governments. Section 93 gives the provinces control over education, subject to certain clauses designed to safeguard the rights of Roman Catholic and Protestant minorities. Finally, although section 95 gives Parliament and the provincial legislatures shared power over agriculture and immigration, in case of conflict the federal government prevails.

Although there is much dispute today as to which level of government is most politically powerful, the terms of the BNA Act suggest that Canada's federal government was intended to be a strong authority. This is certainly true today, given the power of the federal government to raise revenues through various forms of taxation and to determine how to return this money to the various provinces under strict conditions.

Who Speaks for Canada? The Debate over Federal or Provincial Power

As you can see in Table 2.1, the BNA Act assigns a variety of justice-related powers to the federal and provincial levels of government in Canada. For example, the federal government is responsible for criminal law, penitentiaries, and any matters having to do with the promotion of "peace, order, and good government" (*British North America Act*, 1867, s 91). The provinces have been assigned jurisdiction over property and civil rights, liquor licences, and provincial justice systems. At Confederation, the intention was to make as clear as possible the distinction between the two levels of government. Almost from the outset, however, provinces began to challenge the dominance of the federal government in many areas. This defiance, although somewhat muted, re-emerged in a much more public way after the Second World War and the Quiet Revolution in Quebec (see Chapter 3). As Canada was transformed from a rural-agricultural to an urban-industrial society, it became apparent that some provincial areas of jurisdiction—health, education, and social assistance, to name just three—were becoming the most important to Canadian citizens. Provinces have argued increasingly for more flexibility and funding to cope with greater public demand for services.

The federal government, on the other hand, has argued since Confederation that only it can make decisions in the best interests of all Canadians. Allowing provinces too much political power threatens national standards and, possibly, even the rights of citizens now guaranteed under the *Canadian Charter of Rights and Freedoms*. It might also weaken Canada's voice in international affairs, because potentially ten voices—not just one—would speak for Canada. Thus coming to any kind of articulate consensus could prove impossible.[10]

---

10   For further analysis, see Geddes (2001). See also Tindal (2000, pp. 237–271).

Table 2.1   Division of Powers

Federal Government	Provincial Governments	Federal and Provincial Governments
Section 91	**Section 92**	**Section 95**
• Maintenance of peace, order, and good government • Public debt and property • Trade and commerce • Taxes • Borrowing money on the public credit • Postal service • Census and statistics • Militia, military, naval service, and defence • Setting of salaries of officers of the government of Canada • Beacons, buoys, lighthouses, and Sable Island • Navigation and shipping • Marine hospitals • Sea coast and inland fisheries • Ferries between a province and another country and between provinces • Money • Banking • Weights and measures • Bills of exchange and promissory notes • Interest • Patents • Copyrights • Indigenous peoples and their lands • Immigration • Marriage and divorce • Criminal law • Penitentiaries	• Amendment of constitution of province, with the exception of office of lieutenant governor • Direct taxation for provincial purposes • Borrowing of money on provincial credit • Provincial government officers • Public lands belonging to the province • Reformatories • Hospitals, asylums, and charities, other than marine hospitals • Municipal institutions • Shop, saloon, tavern, auctioneer, and other licences • Local works other than shipping lines, railways, canals, and telegraphs that connect provinces or extend beyond provincial borders and any works that, although they operate within a province, are declared by the federal government to be for the general advantage of Canada or of two or more provinces • Incorporation of companies operating only within a province • Marriage ceremonies • Property and civil rights • Provincial justice system • Imposition of fines, penalties, or imprisonment in enforcing provincial laws • Any matters of a local or private nature	• Agriculture and immigration are shared responsibilities
	Section 93	
	Education	

Get Real!

Canada's Big Cities Want More Political Power

Municipal governments fall under provincial jurisdiction in our constitution and must, therefore, seek permission for much of what they do.

If you live in a major Canadian city, you are likely able to recall a time or two when your city's mayor publicly called upon the province to pony up some cash for a particular infrastructure project or municipal service.

In Toronto, the country's largest city with a population approaching almost three million, there's a long history of mayors who have openly expressed frustration with the province (Keenan, 2017). In early 2017, the Ontario government denied the city's request to institute road tolls, a measure local politicians hoped would generate revenue and assist Toronto with some of its fiscal challenges. In frustration, Toronto Mayor John Tory complained:

> It is time that we stop being treated, and I stop being treated, as a little boy going to Queen's Park in short pants to say, "Please, could you help me out with something that I thought was in the *City of Toronto Act* that I could do," and to be told, "No, I'm terribly sorry, go away and come back some other day." (Rider & Pagliaro, 2017)

It's not just Toronto mayors who have expressed frustration with the limited power of cities. In December 2016, the mayors of Vancouver, Ottawa, Calgary, Edmonton, and Toronto wrote an open letter expressing their frustrations with always having to ask permission from the province and the federal government to seek new revenue-generating measures. In their joint communiqué, they stated: "For too long, city governments have been required to rely on property taxes alone to support our growing operating budgets, with dollars stretched thinner and thinner as we serve the growing needs of the public" (Big city mayors, 2016).

For the most part, municipal governments rely on property taxes as their main source of revenue to fund the majority of their operating budgets. For example, fully one-third of Toronto's operating budget comes from taxes on property (Fact sheet, 2016). But big cities want the power to generate revenue from other sources, such as road tolls, as they face increasing financial pressures. Growing populations and aging city infrastructure mean more money has to be spent on, for example, updating or expanding transit, building recreation centres, or managing and maintaining public housing.

So why don't major cities have autonomous powers in the constitution? Well, it could have something to do with where the majority of people lived when Canada first became a country: then a whopping 80 percent of the population resided in rural areas (McGrath, 2017). Nowadays, about 80 percent of the population live in urban centres, so it's really no wonder that there have been growing pains between municipalities and the provinces since Confederation (Population, 2011). Addressing such modifications would almost certainly require amendments to our Constitution, and, as explained in the next chapter, this is not as easy as it might first appear. Do you think municipalities should have greater control over matters that affect them? How might this be done? Should provinces continue to have the final say in municipal affairs? Why?

CHAPTER SUMMARY

Canada is a federation, a government structure that divides political powers between the federal and provincial governments. Confederation grew out of the desire of former British North American colonies to solve the problems posed by a small, scattered population characterized by geographic, cultural, and economic diversity. Our government structure represents an attempt to balance divergent interests for the overall public good. To this day, the challenges associated with such a balancing act—such as the demands of regional interests, bilingualism, Quebec's francophone culture, and Indigenous peoples' desire for self-government, to name

only a few—continue to be the subjects of political debate. The separation of powers between the federal and provincial governments can sometimes lead to conflict, as evidenced in federal–provincial disagreements over the gun registry and differences in approaches to justice. These conflicts can be difficult to follow, because federal and provincial governments may reverse their positions over time, as the federal government did in 2011 when it introduced legislation to end the gun registry, finally passing Bill C-19, *An Act to Amend the Criminal Code (Firearms) and Firearms Act* on April 5, 2012.[11]

KEY TERMS

bicameral legislature, 27

Confederation, 22

Constitution, 27

division of powers, 28

federal system, 24

jurisdiction, 28

legislative union, 27

WEBSITES

Forum of Federation: http://www.forumfed.org/events/enabling-regions-to-set-their-own-taxes-rates/

Intergovernmental Affairs: https://www.canada.ca/en/intergovernmental-affairs.html

Marois Declares PQ Priorities: http://www.cbc.ca/news/canada/montreal/marois-declares-pq-priorities-as-charest-resigns-1.1135451

Orange Crush: http://www.cbc.ca/archives/entry/orange-crush-helps-ndp-become-opposition-in-2011-election

REFERENCE LIST

Big city mayors call for increased revenue powers. (2016, December 13). *The Canadian Press*. Retrieved from http://www.cbc.ca/news/canada/ottawa/big-city-mayors-want-more-revenue-powers-1.3894502

An Act to amend the Criminal Code (firearms) and the Firearms Act, SC 2003, c 8 Department of Justice. Retrieved from http://laws-lois.justice.gc.ca/eng/AnnualStatutes/2003_8/page-1.html

British North America Act, 1867, 30 & 31 Vict, c 3 Department of Justice. Retrieved from http://www.justice.gc.ca/eng/rp-pr/csj-sjc/constitution/lawreg-loireg/p1t13.html

Carrigan, D.O. (1991). *Crime and punishment in Canada: A history*. Toronto: McClelland & Stewart.

Conrad, M., Finkel, A., & Jaenen, C. (1998). *History of the Canadian peoples* (2nd ed., Vol. 1: *Beginnings to 1867*; Vol. 2: *1867 to the present.*). Toronto: Copp Clark Pitman.

Curtis, B. (2001). *The politics of population: State formation, statistics, and the census of Canada, 1840–1875*. Toronto: University of Toronto Press.

Dickason, O. (2002). *Canada's First Nations: A history of founding peoples from earliest times* (3rd ed.). Toronto: Oxford University Press.

11 Public Safety Minister Vic Toews tabled the bill in Parliament on October 25, 2011. For details on immediate provincial reaction, see Fitzpatrick (2011). More recently, the Ontario Superior Court ruled in favour of the federal government (to destroy long-gun registry records in the province), while further litigation in Quebec (an attempt by the province to preserve records) remains ongoing ("Toews applauds Ontario," 2012).

Fact sheet: City revenue. (2016, October). City of Toronto. Retrieved from http://www1.toronto.ca/wps/portal/content only?vgnextoid=c98bf02ab1208510VgnVCM10000071d60f 89RCRD&vgnextchannel=e52b285441f71410VgnVCM10000 071d60f89RCRD

Fitzpatrick, M. (2011, October 25). New long-gun registry would destroy records. *CBC News*. Retrieved from http:// www.cbc.ca/news/politics/story/2011/10/25/pol-gun -registry.html

Francis R.D., Jones, R., & Smith, D.B. (2000). *Destinies: Canadian history since Confederation* (4th ed.). Toronto: Thomson Nelson.

Francis, R.D. Jones, R., & Smith, D.B. (2002). *Origins: Canadian history to Confederation* (4th ed.). Toronto: Thomson Nelson.

Geddes, J. (2001, September 2). Does Ottawa matter? *Maclean's*, 34–37.

Keenan, E. (2017, May 4). Tory is right to raise hell with the province, but must also find a way to fix social housing: Keenan. *Toronto Star*. Retrieved from https://www.thestar .com/news/gta/2017/05/04/tory-is-right-to-raise-hell-with -the-province-but-he-must-also-find-a-way-to-fix-social -housing.html

Matthews, M. (1988). *Lectures on the history of Newfoundland, 1500–1830*. St. John's, NL: Breakwater Books.

McGrath, J.M. (2017, February 10). Cities say they want more money and power. They should be careful what they wish for. *TVO*. Retrieved from http://tvo.org/article/ current-affairs/the-next-ontario/cities-say-they-want -more-money-and-more-power-they-should-be-careful -what-they-wish-for

Population, urban and rural, by province and territory. (2011, February 4). Statistics Canada. Retrieved from http://www .statcan.gc.ca/tables-tableaux/sum-som/l01/cst01/demo62a -eng.htm

Rider, D., & Pagliaro, J. (2017, January 27). Tory challenges Wynne's leadership after she rejects road tolls, but 905 leaders celebrate. *Toronto Star*. Retrieved from https:// www.thestar.com/news/city_hall/2017/01/27/councillors -blast-short-sighted-decision-to-block-tolls-on-gardiner -dvp.html

Sworden, P. (2014). *An introduction to law in Canada*. Toronto: Emond Montgomery.

Tindal, C.R. (2000). *A citizen's guide to government* (2nd ed.). Toronto: McGraw-Hill Ryerson.

Toews applauds Ontario ruling on gun-registry data. (2012, September 21). *The Canadian Press*. *CBC News*. Retrieved from http://www.cbc.ca/news/politics/story/2012/09/21/ pol-cp-toews-gun-registry-ontario.html

EXERCISES
True or False?

_____ 1. Rupert's Land was purchased for $1.5 million.

_____ 2. A federal system of government gives all the power to the federal government.

_____ 3. The BNA Act was the first statute passed by the Canadian government.

_____ 4. The new nation of Canada was a legislative union, a government structure borrowed from Britain.

_____ 5. The federal government is responsible for maintaining peace, order, and good government.

Multiple Choice

1. The original members of Confederation were

   a. Canada West, Canada East, New Brunswick, and Newfoundland

   b. Canada West, Canada East, New Brunswick, and Nova Scotia

   c. Canada West, New Brunswick, Nova Scotia, and Prince Edward Island

   d. Canada East, Newfoundland, New Brunswick, and Nova Scotia

   e. Rupert's Land, Canada West, Canada East, and New Brunswick

2. Confederation promised

   a. economic advantages

   b. transportation advantages

   c. defence advantages

   d. trade advantages

   e. all of the above

3. The Canadian Constitution, embodied in the BNA Act, borrowed from Britain

   a. a legislature composed of two Houses of Parliament

   b. the political party system

   c. the principle of responsible government

   d. b and c

   e. a, b, and c

4. A major departure of Canada from the British system of government was its structure as a

   a. unitary state

   b. legislative union

   c. constitutional monarchy

   d. federation

   e. all of the above

5. The powers of municipal, or local, governments are based in

   a. the Constitution

   b. provincial powers to form and maintain local governments

   c. federal powers to form and maintain local governments

   d. all of the above

   e. none of the above

Short Answer

1. Define "federation."

2. What factors contributed to Canada's formation?

3. What did Confederation's supporters hope to achieve with this union?

4. List some aspects of the Canadian political system that have their roots in Britain.

5. Which aspect of Canada's political system was a major departure from Britain's?

6. If you could rewrite our Constitution, how would you divide federal and provincial authority in the areas of justice and law enforcement? Explain.

The Constitution and the Canadian Charter of Rights and Freedoms

3

LEARNING OUTCOMES

After completing this chapter, you should be able to

- describe the history of the *Constitution Act, 1982*, including attempts to amend it;

- explain the impact of the *Canadian Charter of Rights and Freedoms* on individual and collective rights of people in Canada;

- describe the role of the Canadian judicial system in the political and constitutional process; and

- using recent examples, discuss some of the challenges inherent in balancing the fundamental rights of citizens with the preservation of law and order.

Introduction

This chapter explains how our current Constitution came to be, what that means for our political system, and why constitutional reform continues to be an objective of our federal and provincial governments. The chapter also discusses the significance of the *Canadian Charter of Rights and Freedoms* to Canadians in general and to our judicial system. The discussion serves two purposes: if you think about our Constitution as a kind of instruction manual for running the country, then it makes sense that you acquaint yourself with how its content and character have changed over time, and what this has meant for Canada's evolution as a country. Take into consideration that this document lays out the groundwork for how political power is allocated and how justice is dispensed in order to preserve the rule of law, and therefore legitimate authority, and it becomes readily apparent that a comprehensive understanding of how all of this political machinery fits together requires knowledge of such matters.

The Path to Patriation

As explained in Chapter 2, the source of the Constitution of Canada is the *British North America Act* of 1867, the British statute that united the former British North American colonies to form the Dominion of Canada.

Because the Act was a law that had been passed by the British Parliament, only Britain possessed the legal authority to revise it. Britain had the power to reject Canadian laws, pass laws that affected Canada, and interpret and amend (change) Canadian laws. Thus, when Britain declared war on Germany in 1914, Canada was automatically involved in the First World War as well. The Canadian Constitution could be amended only by Britain, so every time Canada's federal government wanted to amend the Act, it had to ask the British Parliament to pass legislation to do so. As well, Britain's Judicial Committee of the Privy Council served as Canada's last court of appeal. For example, when the federal government and Ontario could not agree on how to draw the Ontario–Manitoba border soon after the latter's creation, the matter was argued before the British Empire's supreme legal authority, which ultimately ruled in Ontario's favour.[1] Even though the Supreme Court of Canada was created in 1875, disputes between Ottawa and the provinces continued to be referred to the Judicial Committee until 1949, when the Supreme Court of Canada finally assumed this responsibility.

The First World War, or the Great War as it was then called, exposed many inner tensions, particularly among French Canadians, a majority of whom viewed the conflict as a foreign one having little or nothing to do with Canada and English Canadians, who tended to view it as a matter of patriotism and an opportunity to prove Canada's loyalty to the British Empire. Tense as these debates were at times, they did get Canadians thinking about Canada's independence as a nation, free from foreign interference.[2]

---

1 An agreement had been reached under federal and Ontario Liberal governments, but before it could be enacted, the federal Liberals lost power. The new Conservative government ignored the previous agreement, and the ensuing legal wrangling eventually led both sides to appeal to the Judicial Committee of the Privy Council for a decision. In 1883, the body ruled that Ontario's western boundary should be fixed at its present-day location. See Francis, Jones, & Smith (2000, pp. 82–83). See also Russell (2002).

2 As discussed later in this chapter, relations between English and French Canadian cultures have had, and will continue to have, major impacts on constitutional issues.

A Primer on French–English Relations in Canadian History

1755 Acadian Expulsion—On suspicion of disloyalty, 10,000 French-speaking inhabitants of Acadia (subsequently renamed Nova Scotia) were forcibly expelled by British troops.

1774 *Quebec Act*—This British law guaranteed the religious freedom of French Canadians (most of whom were Roman Catholics) and confirmed the use of the *French Civil Code* in the courts for non-criminal matters.

1839 Durham Report—This report resulted in the unification of Upper and Lower Canada into a single colony, partly as a means to dominate and eventually assimilate French-speaking culture into English colonial society.

1885 Execution of Louis Riel—Riel was a French Métis political leader who had been instrumental in founding the province of Manitoba. Following a failed Métis uprising, he was tried and eventually hanged for treason, although it was argued that he lacked mental competence to stand trial.

1867 Confederation—This was understood at the time as a partnership between the "two founding races" of French and English nations.

1871, 1890, 1913 The use of the French language was restricted in the public schools of New Brunswick, Manitoba, and Ontario. French Canadians' appeals to the federal government to preserve and protect their rights achieved little.

1917, 1942 Conscription Crises—Mandatory military service legislation was passed during each of the world wars. This was generally opposed in French-speaking Canada and supported in English-speaking Canada.

Source: *Historica Canada* (n.d.).

As a nation, Canada came into its own following the war. Out of a country of just over 8 million people, 625,000 had served in the military, 60,000 of whom died. Stunning victories, such as the Battle of Vimy Ridge, proved to the world that Canada was truly a member of the international community. In 1919, in recognition of Canadian achievements, Canada signed the *Treaty of Versailles* independent of Britain, an event that would have seemed impossible in 1914. In legal terms, however, Canada remained tied to the British Empire.[3]

During the 1920s, further steps were taken to acquire a sense of nationhood. In 1923, Canada signed the *Halibut Treaty* with the United States, marking the first time an international agreement affecting it had not been signed by British officials. At the Imperial Conference of 1926, the dominions and Britain agreed to recognize one another as equal partners united in the British Commonwealth. By the end of the 1920s, Canada established its own diplomatic relations with Washington, Paris, and Tokyo. In addition, London appointed a high commissioner to conduct government-to-government relations with Ottawa, a task that had until then been assigned to the Crown's representative, the governor general.

Canada's growing sense of nationhood caused many Canadians to view the existing constitutional arrangement as both embarrassing and obsolete. Britain, for its part, was happy to comply with a Canadian request for change.

Canada gained more legislative independence from Britain with the passing of the *Statute of Westminster* in 1931. With this statute, Britain aimed to simplify relations with Canada and other members of the British Commonwealth. The statute formally gave

---

3 For further context on the *Treaty of Versailles* and recognition of Canada's achievements, see MacMillan (2001).

Canada authority over its domestic and external affairs and limited the British Parliament to legislating for Canada only when requested to do so by the Canadian government. However, because the federal and provincial governments couldn't agree on a constitutional **amending formula**—a process for changing the BNA Act—Britain retained its authority over Canadian constitutional amendments.

Over the ensuing years, various Canadian federal governments tried to reach agreement on an amending formula with the provinces for the **patriation** of the Constitution—that is, to finally bring the Constitution under the control of Canada. This became increasingly complex because the federal government and the provinces could not agree on an amending formula that would permit changes to the Constitution. The provinces, led initially by Quebec, sought greater control over economic and social policy. They wanted to reverse the trend toward centralization at the federal level of government, which had been particularly strong as a result of the Great Depression and the two world wars. The Quiet Revolution in Quebec, which ushered in significant political, social, and economic reforms after the provincial election of 1960, reawakened a sense that Quebec once more should assert its special place in Canada as one of the two founding partners in Confederation. The transformation reshaped Quebec society in several ways. Quebeckers

> acquired a new confidence in themselves that encouraged them to challenge the inequalities they faced as French-speaking Canadians. They strongly criticized a Canada in which the bureaucracy spoke only English, in which French enjoyed no official recognition in nine provinces, and in which the economy functioned— even within Quebec—largely in English. Here indeed were the makings of a new nationalism. (Francis, Jones, & Smith, 2000, p. 447)

This new, more confrontational era in federal–provincial relations rekindled debates about how Canada should operate—as a highly centralized state or as a loose confederation of autonomous provinces. Prime Minister Lester B. Pearson summed up the challenge in a speech in late 1964:

> National unity does not imply subordination in any way of provincial rights or the alienation of provincial authority. It does require a government at the centre strong enough to serve Canada as a whole; and its full realization demands a strong Canadian identity with the national spirit and pride that will sustain and strengthen it. (October 15, 1964)

As other provinces began to demand more autonomy within Confederation, both levels of government attempted to resolve how this could be accomplished "in house"—that is, within a Canadian constitutional framework that could provide a means of making amendments without having to submit these changes to the British Parliament for approval. Both parties came close in 1964, with the Fulton-Favreau formula, a proposal named after Davie Fulton and Guy Favreau, the two federal justice ministers who had conceived it. Under this plan, unanimous consent would be required to approve any constitutional change of national importance.

Continuing disagreement over the formula prevented its acceptance, but, in 1971, another possible solution emerged. The federal government proposed a formula giving Ontario and Quebec a veto. The provinces agreed to meet in Victoria in June to discuss what had become known as the Victoria Charter. Just before the conference, however, Quebec's Premier Robert Bourassa demanded that the provinces be given substantial control over social programs. As a result, no agreement was reached.

As the decade progressed, the provinces increasingly demanded more powers, which would entail constitutional reform (recall from Chapter 2 that the BNA Act divided powers between the federal and provincial governments, with the federal government retaining the

The official signing ceremony, formally acknowledging the patriating of Canada's Constitution from Britain. Seated are Prime Minister Pierre Trudeau and Queen Elizabeth II.

greatest power). Quebec, for example, continued to demand control over social programs and economic policies. The election in Quebec of the separatist Parti Québécois in 1976, led by René Lévesque, gave greater urgency to these demands.

At the end of the decade, the constitutional debate re-emerged as Prime Minister Pierre Trudeau, seeing no federal–provincial compromise, announced that the federal government would unilaterally patriate the Constitution. Only Ontario and New Brunswick came onside. In September, the Supreme Court ruled that although the federal government could act unilaterally, this action defied the convention of provincial consultation. Meanwhile, the dissenting premiers met in Vancouver to come up with a counterproposal. This group brought its "Vancouver Charter" to Ottawa in November 1981, in hopes of derailing the federal initiative. However, during the early hours of November 5, some provincial representatives worked out a compromise that contained elements of the Vancouver Charter and would include a Charter of Rights and Freedoms, something on which Trudeau had insisted. All of the premiers, save one, were awakened and summoned to the meeting. Quebec's Premier René Lévesque was not invited. The next day, nine provinces and the federal government announced that a deal had been reached. The chain of events became known in Quebec as the "Night of the Long Knives," because it appeared that many of that province's concerns had been sacrificed in order to achieve an agreement. Thus Quebec did not sign the resulting constitutional document. (Although Quebec is still not a signatory to the Constitution, the province benefits from and operates within the Constitution of Canada.) Regardless, on April 17, 1982, Queen Elizabeth II gave royal assent to the new *Constitution Act, 1982*, officially making our Constitution a wholly Canadian document with its own amending formula.

Bringing the Constitution Home

It took another British statute, the *Canada Act* of 1982, to patriate the Canadian Constitution. The *Canada Act* confirmed that British legislation would no longer apply to Canada. Canada's new *Constitution Act, 1982* combines the old *British North America Act* (which was renamed the *Constitution Act, 1867*), the amending formula, and the **Canadian Charter of Rights and Freedoms**.

Canadian Charter of Rights and Freedoms
part of the Canadian Constitution that guarantees certain fundamental rights and freedoms to people in Canada

Constitution Act, 1982

Part V

Procedure for Amending Constitution of Canada

General procedure for amending Constitution of Canada

38.(1) An amendment to the Constitution of Canada may be made by proclamation issued by the Governor General under the Great Seal of Canada where so authorized by

(a) resolutions of the Senate and House of Commons; and

(b) resolutions of the legislative assemblies of at least two-thirds of the provinces that have, in the aggregate, according to the then latest general census, at least fifty per cent of the population of all the provinces.

Majority of members

(2) An amendment made under subsection (1) that derogates from the legislative powers, the proprietary rights or any other rights or privileges of the legislature or government of a province shall require a resolution supported by a majority of the members of each of the Senate, the House of Commons and the legislative assemblies required under subsection (1).

Expression of dissent

(3) An amendment referred to in subsection (2) shall not have effect in a province the legislative assembly of which has expressed its dissent thereto by resolution supported by a majority of its members prior to the issue of the proclamation to which the amendment relates unless that legislative assembly, subsequently, by resolution supported by a majority of its members, revokes its dissent and authorizes the amendment.

Revocation of dissent

(4) A resolution of dissent made for the purposes of subsection (3) may be revoked at any time before or after the issue of the proclamation to which it relates.

Restriction on proclamation

39.(1) A proclamation shall not be issued under subsection 38(1) before the expiration of one year from the adoption of the resolution initiating the amendment procedure thereunder, unless the legislative assembly of each province has previously adopted a resolution of assent or dissent.

Idem

(2) A proclamation shall not be issued under subsection 38(1) after the expiration of three years from the adoption of the resolution initiating the amendment procedure thereunder.

Compensation

40. Where an amendment is made under subsection 38(1) that transfers provincial legislative powers relating to education or other cultural matters from provincial legislatures to Parliament, Canada shall provide reasonable compensation to any province to which the amendment does not apply.

Amendment by unanimous consent

41. An amendment to the Constitution of Canada in relation to the following matters may be made by proclamation issued by the Governor General under the Great Seal of Canada only where authorized by resolutions of the Senate and House of Commons and of the legislative assembly of each province:

(a) the office of the Queen, the Governor General and the Lieutenant Governor of a province;

(b) the right of a province to a number of members in the House of Commons not less than the number of Senators by which the province is entitled to be represented at the time this Part comes into force;

(c) subject to section 43, the use of the English or the French language;

(d) the composition of the Supreme Court of Canada; and

(e) an amendment to this Part.

Amendment by general procedure	42.(1) An amendment to the Constitution of Canada in relation to the following matters may be made only in accordance with subsection 38(1):

(a) the principle of proportionate representation of the provinces in the House of Commons prescribed by the Constitution of Canada;

(b) the powers of the Senate and the method of selecting Senators;

(c) the number of members by which a province is entitled to be represented in the Senate and the residence qualifications of Senators;

(d) subject to paragraph 41(d), the Supreme Court of Canada;

(e) the extension of existing provinces into the territories; and

(f) notwithstanding any other law or practice, the establishment of new provinces.

Exception

(2) Subsections 38(2) to (4) do not apply in respect of amendments in relation to matters referred to in subsection (1).

Amendment of provisions relating to some but not all provinces

43. An amendment to the Constitution of Canada in relation to any provision that applies to one or more, but not all, provinces, including

(a) any alteration to boundaries between provinces, and

(b) any amendment to any provision that relates to the use of the English or the French language within a province,

may be made by proclamation issued by the Governor General under the Great Seal of Canada only where so authorized by resolutions of the Senate and House of Commons and of the legislative assembly of each province to which the amendment applies.

Amendments by Parliament

44. Subject to sections 41 and 42, Parliament may exclusively make laws amending the Constitution of Canada in relation to the executive government of Canada or the Senate and House of Commons.

Amendments by provincial legislatures

45. Subject to section 41, the legislature of each province may exclusively make laws amending the constitution of the province.

Initiation of amendment procedures

46.(1) The procedures for amendment under sections 38, 41, 42 and 43 may be initiated either by the Senate or the House of Commons or by the legislative assembly of a province.

Revocation of authorization

(2) A resolution of assent made for the purposes of this Part may be revoked at any time before the issue of a proclamation authorized by it.

Amendments without Senate resolution

47.(1) An amendment to the Constitution of Canada made by proclamation under section 38, 41, 42 or 43 may be made without a resolution of the Senate authorizing the issue of the proclamation if, within one hundred and eighty days after the adoption by the House of Commons of a resolution authorizing its issue, the Senate has not adopted such a resolution and if, at any time after the expiration of that period, the House of Commons again adopts the resolution.

Computation of period

(2) Any period when Parliament is prorogued or dissolved shall not be counted in computing the one hundred and eighty day period referred to in subsection (1).

Advice to issue proclamation

48. The Queen's Privy Council for Canada shall advise the Governor General to issue a proclamation under this Part forthwith on the adoption of the resolutions required for an amendment made by proclamation under this Part.

Constitutional conference

49. A constitutional conference composed of the Prime Minister of Canada and the first ministers of the provinces shall be convened by the Prime Minister of Canada within fifteen years after this Part comes into force to review the provisions of this Part.

The Constitution contains five different amending formulas, depending on the circumstance and the part of the country affected (see the box on pages 40–41).

Amendments to the Constitution itself require the approval of Parliament and two-thirds (7 of 10) of the provinces that, combined, contain at least 50 percent of Canada's total population. Amendments that affect representation in the House of Commons, the Senate, and the Supreme Court of Canada and those that affect the use of the French and English languages in government affairs require the consent of Parliament and all the provinces (Finkel & Conrad, 1993, p. 585).

The *Canadian Charter of Rights and Freedoms* (see the Appendix) was the most significant amendment to the Constitution and will be discussed in more detail later in this chapter.

Despite patriation, Pierre Trudeau's vision of a unified Canada has yet to be realized. As the following sections explain, almost four decades after patriation Canadians are still debating constitutional issues and attempting to win Quebec's signature to the Constitution.

Ongoing Constitutional Debate

In spite of the events of 1982, the Quebec separatist movement could not galvanize public opinion sufficiently to achieve independence. After coming to power in 1976, the Parti Québécois had focused on social issues rather than pursuing its separatist objectives. As well, a 1980 referendum on the issue of "sovereignty association"—only a step toward full nationhood—was lost when 60 percent of Quebeckers voted against the proposal. When the provincial Liberal Party won the election of 1985, it seemed as though the Quebec separatist movement was dead. In federal politics, Pierre Trudeau had retired and, in September 1984, Canadians elected the Progressive Conservatives led by Brian Mulroney. A Quebecker himself, Mulroney wanted to bring Quebec back into the constitutional family.

The Meech Lake Accord

An apparent agreement was reached between Mulroney and the ten provincial premiers at a first ministers' conference at Meech Lake, Ontario, in April 1987. The proposed

The Meech Lake Accord stirred widespread debate across Canada, both among supporters and detractors.

amendments of the Meech Lake Accord met Quebec's minimum demands for signing the Constitution (Wagenberg, 1992, p. 102):

- Quebec would be recognized as a distinct society.
- Quebec would have a veto on any future constitutional changes.
- All provinces would have increased powers over immigration.
- All provinces would be able to opt out of any federal cost-sharing programs (e.g., medicare, child care).
- Justices of the Supreme Court of Canada would be appointed from lists provided by the provinces.

In addition, the concerns of the other provinces were addressed with the following amendments:

- Provincial demands for Senate reform would be met by giving the provinces the right to provide the federal government with a list of individuals from which to choose senators.
- Future constitutional amendments would be discussed at annual first ministers' meetings.
- All provinces—not just Quebec—would have the power to veto amendments.

Mulroney then announced that no amendments to the Meech Lake Accord would be considered; the Accord had to be ratified within three years by Parliament and by all ten provincial legislatures. Not a word could be changed (Finkel & Conrad, 1993, p. 593).

Despite the agreement of the politicians, many groups opposed the Meech Lake Accord. Some people were unhappy that ordinary Canadians had not been involved in the reform process in any way, arguing that the future of the nation should not be decided by only 11 individuals. People who were in favour of a strong federal government believed that the Accord gave too much power to the provinces. First Nations' hopes for a guarantee of the right to self-government were dashed. Many people, including Quebeckers, wanted to know exactly what "distinct society" meant in the legal sense, a definition that was not provided in the Accord. Many people were concerned about how this recognition of Quebec might affect the provisions of the *Canadian Charter of Rights and Freedoms* and how it would be interpreted by the Supreme Court when deciding issues related to the Charter. Mulroney countered that "distinct society" was mainly a symbolic term, thus basically confirming that it had little constitutional worth. Critics, many of them from Quebec, disagreed. Other critics of the Accord included women's groups and groups that were concerned that the ability of provinces to opt out of proposed shared-cost programs (e.g., a national child-care program) would lead to the abandonment of such programs.

The three years allowed for legislative approval witnessed political party changes in several provinces. When the deadline was reached, two of the ten provinces had still not approved the agreement: Newfoundland and Manitoba. Newfoundland's Premier Clyde Wells, a lawyer and constitutional expert, was in favour of a strong federal government and an elected Senate with equal representation from all the provinces, and he was opposed to recognizing Quebec as a distinct society. In Manitoba, a member of the Legislative Assembly, Elijah Harper, in a stand for First Nations' rights, managed to delay a vote on the passage of the Accord.

Hopes of obtaining Quebec's approval of the Constitution died with the Meech Lake Accord in 1990. In the end, the effort to achieve national unity actually stirred up pro-separatist feelings. Quebeckers felt betrayed by the opposition to the distinct society clause and the switch from addressing Quebec's constitutional concerns to addressing the concerns of other groups. As a result, several Quebec members of the National Assembly formed a new federal political party—the Bloc Québécois, led by one of Mulroney's most senior Cabinet ministers, Lucien Bouchard—to defend Quebec's rights in Ottawa. Quebec's Premier Robert Bourassa announced plans for a referendum on separation for 1992. Facing growing support for Quebec separation, the federal and provincial leaders decided to resume negotiations toward a new accord before the referendum deadline (Finkel & Conrad, 1993, pp. 592–598).

The Charlottetown Accord

The federal government began by announcing a Citizens' Forum on Canada's Future in November 1990. Sensing a looming national crisis, Prime Minister Mulroney wanted to consult a broad range of Canadians about how to deal with the situation. He described the commission as a way to create "a dialogue with people across the country and help create a consensus about Canada and our future" (Maton, 1996). The commission's subsequent report contributed to a larger effort at constitutional reform already under way.

The Charlottetown Accord of August 1992 was two years in the making and included something for everyone: special status for Quebec in exchange for equal provincial representation in the Senate, recognition of Indigenous rights to self-government, a social charter guaranteeing that existing social programs would be maintained by government, and more provincial powers. In addition, all Canadians would be involved in ratifying the Accord in a referendum scheduled for October 1992.

Despite polls suggesting that most Canadians would support the new Accord, six of the ten provinces voted against it. It seemed that in trying to please everyone, the Accord managed to please no one and only fuelled Quebec separatist sentiments. Everyone was tired of constitutional wrangles and wanted to turn to other pressing concerns, such as the serious economic recession and rising unemployment. Meanwhile, separatists in Quebec seized on the Charlottetown Accord as additional proof to back their cause. Quebec finally held its referendum on separation in 1995, which was only narrowly defeated when 49.4 percent of Quebecers said "Yes" to separation from the rest of Canada (Finkel & Conrad, 1993, pp. 598–602).

Recent Constitutional Issues

Canada has experienced some difficult economic and social ills since the attempt to amend the *Constitution Act*. Constitutional issues and the threat of Quebec separation, although important, have taken a back seat to other priorities—national security, external threats, and the state of the economy among them. When former Bloc Québécois leader Lucien Bouchard was re-elected premier of Quebec in 1998 with less than 43 percent of the popular vote, his government decided that there was no pressing need for another referendum on separation. The Quebec Liberal Party, led by Jean Charest, won the provincial election of April 2003 and stated that, for then at least, it saw no need to revisit constitutional reform. Meanwhile, the provinces and the federal government have continued to discuss various constitutional issues.

One result of subsequent meetings discussing constitutional reform was the Calgary Declaration of September 1997, in which the federal government and all provinces except Quebec (which boycotted the meeting) agreed to a set of seven principles that, it was hoped, would bring Quebec into the Constitution. Unlike the Meech Lake and Charlottetown accords, the Calgary Declaration was mostly a goodwill gesture that expressed some general principles rather than specific constitutional amendments. For example, Quebec was described as having a unique character, but this was alongside statements about the diversity and equality of all the provinces. The Calgary Declaration emphasized cooperation, multiculturalism, and the partnership between the federal and provincial/territorial governments. To date, little has come of this effort.

In the same year, the federal government decided to pursue the issue of separation by challenging Quebec's right to separate. The government asked the Supreme Court of Canada to address whether Quebec can legally make a unilateral decision (i.e., decide on its own) to separate under the Canadian Constitution, whether Quebec can unilaterally separate under international law, and which law—Canadian or international—would apply if there were a conflict between the two.

In August 1998, the Supreme Court decided that Quebec had no unilateral right to separate under Canadian or international law but that the rest of Canada could not deny Quebec's right to pursue separation if a majority of Quebeckers chose to do so. The court also decided that if a clear majority of Quebeckers voted for separation in a referendum, then the federal government had a "constitutional duty to negotiate" (Newman, 1999, Chapter 4) with Quebec. Note that the latter puts a reciprocal obligation on Quebec to negotiate. After the Court's ruling, the federal government introduced legislation in 1999 outlining how any separation vote must be conducted. The Quebec government countered with legislation of its own. The debate continues, as does the desire of some Quebeckers to secede.

Passions flared anew in 2006, when then Prime Minister Stephen Harper introduced a motion in the House of Commons stating that Quebec forms a nation "within a united Canada." The motion was intended to pre-empt a looming Bloc Québécois motion that would call for Quebec to be recognized as a nation but would not include any reference to Canada. The prime minister's motion passed by a vote of 266 to 12 but not without repercussions for his minority government: a Cabinet minister resigned in protest of what he called Harper's "ethnic nationalism" (Benzie, 2004, p. A6). Although the nation debate has faded off the political radar, the larger issue of Quebec's place in Canada will remain one of the more challenging constitutional quandaries facing Canada's politicians.[4]

The Canadian Charter of Rights and Freedoms

As mentioned earlier in this chapter, probably the most significant aspect of the *Constitution Act, 1982* was the inclusion of the *Canadian Charter of Rights and Freedoms*. Since Confederation, Canadians had enjoyed rights such as freedom of speech under **common law** (law based on past legal decisions, or precedents) and custom, but these rights were not entrenched in the BNA Act. In 1960, Prime Minister John Diefenbaker created the *Canadian Bill of Rights*, prohibiting discrimination according to race, national origin, colour, religion, or sex. However, because it was passed as a normal piece of legislation, it remained vulnerable to change or repeal by any successive government. As a federal statute, it only applied to matters under federal jurisdiction. The provinces could do as they wished.

common law
a body of law that has grown out of past court cases and is based on precedent or custom

---

4 Jean Charest's long-reigning Liberals were defeated in the September 2012 Quebec provincial election by a resurgent Parti Québécois (PQ). The PQ's unanticipated victory (in light of Quebec's federal "Orange Crush" in May 2011) has threatened to put the sovereignty debate at the forefront of national politics once more. For a broader analysis of recent federal government initiatives with regard to constitutional matters, see Hébert (2007).

The Charter, the brainchild of then Prime Minister Pierre Trudeau, gave constitutional authority to a list of fundamental rights and freedoms enjoyed by all people in Canada (see the Appendix for the full text of the Charter).

With the addition of the Charter, Canada saw its government structure shed some of its British tradition—in which Parliament is supreme and its decisions cannot be challenged—and take on more of the American tradition, where the Supreme Court is the highest power because of its right to interpret the terms of the Constitution (Wagenberg, 1992, p. 112). The Charter guarantees certain fundamental freedoms and democratic rights to all Canadians, thereby expressing the basic values of our nation, and sets out rules that all levels of government must follow.

Section 2 of the Charter sets out the fundamental freedoms:

- freedom of conscience and religion;
- freedom of thought, belief, opinion, and expression, including freedom of the press and other media;
- freedom of peaceful assembly; and
- freedom of association.

The other sections set out various rights, declare Canada's official bilingualism, explain how rights and freedoms are enforced, and describe how the Charter applies to all levels of government. Sections 7–14 set out legal rights, which apply to anyone in Canada and are particularly relevant to law enforcement. These legal rights include

- the right to life, liberty, and security of the person;
- the right to be secure against unreasonable search and seizure;
- the right not to be arbitrarily detained or imprisoned;
- on arrest or detention, the right to be informed promptly of the reason for arrest and the specific offence;
- the right to retain counsel;
- the right to be tried within a reasonable time; and
- the right to be presumed innocent until proven guilty.

The Charter is a fundamental piece of legislation that law enforcement officers need to understand and apply conscientiously. As part of the Constitution, the Charter must be considered in concert with other Canadian criminal and civil laws and also applies to the actions of government and its representatives—for example, law enforcement officers. Thus anyone who believes that Charter rights are being contravened by any federal or provincial law can dispute that law in court and, conceivably, have it declared unconstitutional by the court. Similarly, if a court finds that an accused person's rights have been contravened at any step in the judicial process by any agent of the state, such as a law enforcement officer, the charge against the accused may be stayed.

Limits on Charter Rights

Included within the Charter's guarantees of rights are some limits to those rights. Two of the most important qualifiers are discussed here. First is the "reasonable limits" clause in section 1:

> 1. The *Canadian Charter of Rights and Freedoms* guarantees the rights and freedoms set out in it subject only to such reasonable limits prescribed by law as can be demonstrably justified in a free and democratic society.

This means that Charter rights can be overridden if the government can prove that an apparent Charter violation is a reasonable limit. For example, when police officers conduct a RIDE (Reduce Impaired Driving Everywhere) program, they are allowed to detain motorists because doing so is seen as a reasonable limit that can prevent motorists and others from harm caused by drunk drivers. Similarly, the right of freedom of speech does not extend to spreading hate literature against a particular person or group in our society.

The "notwithstanding clause" in section 33 is another limit in the Charter and one that has been the subject of much controversy:

> Parliament or the legislature of a province may expressly declare in an Act of Parliament or of the legislature, as the case may be, that the Act or a provision thereof shall operate notwithstanding a provision included in section 2 or sections 7 to 15 of this Charter.

What this means is that a government can override a section of the Charter with one of its own laws by passing legislation declaring that it is doing so. Section 33 goes on to explain the time limits on such an action. This clause seems to have been a way for Pierre Trudeau to secure the provincial premiers' approval of the Charter. Shortly after the passage of the Constitution in 1982, Quebec used the notwithstanding clause to exempt all of its legislation from the Charter, claiming that its provincial human rights code protected Quebeckers adequately. This has allowed Quebec, for example, to override the minority-language education rights that are set out in section 23 of the Charter. The province also invoked the clause in the late 1980s in order to exempt Bill 178, Quebec's French-only sign law, from a Supreme Court decision declaring it unconstitutional.

An Expanded Role for the Courts

The Charter has effectively shifted some power from the government to the courts, whose role now includes interpreting the impact of any legislation on Charter rights. Individuals as well as special interest groups are challenging legislation and government policy in ways that were not possible before 1982. What were once political issues are increasingly becoming legal issues, and some people see this new power of the courts—and of the people who challenge the Charter—as dangerous. In a democratic system that is based on representatives being elected by citizens, should judges, who are appointed, have the right to overturn laws and policies made by our elected representatives?

This complex question has no simple answer, and it is being hotly debated by academics, lawyers, and concerned citizens. Some believe that the courts, particularly the Supreme Court of Canada, have too much political power, while others believe that this new role of the courts is exactly what is needed to make sure our politicians uphold the laws of the land, including the rights of citizens.

Get Real!

Freedom Versus Security

The *Canadian Charter of Rights and Freedoms* is intended to protect Canadians from governments and their representatives. It formed a key part of former prime minister Pierre Trudeau's vision for a "just society" (Axworthy & Trudeau, 1990; "Canada Must Be a Just Society," September 9, 1968)—a place where individual difference could be accommodated within a larger framework of communal values. While this sounds reasonable, in practice it is often difficult.

Take, for example, six-year-old Canadian-born Syed Adam Ahmed from Markham, Ontario, who ran into trouble at Toronto's Pearson International Airport one December morning as he and his dad were on their way to Boston to catch the NHL Winter Classic. The young boy had to go through an extra security check because he was identified as "DHP"—Deemed High Profile—on Canada's no-fly list—known as the Passenger Protect Program. While Ahmed has encountered the same problem numerous times since he was a toddler, it wasn't until his father, Sulemaan Ahmed, tweeted out a picture of an airport computer monitor showing his son's DHP status on December 31, 2015, that the situation garnered media attention ("Markham boy," 2016).

While it is clearly a mistake that the young Ahmed was included on the list, the problem hasn't gone away. In fact, a group called the #NoFlyListKids was created by a group of concerned Canadian families who say it represents more than 60 children who get flagged as on the list (#NoFlyListKids, 2017). The group wants changes made to Canada's travel and security regulations so this type of situation stops. "The current system results in false-positives and unnecessary secondary screening for children whose names match those on Canada's no-fly list, also known as the Passenger Protect Program," reads the group's website page (#NoFlyListKids, 2017).

The Passenger Protect Program was first created in 2007 in response to a growing number of terrorist attacks occurring aboard airplanes. At that time, people on the no-fly list were those deemed "immediate threats" to security—although even that definition proved challenging for authorities to define (Friscolanti, 2015). What exactly constitutes an immediate threat?

In 2015, the federal government made amendments to the Passenger Protect Program with legislation called the *Anti-Terrorism Act*. Among a number of controversial elements of the act was a broadened scope of those included on the no-fly list. Some critics pointed out that these changes were an overreaction to an attack months earlier when a lone gunman shot and killed Corporal Nathan Cirillo, who was standing sentry down the street from Parliament. Immediately afterward, the assassin entered Parliament, where he was shot and killed. With the legislation, a person can now be added to the list if there are "reasonable grounds" that the individual will engage or attempt to engage in an act that would threaten transportation security, or if there are reasonable grounds that the person is attempting to travel abroad to commit terrorism ("Safeguarding Canadians," June 20, 2016).

While the government won't reveal how many names are now on the list, there are a growing number of complaints documented in media reports from adults and families of children who are affected by faults in the no-fly list. A person whose name matches that of someone on the no-fly list who attempts to board a plane can be flagged for security reasons. If that happens, the airline has to confirm the passenger's identity and inform Transport Canada, causing delays and discomfort for those falsely implicated by the list.

Although promises have been made by the federal government to fix the problem, including the creation of a Passenger Protect Inquiries Office, the fix is slow in coming for those who face delays when boarding (Elkaim, May 31, 2017). While it is obvious that all travellers want to know that safety is a primary concern for the services being used, this experience provides a poignant example of how easy it is to trade off aspects of our democratic freedoms in our haste to feel more secure. What if your name were flagged by the list every time you tried to board a plane in Canada? To what lengths do you think governments should be able to go in order to protect people from potential security threats? Is it acceptable to inconvenience or limit the freedoms of fellow Canadians to do so?

CHAPTER SUMMARY

More than 100 years after Confederation, Canada finally brought home its Constitution in 1982. The central documents of our current *Constitution Act, 1982* are the *British North America Act*, now called the *Constitution Act, 1867*, and the *Canadian Charter of Rights and Freedoms*. However, we are still struggling as a nation to reach a consensus on many related issues, particularly Quebec's assent to the Constitution.

Several attempts have been made to incorporate the conditions that Quebec believes are necessary prerequisites to signing the Constitution. These attempts included the Meech Lake and Charlottetown accords, both of which failed to win the support of a majority of provinces. Attempts at constitutional reform continue but have taken a back seat to other issues in recent years.

The Charter has significance in our everyday lives and in the institutions of government. The Charter enshrines rights and freedoms in the Constitution that previously existed only as part of Canadian common law and custom. As a result, it has had significant implications for our political system, particularly in terms of the increased power of the judiciary, which has, many argue, become a third branch of government (a topic that is discussed in more detail in Chapter 4). In a post-9/11 world, the challenge for Canadian government officials is to strike a balance between preserving Charter rights and freedoms and ensuring national security.

KEY TERMS

amending formula, 38

Canadian Charter of Rights and Freedoms, 39

common law, 45

patriation, 38

WEBSITES

1981: Aboriginal People Fight for Constitutional Protection. CBC Digital Archives. Retrieved from http://www.cbc.ca/archives/entry/1981-native-people-fight-for-constitutional-protection

1982: Trudeau Brings Home the Constitution: http://www.cbc.ca/archives/entry/proclamation-of-canadas-constitution

1995 Quebec Referendum: http://www.cbc.ca/archives/tag/1995+quebec+referendum/

Canadian Charter of Rights and Freedoms: http://laws-lois.justice.gc.ca/eng/Const/page-15.html

Constitution Act: http://laws-lois.justice.gc.ca/eng/Const/page-15.html

Forum Questions Trudeau on his criticism of the Meech Lake Accord: http://www.cbc.ca/player/play/1766147078

Meech Lake Accord: http://www.cbc.ca/archives/tag/1995+quebec+referendum/

The Road to Patriation: http://www.nfb.ca/film/road_to_patriation/

Supreme Court of Canada: http://www.scc-csc.ca

Supreme Court of Canada for Quebec Secession: https://www.canlii.org/en/ca/scc/doc/1998/1998canlii793/1998canlii793.html

REFERENCE LIST

Axworthy, A., & Trudeau, P.E. (Eds.). (1990). *Towards a just society: The Trudeau years*. Toronto: Viking Books.

Benzie, R. (2004, December 6). Premiers hail birth of council of the federation. *Toronto Star*, p. A6.

Canada Act 1982 (UK), 1982, c 11

Canada must be a just society. (1968, September 9). CBC Digital Archives. Retrieved from http://www.cbc.ca/player/play/1797431608

Canadian Charter of Rights and Freedoms, Part I of the *Constitution Act, 1982*, being Schedule B to the *Canada Act 1982* (UK), 1982, c 11.

Elkaim, A.V. (2017, May 31). Canadian executives demanding action on no-fly list glitches. iPolitics. Retrieved from http://ipolitics.ca/2017/05/31/canadian-executives-demanding-action-on-no-fly-list-glitches/

Finkel, A., & Conrad, M. with Strong-Boag, V. (1993). *History of the Canadian peoples* (Vol. 2: *1867 to the present*). Toronto: Copp Clark Pitman.

Francis, R.D., Jones, R., & Smith, D.B. (2000). *Destinies: Canadian history since Confederation* (4th ed.). Toronto: Thomson Nelson.

Friscolanti, F. (2015, February 5). Canada's evolving no-fly list—and why changes to it were inevitable. *Maclean's*. Retrieved from http://www.macleans.ca/news/canada/the-evolution-of-canadas-no-fly-list-and-why-it-was-inevitable/

Graham, R., (2011). *The last act: Pierre Trudeau, the gang of eight, and the fight for Canada*. Toronto: Allen Lane Canada.

Hébert, C. (2007). *French kiss: Stephen Harper's blind date with Quebec*. Toronto: Knopf Canada.

Historica Canada. (n.d.). Retrieved from http://www
.thecanadianencyclopedia.ca/en/

MacMillan, M. (2001). *Paris 1919.* New York: Random House.

Markham boy, 6, on no-fly list, parents say. (2016, January 3).
CBC News. Retrieved from http://www.cbc.ca/news/canada
/toronto/markham-security-travel-watchlist-1.3387890

Maton, F. (1996). In Spicer Commission 1991: Citizens'
Forum on Canadian Unity. Retrieved from http://www
.solon.org/Constitutions/Canada/English/Committees
/Spicer/spicer_1.html

Newman, W.J. (1999). *The Quebec secession reference: The rule
of law and the position of the attorney general of Canada.*
Toronto: York University Centre for Public Law and Public
Policy.

#NoFlyListKids. Accessed June 4, 2017. Retrieved from http://
noflylistkids.ca/en/

Pearson, L.B. (1964, October 15). First among equals: The prime
minister in Canadian life and politics. Address to the Empire
Club at the Royal York Hotel, Toronto. Library and Archives
Canada. Retrieved from http://www.collectionscanada.gc
.ca/2/4/h4-4086-e.html

Roach, R. (2003, July 15). A "Council of the Federation" is just the
beginning. *The Globe and Mail,* p. A15.

Russell, P.H. (2002). Provincial rights. In R.D. Francis & D.B. Smith
(Eds.), *Readings in Canadian history: Post-Confederation*
(6th ed., pp. 21–33). Toronto: Thomson Nelson.

Safeguarding Canadians with passenger protect. (2016, June
20). Public Safety Canada. Retrieved from https://www
.publicsafety.gc.ca/cnt/ntnl-scrt/cntr-trrrsm/pssngr-prtct
/index-en.aspx

Statute of Westminster. (1931). 22 Geo V, c 4 (UK).

The Constitution Act, 1982, Schedule B to the Canada Act 1982
(UK), 1982, c 1

Wagenberg, R.H. (1992). The institutions of the Canadian state.
In Pryke, K.G. & Soderlund, W.C. (Eds.), *Profiles of Canada.*
Toronto: Copp Clark Pitman.

EXERCISES
True or False?

_____ **1.** Under the BNA Act, the Canadian government
simply passed legislation when it wanted to amend
the Act.

_____ **2.** Canada's current Constitution is called the *Canada Act.*

_____ **3.** Before the *Canadian Charter of Rights and Freedoms*
was added to the Constitution, Canadians enjoyed
rights under common law and by custom.

_____ **4.** The Charter has no effect on the justice system or on
how law enforcement officers do their job.

_____ **5.** The Charter grants unlimited fundamental rights and
freedoms to all Canadians.

Multiple Choice

1. Since 1982, government constitutional negotiations have
centred on

a. redefining federal and provincial government powers

b. obtaining Quebec's signature to the *Constitution Act, 1982*

c. reforming the Senate

d. addressing the concerns of various groups in Canadian
society

e. all of the above

2. The Charter is a significant part of our Constitution because it

a. changed the Canadian political system from one based
in British tradition to a system more like that of the
United States

b. is above all other law

c. enshrines specific rights for all Canadians

d. limits government legislation and policies

e. all of the above

3. The rights and freedoms set out in the Charter

a. can be limited by the federal and provincial
governments

b. can be limited by the "reasonable limits" and
"notwithstanding" clauses

c. have no limits

d. can be ignored by the courts

e. a and b

4. The *Canadian Charter of Rights and Freedoms* is relevant to
law enforcement because it

a. defines the rights of citizens, including those of persons
accused of committing offences

b. limits the actions of government and its agents in
maintaining public order

c. gives law enforcement officers the right to decide what
constitutes reasonable limits on citizens' behaviour

d. all of the above

e. a and b

5. The expanded role of the Canadian courts since the passing of the Charter is controversial because now

   a. the courts are more powerful than the government

   b. appointed judges interpret the Charter and make decisions that affect laws and policies created by elected politicians

   c. the courts are responsible for making laws

   d. the courts can overturn any law or policy they don't like

   e. all of the above

Short Answer

1. Explain why Quebec has not signed the *Constitution Act, 1982*. What are its main concerns?

2. In order to amend the Constitution, what has to happen first?

3. Why have the federal and provincial governments attempted constitutional reform? What are they trying to achieve?

4. List some advantages and disadvantages of having a powerful judiciary as part of our political structure.

5. Describe how the *Canadian Charter of Rights and Freedoms* affects you now and will affect you in a future career in law enforcement.

Welcome to the Machine: Canadian Political Structure and Its Operation

4

LEARNING OUTCOMES

After completing this chapter, you should be able to

- define and differentiate the terms "representative government" and "responsible government";
- understand the structure and roles of the three levels of government;
- explain how laws are enacted at the three levels of government; and
- describe the status of First Nations within our political structure.

Introduction

Chapter 3 discussed the historical context underlying Canadian politics and how the country's evolution informs current government action. This chapter focuses on the "nuts and bolts" of political structure—that is, how various people and groups organize themselves within government to achieve political aims. What democratic traditions underlie Canada's parliamentary tradition? How are laws created and debated? What is the relationship among various systems of government, and how do they compare with one another? How does Indigenous government function in the Canadian political context? This chapter addresses these and other questions.

Parliament Hill, Ottawa

What Is Representative Government?

Imagine for a moment that your college has decided to allow students to choose the colour to paint the classrooms. What is the most democratic way the institution could arrive at a decision? Your response might be, "Ask every student." This sounds straightforward, but in schools where enrollment is literally in the thousands, it would take a very long time, and, worse, some students might change their minds. Further, by the time the entire student body had been consulted, the school year might be over, with an entirely new group of students arriving in the fall. In short, democracy taken to an extreme is simply too time-consuming and achieves little in the way of results.

So what is the most efficient way to decide what colour to paint the classrooms? Well, you could decide based on your individual preference, but this would be seen as blatantly undemocratic and would therefore lack the support of your fellow students. Another solution might be to select a number of students—say, one from each program—to poll their respective peers and bring the results to a meeting where a vote could be held on each colour. In this way, democratic consultation and administrative efficiency would be accommodated to an acceptable degree. Voila! You have just created a representative system of consultation. Representative government works on the very same principle.

In a **representative government**, people are elected by geographic area to represent the concerns of the people living in that area. It is a fundamental principle of democracy. Canada has a representative government that is based on members elected by citizens to represent their interests. Similarly, the provincial and territorial governments have members elected by citizens to represent their interests.

Critics of Canada's system of representative forms of government argue that the tradition of party loyalty (whereby each leader can instruct members of his or her party whether to vote for or against a particular bill) deters representatives from reflecting the views of their constituents on political issues. Further, they argue, the tendency of senior politicians (prime ministers, premiers, and Cabinet ministers) to dominate policy-making and the legislative agenda subverts the original spirit of representative democracy. This, they contend, is responsible for growing public apathy about elections and a lack of respect for the functions of government. As you will see, this has also led to calls for reforms to Canada's electoral system.

As discussed in Chapter 1, a move in this direction is very dangerous because it has a direct impact on respect for the rule of law and those who defend it (police and the courts). Recent moves by provincial and federal governments to address the "democratic deficit" suggest that they recognize the importance of protecting political integrity.[1] These initiatives are an encouraging sign, but whether they will reinvigorate public attitudes remains to be seen.

representative government
government that is based on members elected by citizens to represent their interests

Elections in Canada

In Canada, elections can be called at the discretion of the prime minister on the advice of the governor general at the federal level, and at the discretion of premiers in consultation with their respective viceregal representatives at the provincial level.

However, in 2007, federal legislation was passed that fixes a date for an election every four years, on the third Monday of October. For example, because the last federal election was held on Monday, October 19, 2015, the next one is currently scheduled for Monday, October 19, 2019. This follows similar legislation passed by all provinces and territories, excluding Nova Scotia, Nunavut, and Yukon, that began with British Columbia in 2001. Of course, exceptions can be made to these fixed dates in times of public emergency, such as war or domestic and regional crises.[2] Municipal election schedules vary from province to province. Municipal elections in Ontario used to be held every three years; however, in 2006 and 2009, the province made amendments to the *Municipal Elections Act* (1996) that changed this practice. Now municipal elections are to take place every four years, on the fourth Monday of October (the first election under these rules took place in 2010).[3]

---

1   Former prime minister Paul Martin made the "democratic deficit" a key issue for his government ("Martin urges parliamentary reform," 2002). Former prime minister Stephen Harper, for his part, focused on Senate reform, election timing, and government accountability ("Harper promises bill," 2006). Responding to similar concerns, the Ontario government commissioned a panel to examine options for electoral reform, which released its report in 2007. The panel's recommendation for the introduction of a system of election based on proportional representation was rejected by a solid majority of Ontario voters in a referendum on the issue in the fall 2007 election. For report details, see Ontario Citizens' Assembly on Electoral Reform (2007).

2   For further details and the complete list of fixed federal and provincial election dates across Canada, see Parliament of Canada (n.d.).

3   For a schedule of municipal elections dates, see Muniscope (n.d.).

One of the major players in an election is the candidate who is running for office. (The other major player, the constituent or voter, is discussed in Chapter 11.) The rules and regulations governing candidacy are contained in the *Canada Elections Act* (1985) and its counterparts at the provincial and territorial levels. With a few exceptions, the rules are similar. You must be a resident of Canada and be eligible to vote. You cannot currently be serving as a political representative at another level, and you must be innocent of any corrupt political practices for the previous five years. You are also disqualified if you are imprisoned or are an election officer. Most judges and some Crown attorneys are also prohibited from running.[4] Federal candidates must collect 100 signatures of fellow electors and give a deposit of $1,000. In Ontario, only 25 signatures are required, and there is no fee; for municipal elections, no signatures are required, but there is a fee of $100 (the fee is $200 for candidates seeking leadership positions such as mayor or reeve[5]).

What Is Responsible Government?

responsible government
government that is responsible to the wishes of its citizens, as embodied in their elected representatives

The concept of responsible government is another central principle characterizing democratic countries such as Canada, where the system of government is based on a parliamentary model. The principle of **responsible government** requires that the government may govern only as long as it has the support (or confidence) of a majority of the state's elected representatives.

Majority or Minority?

member of Parliament
an elected representative in the House of Commons who represents a riding

If a majority votes against the government on a bill of major importance, then that government must resign, thus dissolving Parliament. In almost all cases, this results in an election call to allow voters to decide which party will form the next government. In Canada's 338-seat House of Commons, for example, a simple majority of 169 **members of Parliament** (MPs) voting against a major government bill would trigger this event. (The Speaker of the House does not cast a vote unless there is a tie.)

party loyalty
the requirement that all members of a political party vote according to the wishes of their leader

In reality, however, this rarely happens because of another parliamentary tradition called party loyalty. **Party loyalty** (discussed earlier) demands that all members of a particular political party vote according to the wishes of their leader. In other words, they are not free to vote as they wish, unless expressly permitted to do so by their leader. Of course, members may break with their party by refusing to vote along party lines, but they do so at the risk of being thrown out of their party. This means that as long as the government—that is, the political party with the most elected representatives—can convince 169 or more MPs in the House of Commons to vote in its favour, it can continue to hold power.

majority government
a government whose members make up more than half of the total MPs in the House of Commons

Observing the principle of responsible government is particularly easy when 169 or more MPs belong to the same party. In this situation, the party forms what is called a **majority government**, because its members constitute a majority in the legislature.

---

4 For more details, see Elections Canada (2017).

5 For information about candidacy in federal elections, see Elections Canada (n.d.). For Ontario, see Ontario Ministry of Municipal Affairs and Housing (2016).

But what happens when a federal political party ends up with more MPs than the other parties but fails to achieve the number required for a majority? In this case, a **minority government** is formed. As you can probably tell, minority governments are much more unstable because opposition MPs outnumber, and can therefore outvote, the government on any bill.

There are advantages and disadvantages to each situation. Majority governments tend to be more productive because they can use their greater numbers, through party discipline, to outvote opposition members as a bill makes its way through the legislative process (discussed later in this chapter). They also don't need to worry about losing their mandate through an opposition-sponsored, non-confidence vote—a vote to replace the government because it has lost the confidence of the majority of the House. Thus, within the five-year limit required by the Constitution, majority governments are free to decide when the next election will be held. Most governments typically wait about four years before issuing an election call. The four-year election cycle mentioned earlier operates only when a sitting government hasn't called an election or some other unforeseen event, such as the proroguing of Parliament (the ending of a parliamentary session), disrupts the timeline. Majority governments are often criticized for being insensitive to different viewpoints and may be perceived by constituents as being arrogant and undemocratic.

Minority governments face almost the opposite set of challenges. They are forced to listen to opposition concerns, which often lead to political compromises or further consideration. This situation makes minority governments inherently unproductive and short-lived. The cooperative consultative practices inherent in minority governments can bog down the legislative process, and the opposition parties may outvote—and thus defeat—the government at any time. The result is an unpredictable session. Despite recent trends, Canadians historically tend to elect majority governments. The minority Liberal government elected in June 2004 was the first one in 25 years. It was dissolved in 2005, after a non-confidence vote, and replaced by successive Conservative minority governments in 2006 and 2008. Before this, the last minority government, led by Joe Clark, was elected in 1979 and lasted less than a year—from May 1979 to February 1980—before it was defeated.

> **minority government**
> a government that has the greatest number of MPs in the House of Commons but not more than half of the total MPs

Electoral Reform

We often hear candidates on election day say that voters will make their opinions known at the ballot box and the results will express their collective wishes. While this is certainly true, the political outcome of any election depends in large part upon the type of system that is used to calculate votes and reflect voter preferences. Traditionally, Canadians have voted using what is known as the "first-past-the-post" (FPTP) approach, where the candidate receiving the most votes wins. One manifestation of what are known as "majoritarian" voting systems, this formula does produce one clear winner. However, critics argue that it often distorts overall electoral results and does not accurately reflect democratic will (Fair Vote Canada, n.d.). Figure 4.1 illustrates how this can occur. Say you live in a community of 1,000 eligible voters. At the end of the night, candidate A has received 350 votes (35 percent), candidate B 300 votes (30 percent), candidate C 250 votes (25 percent), and candidate D 100 votes (10 percent). In this scenario, candidate A wins—that is, takes 100 percent of the political power—even though 65 percent of the electorate voted against him or her. These voters' political viewpoints have, for all intents and purposes, been sidelined.

Because of this characteristic, most modern democracies are moving to some form of **proportional representation** (PR) voting system, which seeks to distribute political

> **proportional representation**
> a distribution of political power in direct proportion to votes cast

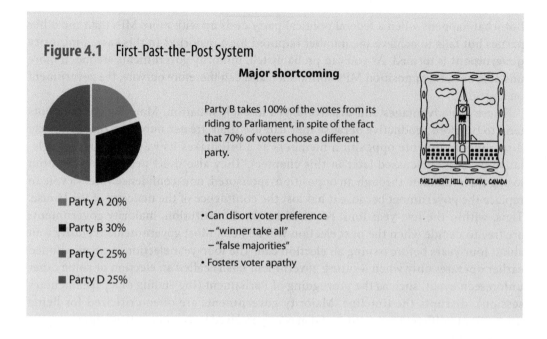

Figure 4.1   First-Past-the-Post System

Major shortcoming

Party B takes 100% of the votes from its riding to Parliament, in spite of the fact that 70% of voters chose a different party.

PARLIAMENT HILL, OTTAWA, CANADA

■ Party A 20%

■ Party B 30%

■ Party C 25%

■ Party D 25%

• Can disort voter preference
  – "winner take all"
  – "false majorities"
• Fosters voter apathy

power in direct proportion to votes cast. So, using the same results as above, each candidate's party would receive its respective percentage of seats in the legislature in accordance with the percentage of voters supporting it. Moving to this form of electoral system would require a major overhaul of Canada's existing system, requiring parties to draw up lists of candidates not tied to any particular geographic area, as well as the redrawing of constituency boundaries to accommodate multiple members—which explains, in part, why doing so appears to have unnerved politicians and voters alike. For example, one of the central planks of the federal Liberal 2015 campaign pledged to end the FPTP system of voting, but just a year later, the government announced it was abandoning the initiative. Similarly, referendums have been held in the provinces of British Columbia and Ontario to introduce electoral reform measures, and neither jurisdiction garnered the required voter support.[6]

As with majoritarian systems, there are also many variations to proportional representation formats, but a quick comparison of the 2015 federal election showing actual (FPTP) results and a simple allocation of seats by PR underscores how different systems configure the political landscape (see Figure 4.2).

Structure of the Federal Government

In democratic countries such as Canada, power is usually separated into three main categories: executive, legislative, and judicial. The federal government is organized according to these three branches, and this structure informs its day-to-day operations (see Figure 4.3).

---

6 Voters in British Columbia were asked in 2005 and 2009 to consider adopting a single-transferable-vote (STV) format as part of a general provincial election ("Final referendum results," 2005; "British columbia votes," 2009). In 2007, Ontario voters failed to support a proposal to consider moving to a system of mixed-member proportional representation ("Ontario rejects electoral reform," 2007).

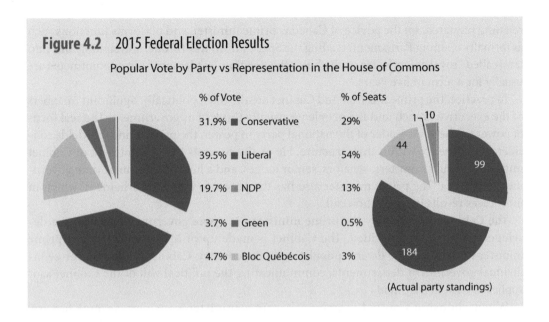

Figure 4.2   2015 Federal Election Results

Popular Vote by Party vs Representation in the House of Commons

% of Vote		% of Seats
31.9%	■ Conservative	29%
39.5%	■ Liberal	54%
19.7%	■ NDP	13%
3.7%	■ Green	0.5%
4.7%	■ Bloc Québécois	3%

(Actual party standings)

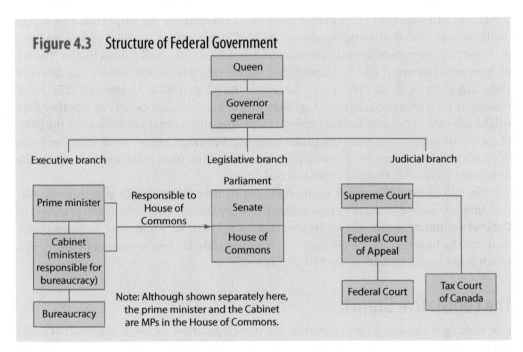

Figure 4.3   Structure of Federal Government

Note: Although shown separately here, the prime minister and the Cabinet are MPs in the House of Commons.

The Executive Branch

The **executive branch** of the federal government includes the current reigning British monarch (e.g., Queen Elizabeth II), the governor general (the monarch's representative in Canada), the prime minister, the Cabinet, and the ministries and departments that provide government goods and services. In a parliamentary system, the power to govern rests here.

Although the British sovereign is officially Canada's head of state, this role includes no active responsibilities apart from the formal appointment of the governor general, who is always chosen by the prime minister. The governor general acts as the Crown's representative in Canada, although the relationship is entirely ceremonial in nature, hearkening back to our colonial ties to the British Empire. The governor general is appointed by the

executive branch (federal)
the branch of government that includes the monarch's representative (governor general), the elected head of state (prime minister), and Cabinet

reigning monarch, on the advice of Canada's prime minister, and performs functions such as formally opening Parliament, reading the Speech from the Throne, and signing bills into law (called "royal assent"). He or she holds the position "at pleasure," but appointments are usually for a term of five years.

In practice, the prime minister and Cabinet are the most politically significant members of the executive branch and the people we usually think of as government. The real locus of power lies here. As leader of the national party in power, the prime minister wields considerable influence within this structure. He or she controls the appointment of Cabinet ministers, deputy ministers, senators, senior judges, and a host of other important government positions. The prime minister also has the power to dissolve Parliament, which in most cases results in an election call.

The **Cabinet**—chaired by the prime minister—is where government policies are developed, debated, and decided. The Cabinet is made up of MPs selected by the prime minister to represent the diverse population of the country. Cabinet ministers oversee individual government departments, communicating the political will of the Cabinet as it applies to each department.

When choosing Cabinet members, a prime minister considers several factors. Primary among these (although not legally required) is that the person be elected to the House of Commons. This expectation helps underscore the importance of direct public accountability through elections. As well, a person's education, career, and experience in government are also considered. Choices are also influenced by the "theory of representativeness," which dictates that public officials should reflect the diversity and complexity of those they serve. Therefore, the geographical location of MPs' main residence, their ethnic background, gender, and other traits are factors in whether they will be selected to become Cabinet ministers. Finally, individuals are chosen on the basis of their past relationship with the prime minister. Because Cabinet represents the locus of power in a parliamentary democracy, it is vital that the team work together under the direction of its leader, in good times and bad.

Although individual Cabinet ministers may privately disagree with government policies, they are bound to support government action publicly. This reflects the principle of **Cabinet solidarity**, which allows the government to speak with one voice on given policy matters. The bureaucracy, or civil service, is responsible for implementing political will, which is examined in detail in Part III of this text.

Cabinet
the government body that consists of MPs, appointed by the prime minister, who oversee government departments and act as advisers in major policy areas

Cabinet solidarity
the united front that Cabinet presents on given policy matters, although individual Cabinet ministers may privately be opposed

The Legislative Branch

Law-making is a major government role, and most legislation, or law, is the result of political initiatives that are designed to implement the political wishes of those we have elected to represent us in Parliament. The **legislative branch** consists of those government bodies that are responsible for passing legislation. At the federal level, this branch includes the two Houses of Parliament: the House of Commons (the lower chamber) and the Senate (the upper chamber).

legislative branch (federal)
the law-making branch of government (House of Commons and Senate)

Proceedings in each chamber are overseen by the Speaker, who is elected from among the current MPs or, in the case of the Senate, selected by the prime minister. Once in that position, the Speaker assumes a neutral, non-partisan role, maintaining order and ensuring respect for the rules of Parliament.

House of Commons

The House of Commons is currently made up of 338 MPs representing the 338 geographic areas—called ridings or constituencies—into which Canada has been divided. Ridings vary in size according to population, with each containing approximately 100,000 Canadians. When an election is held, candidates in each riding compete to get the most voter support. The candidate with the most votes becomes the MP for that riding. As has already been noted, this is known as a "first-past-the-post" system of election.

The party with the second-highest number of MPs elected forms the official Opposition. These MPs, along with the other non-government members of the House, hold the governing party publicly accountable and responsible for its actions. They also participate in passing legislation and represent their respective constituencies.

Senate

Unlike the elected members of the House of Commons, senators are appointed by the governor general on the advice of the prime minister and Cabinet. Senators can introduce certain types of bills and also review and, if they deem necessary, amend legislation that has been approved by the House of Commons. The Senate also reviews proposed legislation and may choose to reject it. For this reason, the Senate is known as the chamber of "sober second thought." Senators must be at least 30 years old, and they may hold office until aged 75. Of the 105 seats in the Senate, Ontario and Quebec have 24 each; Nova Scotia and New Brunswick have 10 each; Alberta, British Columbia, Manitoba, Newfoundland and Labrador, and Saskatchewan have 6 each; Prince Edward Island has 4; and the Northwest Territories, Nunavut, and Yukon have 1 each.

The Senate's representative scope and powers were the subject of much debate going into Confederation; in fact, Senate reform proposals are one of the oldest themes in Canadian political history. Most recently, this debate has focused on the fact that members of the Senate are not elected and therefore not directly accountable to the Canadian public. As well, the Senate has become a patronage reward for friends of the prime minister and those loyal to his or her party. A general perception exists that as long as senators are appointed, this House has no legitimacy. Alleged financial mismanagement and the questionable behaviour of some senators during the past few years have only deepened public mistrust. This has led to calls for what has become known as a **triple E Senate**—one that is equal, elected, and effective. The logic is that if an equal number of senators were elected from each province, then the Senate would function as it was originally intended and its integrity would thereby be restored. In the United States, for example, voters in each state, regardless of size or population, elect two senators to Congress to counterbalance the House of Representatives, where state representation is determined by population. At present, Alberta is the only province to have passed provincial legislation to introduce a framework for electing its senators. Some politicians in other provinces have also declared their support for such legislation, while still others have called for the abolition of the upper chamber altogether. The long-standing debate over Senate reform will likely continue.[7]

triple E Senate
a Senate that is equal, elected, and effective

How Federal Law Is Made

A proposed law is called a **bill**. There are three different kinds of bills: government, private members', and private. All bills are not created equal: successful navigation through Parliament's legislative labyrinth depends to a large extent on who has sponsored the voyage.

bill
a proposed law

---

7   For a detailed analysis of past Senate reform proposals, see Barnes, Bédard, Hyslop, Spano, Paré, & Robertson (2011).

government bill
a bill proposed by a member of Cabinet

Government bills are introduced by Cabinet members and concern national matters. Only this category of bill can involve spending public money or imposing taxes. Not surprisingly, government bills almost always pass. This is because the legislation in question has the support of the governing party, which can take advantage of the principle of party loyalty to ensure passage.

private member's bill
a bill proposed by a non-Cabinet MP

Private members' bills are sponsored by either backbench MPs (members of the governing party who do not sit in Cabinet) or opposition MPs. These bills are normally used to propose an alternative to existing government policy or to embarrass the government into action, so they are usually defeated or sidelined by the governing party. It is only because of parliamentary reforms approved in 1998 that these bills are even allowed to be discussed. For a private member's bill to pass into law, it must have strong public support and relate to a national concern. For example, for years some people have believed that Canada should have a national holiday in February called Heritage Day. Every now and then, a private member's bill surfaces to propose such a holiday.

private bill
a bill proposed by a senator

Private bills are always introduced in the Senate and almost always pass. They deal with minor issues, such as professional designations, that concern a person or a group of people—for example, authorizing the Chartered Professional Accountants of Canada to use the professional designation of "chartered professional accountant."

The overwhelming power of a governing party to control the legislative process has caused many MPs and members of the public to criticize this practice and has led to some parliamentary reform, but the Cabinet remains a dominant force in setting the legislative agenda.

Former Canadian Governor General Michaëlle Jean meeting former US President Barack Obama.

The various kinds of bills must all pass through Parliament and the Senate for approval before becoming law. Figure 4.4 summarizes the process. Once a bill receives royal assent, the bill becomes an act and is given a statute number. In theory, the Queen, through the governor general, could withhold assent and refuse to sign the bill, preventing it from becoming law. This has never happened in Canada. The Queen could also withdraw her assent within two years, but this, too, has never happened. The relationship of the Crown to the political leader was clarified in 1926 through a series of events that became known as the King–Byng Affair. Prime Minister William Lyon Mackenzie King, leading a new minority government, asked Governor General Lord Byng to dissolve Parliament after losing the support of the Progressive Party over a Custom Department scandal. Byng refused and instead asked Conservative leader Arthur Meighan to form a government. Within days, the Meighan administration was defeated on a motion of non-confidence. In the election that followed, King's Liberals were vaulted into a majority. The incident ended any uncertainty regarding the deference of governors general to the wishes of Canada's elected representatives and led to the passage of the *Statute of Westminster* (discussed in Chapter 3).[8] As a result, royal assent is only a formality. The governor general's role is merely ceremonial and carries no political power.

---

8   For a brief summary, see Bélanger (2001).

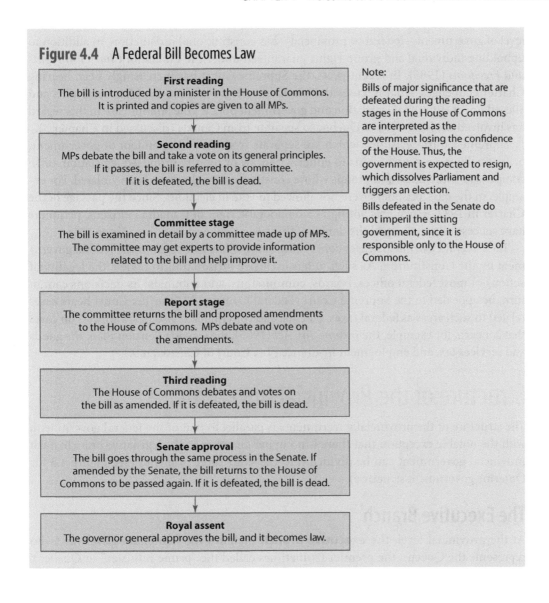

Figure 4.4   A Federal Bill Becomes Law

First reading
The bill is introduced by a minister in the House of Commons. It is printed and copies are given to all MPs.

Second reading
MPs debate the bill and take a vote on its general principles. If it passes, the bill is referred to a committee. If it is defeated, the bill is dead.

Committee stage
The bill is examined in detail by a committee made up of MPs. The committee may get experts to provide information related to the bill and help improve it.

Report stage
The committee returns the bill and proposed amendments to the House of Commons. MPs debate and vote on the amendments.

Third reading
The House of Commons debates and votes on the bill as amended. If it is defeated, the bill is dead.

Senate approval
The bill goes through the same process in the Senate. If amended by the Senate, the bill returns to the House of Commons to be passed again. If it is defeated, the bill is dead.

Royal assent
The governor general approves the bill, and it becomes law.

Note:
Bills of major significance that are defeated during the reading stages in the House of Commons are interpreted as the government losing the confidence of the House. Thus, the government is expected to resign, which dissolves Parliament and triggers an election.

Bills defeated in the Senate do not imperil the sitting government, since it is responsible only to the House of Commons.

The Judicial Branch

Courts exist to enforce the principle of the rule of law. This means that all government actions must be authorized by law and there must be specific legal authority for the actions taken by government. As explained in Chapter 1, this principle is essential to our democratic system and ensures that no government official is above the law.

The **judicial branch** of government consists of the court system, which helps to legitimize the rule of law and supports the powers of the federal and provincial governments as identified in the *Constitution Act* (1982). At the federal level, the judicial branch comprises the Supreme Court of Canada, the Federal Court of Appeal, the Federal Court, and the Tax Court of Canada.

The Supreme Court consists of nine judges, including the chief justice, who are appointed by the federal government. Three judges must come from Quebec, but appointment of the rest is based only on custom: three are usually from Ontario, two from the West, and one from the Atlantic provinces. The judges may serve until they are 75 years old.

The Supreme Court is the final court of appeal in Canada, and its decisions are binding on all the lower courts, including those of the provinces. The Supreme Court also serves a political purpose in that it facilitates the operation of the federal system by deciding which

judicial branch
the branch of government that consists of the court system

level of government—federal or provincial—has constitutional jurisdiction, in addition to upholding individual and group rights guaranteed under the *Canadian Charter of Rights and Freedoms* (1985). In recent years, the Supreme Court has increasingly been hearing Charter challenges—that is, cases that deal with alleged violations of Charter rights and alleged unconstitutional legislation and government policy. One famous case in this regard has involved the legal right of Quebec to separate from Canada (discussed in Chapter 3).

Supreme Court decisions, which are separate from and independent of government, occasionally force governments to either withdraw or modify proposed legislation, or to compensate individuals and groups whose constitutional rights have been violated. For example, in the past, prisoners were not allowed to vote in elections. Since the passage of the Charter in 1982, which lists voting as a democratic right of Canadian citizens, prisoners have successfully challenged the denial of this basic right and won the right to vote.

The Federal Court hears cases concerning areas of law conferred to the federal government by the Constitution. As such, it has exclusive jurisdiction to review the legality of actions of most federal offices, boards, commissions, and tribunals. Its decisions can, in turn, be appealed to the Supreme Court (Federal Court, n.d.). The Tax Court hears cases related to such areas as federal taxes, patents, and copyrights. It also hears appeals on cases that concern, for example, the *Income Tax Act* (1985), the Canada Pension Plan, the goods and services tax, and employment insurance (Tax Court of Canada, n.d.).

Structure of the Provincial Governments

The structure of the provincial governments is parallel to that of the federal government, with the notable exception that there is no upper chamber in the legislative branch. Each provincial government can be divided into the same three branches (see Figure 4.5 for Ontario's government structure).

The Executive Branch

executive branch (provincial)
the branch of government that includes the monarch's representative (lieutenant governor), the elected head of state (premier), and the Cabinet

At the provincial level, the **executive branch** includes the lieutenant governor (who represents the Queen), the premier (sometimes called the "prime minister" in Quebec),

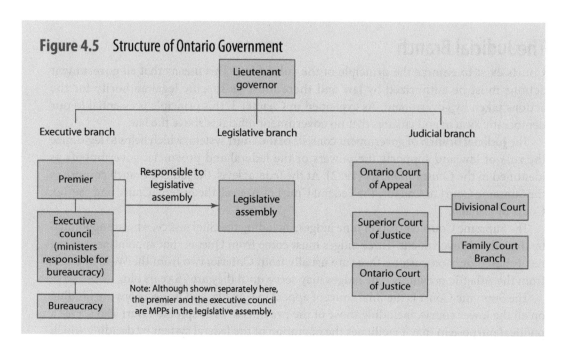

Figure 4.5 Structure of Ontario Government

and the Cabinet (sometimes called the executive council in Ontario). Cabinet members are chosen by the premier and must be elected members of the provincial legislative assembly. The lieutenant governor is formally appointed by the governor general, but the prime minister actually chooses the person for this position. The method of appointment hearkens back to Confederation. Federal politicians such as Prime Minister John A. Macdonald thought that by choosing the Crown's representative in each province, the federal government would be able to prevent provinces from acting contrary to the wishes of Ottawa. Under the *British North America Act* (BNA Act) (1867), lieutenant governors were given the power to reserve (hold) or disallow laws passed by provincial legislatures. However, provinces increasingly challenged this view, arguing that their relationship with the Crown gave them political power that was similar, rather than subordinate, to that exercised by the federal government.[9]

Again, the lieutenant governor's role is mostly ceremonial (e.g., he or she opens the Legislative Assembly), and key political decisions are made by the premier and Cabinet.

The three territories are officially administered by the federal government, which is represented by a commissioner for each territory. In reality, the commissioner has much the same role as that of the lieutenant governor of a province. Each of the territories has an elected Legislative Assembly made up of a premier and members of the Legislative Assembly (MLAs), but these governments operate on the basis of consensus rather than on party-based confrontation. The premier and Cabinet are chosen by fellow members of the Legislative Assembly by secret ballot.

The Legislative Branch

The provincial **legislative branch** is called the National Assembly in Quebec and the Legislative Assembly in all other provinces. The provincial governments differ from the federal government in that they have a unicameral (or one-House) legislature. The Legislative Assembly has its counterpart in the federal House of Commons but has no upper chamber that corresponds to the Senate.

Elected representatives of provincial governments are known as members of the Legislative Assembly (MLAs), with two exceptions. In Ontario, each representative is known as a member of provincial Parliament (MPP), and in Quebec, the term member of the National Assembly (MNA) is used. The number of sitting members in each of the provinces and territories varies in proportion to the population of the province or territory. In 2004, changes were made to provincial riding boundaries to reflect federal electoral boundary changes. This resulted in an increase in the total number of MPPs, from 103 to 107, going into the 2007 provincial election.

legislative branch (provincial)
the law-making branch of government, called the National Assembly in Quebec and the Legislative Assembly in all other provinces

How Provincial Law Is Made

The legislative assemblies of the provinces pass laws using much the same process as Parliament, except that there is no provincial equivalent to the Senate: there are three readings; a committee stage; final debate; final vote; and, finally, royal assent by the lieutenant governor. Government bills concern provincial matters and are introduced by Cabinet ministers. Private members' bills also concern provincial matters and are introduced by any other MPP. Private bills usually concern a person or corporation and

---

9 Much of the early impetus for the provincial rights movement came from Ontario Premier Oliver Mowat. For example, see Russell (2002) and Miller (2002). For a general overview, see Francis, Jones, & Smith (2000).

can be introduced by any MPP, but are often introduced by the MPP for the particular person's or corporation's riding.[10]

The Judicial Branch

This branch of government consists of the provincial courts, which do not have any real political power but uphold the laws made by the legislative branch. The judicial branch structure varies from province to province, so the names of individual courts and divisions also vary. Each province has a Superior or Supreme Court that has trial and appeal divisions. The trial division often includes small claims, family, and other courts. There may also be civil and criminal divisions. As well as the Superior Court, there are provincial courts, which may also include family, small claims, youth, and other courts. Judges are appointed by the provinces.[11]

Structure of Municipal Governments

The third level of government is municipal or local government. As mentioned in Chapter 2, the Canadian Constitution gives the provinces the responsibility for municipal governments—the municipalities themselves have no constitutional powers. It is at each province's discretion whether to create local governments and to determine what responsibilities municipal governments will have. Usually local governments are responsible for such services as roads, police, firefighting, sewers, water, and garbage collection. Schools are usually maintained separately by a school board. In Ontario, local governments are managed by a provincial law called the *Municipal Act* (1990).

municipal council
the governing body of a municipal government

Because municipal governments are a provincial responsibility, their structure varies widely. However, most tend to have a simple structure that includes only one elected body of representatives (generally with no political party affiliation)—the **municipal council**—which combines legislative and executive roles. Typically the municipal government consists of this council and its staff. The size of the council depends on the size of the municipality. There are several categories of municipality: city, town, village, rural municipality, county, or regional, district, or metropolitan municipality. Some councils have as few as 3 members, while Toronto's council currently has 1 mayor and 44 councillors, for a total of 45 members. Generally a mayor heads the council, although he or she may also be a reeve (in rural municipalities), a warden (in a county), or a chair (in a regional municipality). Council members are elected by ward (the municipal equivalent of a riding) and are known as councillors or aldermen (the term "aldermen" is falling out of favour because many are women). Municipal governments pass local laws, called **by-laws**, as well as supervise local services and hire staff for those services.

by-law
a local or municipal law

In recent years, several provinces have taken measures to decrease the number of municipalities in an effort to cut costs and reduce duplication of services. Ontario is one province that is significantly decreasing the number of municipalities, as witnessed by the formation of the Toronto "megacity" by amalgamating seven municipal governments in 1997.

---

10 For information about current and past legislation, as well as how bills become law, see Legislative Assembly of Ontario (n.d.).

11 To view the 2001 *Municipal Act* and subsequent suggestions for amendment, see Ontario Ministry of Municipal Affairs and Ministry of Housing (n.d.).

Figure 4.6 Example of Municipal Government

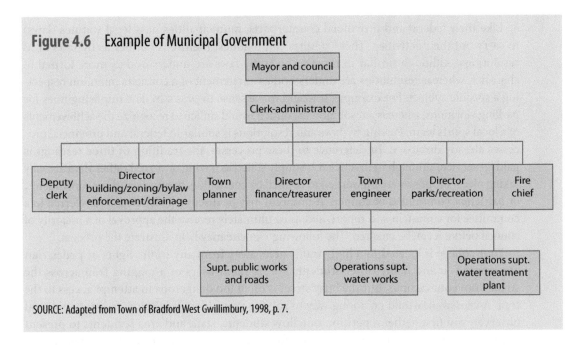

SOURCE: Adapted from Town of Bradford West Gwillimbury, 1998, p. 7.

Councils can appoint citizens to various committees to make decisions on specific responsibilities, such as local roads, recreation, libraries, water, sewers, garbage collection, firefighting, police services, and public transportation. The day-to-day running of the local government is generally handled by staff organized into various departments, which are managed by department heads reporting to either a clerk or chief administrative officer (CAO) of the municipality. The departments, for example, could be the recreation department, public works department (water, sewers, and roads), and fire department. The clerk or CAO reports directly to the council (see Figure 4.6).

Local governments can be a significant factor in our quality of life because they are responsible for administering the services and programs we enjoy every day. In recent years, some provincial governments have downloaded more and more responsibility for services to local governments without making sure that they have adequate money to provide these services. Examples of areas in which this downloading has occurred include local roads, transportation, public housing, and emergency services such as ambulances. Unfortunately, despite their importance in our everyday lives, local governments are rarely given the credit and attention they deserve.

This may be due, in part, to the tendency of mass media to focus on provincial and federal issues, in spite of the fact that the day-to-day operation of these levels of government remains at a distance from most citizens. Consider the impact that municipal services have on you every day. Did you shower this morning? The heat, electricity, and water you use most likely are managed by a local utility. By what routes do you travel to class each day? Most of the roads, traffic lights, and signs in municipalities have been established and maintained by them. Do you plan to clean the house or go for a bike ride in the park this evening? Garbage pick-up and the maintenance of local parks also constitute a significant part of the services provided by your municipality. Ironically, of the three major levels of government, municipal elections draw the lowest voter turnout. Consider this the next time municipal elections are held.

How Municipal By-Laws Are Made

The process of passing by-laws is not nearly as complicated as the process of passing federal and provincial laws. The municipal council votes on by-laws proposed by its members and municipality staff, and passes those that have the support of a majority of council members.

Like their federal and provincial counterparts, municipalities pass legal statutes (laws) to carry out their activities. These statutes can manifest themselves either as by-laws or as resolutions. Although similar in most respects, by-laws are understood as more formal in character, whereas resolutions are understood as a statement of a council's intention respecting a specific subject. For example, it would make sense to pass a by-law imposing fines for parking violations, whereas a resolution of council would suffice to recognize the achievements of a local sports team. Passing by-laws and resolutions is similar to federal and provincial processes already discussed. In deference to these processes, the tradition of three readings is paid lip service, although in practice it is simply stated as having occurred rather than actually taking place. Proposals are forwarded to council by councillors themselves, their constituents, or particular committees of council. A proposal may be discussed, debated, and referred to a committee for comment and report, and must ultimately receive the approval of a majority of council before it can be enacted. The following vignette may help illustrate the process.

Your college is located in a high-traffic area, away from any traffic lights or pedestrian crossings. You and many other students are frequent users of a jogging trail across the street from your campus, but the busy street is often too dangerous to attempt access to the trail. A crosswalk would go a long way to solving your dilemma. Being an astute political observer, you first gather a petition of fellow students, staff, and area residents to present to your local councillor. He or she, in turn, forwards the request to the city clerk, who places it on the agenda for the upcoming council meeting. Council, at the meeting, directs the department head of public works and roads to study the feasibility and cost of completing this project. Once completed, the report and its recommendations are sent back to council, and the matter is tabled for discussion at the next council meeting. It is budget-setting time and some councillors object to the cost, but your councillor points out that the popularity of the jogging path means that more and more students are crossing the road, and that their safety should be paramount in council's mind. At the same meeting, council hears a deputation from a local trucking firm opposed to the crosswalk, saying it will impede traffic flow in the area. Council agrees to refer the matter back to the roads department so that it can study whether, in fact, this is the case. Will the bureaucracy never end?

After much passionate debate, and amid the din of cheering students, council approves the crosswalk. A by-law is then prepared, establishing the crosswalk, setting out the offence if motorists do not obey the new law, and stating that the penalty will be pursuant to the *Provincial Offences Act* (1990). Once the by-law is presented to council, given three readings, and passed, the public works and roads department is instructed to install the appropriate signs and markings, and the police service is advised that this new law is in place and enforceable.[12]

Although fictitious, this example demonstrates the ability of municipal politics to accommodate and respond to local concerns and its receptiveness to grassroots participation, whether by individuals or groups. All the same, it remains political.

First Nations in the Canadian Political Structure

Members of First Nations in Canada have a unique, and many would say extremely disadvantaged, status in our current political structure.

In Chapter 2, in the section on the division of powers, you may have noticed that Indigenous peoples came under federal jurisdiction. Otherwise, the *British North America Act* made no mention of First Nations. In recent decades, Canadians have witnessed

---

12 This anecdote was put together with the assistance of Laura S. Lee, Clerk, Council Services, City of Orillia.

First Nations' growing frustration with government, sometimes erupting into violent confrontations when peaceful negotiations have been unsuccessful. The idea of Indigenous self-government has been steadily gaining support and has been instituted in parts of Canada (e.g., Nunavut and Labrador). This topic is discussed further in Chapter 5, but here some of the relevant history and context of First Nations' relationship with the federal government and the rest of Canada are outlined.

> According to the *Indian Act*, a "band" is a body of First Nations for whom the government has set aside lands for their common use and benefit; for whom the government is holding moneys; and who have been declared a band by the governor in council for the purposes of the Act. (Note: The federal government does not recognize the term "First Nations" but identifies native communities as "bands.") (Williamson & Roberts, 2004, p. 120)

Keep in mind as you read this section that the term "Indigenous" covers diverse peoples, cultures, and traditions and that it is dangerous—as well as naive—to assume that all these groups are the same and have the same goals. Canada has over 634 Indigenous communities within its borders (Assembly of First Nations, n.d.). As well, since detailed coverage of the status of these groups in the Canadian political structure is beyond the scope of this book, this section greatly simplifies the history and issues that have led to their current status.

Historical Background

The history of Canada's Indigenous cultures since colonial times is a history of steady erosion of their rights and independence and of broken promises on the part of government. When the European colonists no longer relied upon the once crucial support of their native allies in war and trade, they began to see these same peoples as liabilities and obstacles to expansion and development. Government initiatives in relation to first peoples turned to assimilating them into the non-Indigenous culture and "protecting" native land by creating and controlling reserves on which they were to live. With the *Royal Proclamation of 1763*, Britain attempted to organize its newly acquired territory in North America after the defeat of the French in 1760. In this statute, the British government declared itself the only party that could make treaties with the many independent Indigenous nations living within this area, and it also set down a treaty-making process (Williamson & Roberts, 2004, pp. 69–80). This process accorded "nation" status to Indigenous peoples, in essence, employing a long-held European custom of international law to legally recognize them as autonomous, self-governing states.

This mutual understanding began to erode as British military interests during the early 1800s gave way to concerns over settlement and expansion westward. Legal responsibility was gradually transferred to colonial authorities, and after the new Canadian government was given full responsibility for Indigenous peoples under the BNA Act, the relationship became even more lopsided. In 1876, the federal government passed the *Indian Act* (1985), a statute that confirmed its control over native lands, the resources on those lands, and the lives of the people themselves. Under it, Indigenous people became "wards of the Crown," diminishing their legal status to that accorded to children and the mentally incompetent. Until the passing of this Act, these communities had governed themselves and made their own decisions. Under the Act, the federal government imposed changes on how chiefs and councils were to operate, how bands were to select their leaders, and so on. Basically, the government disregarded traditional customs and replaced them with laws that were made without consulting the people they affected (Williamson & Roberts, 2004, pp. 106–108). In addition, Indigenous peoples were subject to the legislation of the province in which they resided.

The *Indian Act* covered only registered or status Indians—the descendants of those people who were considered Indians when the Act was passed, a definition that excluded the Métis and Inuit peoples. Status Indians were entitled to certain services provided by the federal government (e.g., in the areas of health and education), but they could not vote in federal elections until 1961, when this condition was finally changed. Status could also be lost, as discussed below, with the result that some people were and still are excluded from the Act.

Revisions to the *Indian Act* in 1951 further restricted who was eligible for status. Status Indian women who married non-status men—even men of Indigenous ancestry—automatically lost their status. The same condition did not apply to men who married non-status women. Losing status meant losing certain federal services, any private property on a reserve, and even the right to live on a reserve. This discriminatory condition was abolished in 1985 after much protest, and some people have regained their status (Hedley, 1992, p. 78).

Over the years, there have been many revisions to the *Indian Act*, but it continues to apply only to those people defined by the government as status Indians. It is no longer possible for status Indians to lose their status. You might think that abolishing this status would be welcomed by the many communities that have lived under these restrictions for so long, but, in fact, most oppose eliminating it because they believe that doing so would ultimately erase their unique identity in Canada and lead only to more hardship for people who already face much higher levels of poverty, unemployment, and other socio-economic problems than the non-Indigenous population.

Treaties

In addition to federal statutes, Indigenous rights are based on the peoples' historical occupation of the land and on treaties signed with first the British and then the Canadian governments. These treaties—agreements between Indigenous communities and the government of the day—first established peace and trade between the parties, and later increasingly involved transferring land to the government. With this loss of land—and the livelihood they made from this land—these First Nations lost much of their autonomy.

Treaties fall into three main categories: pre-Confederation treaties, numbered treaties, and modern treaties. Pre-Confederation treaties were made with the British government before Canada became a nation. Many of the original documents have been lost or were poorly recorded. Eleven numbered treaties were made between 1871 and 1921 as Canada grew as a nation and built a national railway, and these required Indigenous leaders to accept settlement on reserves. Most of these treaties also promised schools, farming equipment, money, and other benefits, much of which never materialized. Modern treaties are land claim agreements that have been signed since 1973 (Williamson & Roberts, 2004, pp. 80–82).

As you can imagine, the result is a patchwork of treaties across Canada, some of them dating back to the 1700s. And, in spite of the fact that many government obligations have been ignored, the rights guaranteed in these treaties remain legally binding by our judicial system. Treaty disputes continue to this day and must be resolved on a treaty-by-treaty basis. Individual treaties are not always clear about the rights and responsibilities that they confer. Further complicating matters are the following circumstances: some treaties contradict provincial regulations, written treaty provisions must be interpreted, unwritten promises that have survived as oral history have to be considered, and some provisions have since been overridden by federal legislation. These are only some of the factors that make settling disputes over land, Indigenous rights, and other issues so complex (Williamson & Roberts, 2004, pp. 82–84; Hedley, 1992, pp. 75–77).

Funding

Most of the funding for services and programs provided to Indigenous peoples comes from the federal government, the majority of it from Indigenous and Northern Affairs Canada. Some examples include educational programs (such as band schools and native culture and language programs), health care programs (such as alcohol and drug awareness and mental health), child welfare, and economic development (such as support for small businesses). Over the years, some communities have been permitted some control over the day-to-day administration of these services, services that other Canadians receive through their provincial and municipal governments. However, funding for many of these programs—for example, in the area of health care—still lags behind the level of funding that other Canadians enjoy (Williamson & Roberts, 2004, Chapter 6).

First Nations Rights

It is clear that the government's attempts over the years to assimilate Canada's Indigenous peoples into the non-native population have failed (Hedley, 1992, p. 79). Distinct cultures and communities still exist across Canada, just as the wider Canadian mainstream society is made up of distinct ethnic groups. After many years of Indigenous peoples' resistance to, and criticism of, federal policy regarding their unique place in Canada's history and heritage, their treaty rights were enshrined in 1982 in the *Canadian Charter of Rights and Freedoms* (section 25), although the nature of these rights and the definition of who is covered by this section of the Charter are still being worked out. The Meech Lake Accord and then the Charlottetown Accord—attempts at constitutional reform—proposed self-government for Indigenous communities, but, as discussed in Chapter 3, both accords were defeated. A guarantee of the right to self-government—a major aim of many Indigenous communities—is yet to be won.

Settling land claims is seen as a way for Indigenous people to gain some independence from the federal government and benefit from the resources of the land, thus making some social and economic gains. The ability to make decisions at the band level, free of federal interference, is an important prerequisite to this independence. The desire for independence does not mean that Indigenous people want to separate from Canada, but that they seek a renewed relationship with government that allows them to pursue their interests. Several local, regional, and national associations have been created to lobby for native rights and to pursue the resolution of land and treaty claims. At the national level, the Assembly of First Nations is perhaps the most familiar to Canadians. Some progress has been made, but much remains to be done for Canada's Indigenous citizens to achieve political, economic, social, and cultural independence (Williamson & Roberts, 2004, Chapter 7; Hedley, 1992, p. 76).

First Nations Government

The federal government recognizes Indigenous government only at the band level and defines what constitutes a band. The chief and band council make by-laws—called band council resolutions—for the community on a reserve.

Under the *Indian Act* (1985), councils make decisions for the reserve in such areas as, for example, health, traffic, law and order, road and building construction, and other local works. However, council resolutions may be denied by the federal government or negated by provincial laws. Enforcing resolutions is also difficult when there is no native police force or other enforcement agency on a reserve (Williamson & Roberts, 2004, Chapter 7). For these and other reasons, the Assembly of First Nations and other like-minded organizations have made self-government their major goal.

Get Real!

Keeping Government Honest

What would you think if a politician paid $16 for a glass of orange juice and got taxpayers to foot the bill? Well, in 2012 a Canadian Press reporter filed an access to information request for the expenses of then Minister Bev Oda's trip to London, England for a conference, and found that the minister did exactly that (Ditchburn, 2012). When the news was reported, Oda agreed to pay back the expense, as well as a portion of the thousands of dollars spent on the trip for a luxury car with chauffeur and a $665-per-night stay at a hotel.

Would the taxpayers have ever found out if it weren't for a reporter making use of the *Access to Information Act* (1985)? Would Oda have paid back the money if the expenses were never exposed? "Information itself—or the possibility of information coming to light—acts as a check on abuse of powers," said Chief Justice Beverley McLachlin (2009), adding that the right to access is considered a quasi-constitutional right by the Supreme Court of Canada. "Citizens cannot challenge unlawful government action unless they know about it" (McLachlin, 2009).

It was on July 1, 1983 that the Government of Canada adopted the *Access to Information Act* and *Privacy Act* (1985). Passed not long after Canada adopted the *Canadian Charter of Rights and Freedoms*, the two acts have been critical components of democracy, balancing the right to obtain information from government bodies with the protection of individual privacy.

Under the *Access to Information Act*, any member of the public can request a variety of government records from different departments and publicly funded agencies by submitting $5 and a form outlining the request. By law, those departments have to respond to the request within 30 days. While the law doesn't allow for access to certain public records, such as those coming from the Prime Minister's Office and Cabinet ministers' offices, those restrictions are under review and the Liberal government of Justin Trudeau has proposed updating the Act to increase government transparency (Smith, 2016).

It's not just federal government officials who are subject to the *Access to Information Act*, municipalities and provinces also abide by similar acts.

Some requests, mostly by journalists, have exposed major flaws or problems within Canadian government bodies and agencies, including police forces that are federal, provincial, and municipal. In 2017, *The Globe and Mail* reporter Robyn Doolittle released an exhaustive examination into the 870 police services across the country. After filing hundreds of access to information requests, she was able to get a look into how Canada's police services respond to sexual assault complaints. The 20-month-long investigation exposed flaws in how police handle complaints and discovered that one in five sexual assault claims are considered by police to be baseless and categorized as "unfounded" (Doolittle, 2017). The response by police services to the investigation was immediate (Rodan, 2017). Many police services committed to reviewing cases that were considered to be unfounded. Officials from the Ontario Provincial Police said they would review 4,000 unfounded cases from across the province. The London Police Service, which had one of the highest unfounded rates, said it would audit cases dating back to 2010. Others such as the Calgary Police Service and the RCMP also promised to review cases.

The *Access to Information Act* and *Privacy Act* are important tools used by journalists, regular citizens, researchers, academics, and even political parties to expose irregularities or wrongdoings in how the big machine of government and public bodies operate. Can you think of a news story that used access to information to expose a problem? Do you think governments would be as accountable without the acts? Why or why not?

CHAPTER SUMMARY

Representative and responsible government are two fundamental principles of parliamentary democracy. These concepts manifest themselves in the structure of the federal and provincial governments, with their executive, legislative, and judicial branches of authority. Municipal governments are much simpler, though they affect our everyday lives more directly. Through the electoral process, Canadians have an opportunity to choose the party, platform, and person that they feel will best represent their needs in the Canadian federation.

At the federal and provincial levels, proposed laws are called bills. There are various categories of bills, and the successful passage of a bill into law depends mainly on who initiates it.

Similarly, municipalities enact by-laws and resolutions to put council decisions into action.

First Nations have a unique relationship with the federal government and position in Canada's political structure, a relationship that has its roots in colonial history. Years of attempts to control Indigenous peoples and assimilate them into the non-Indigenous population have contributed to high levels of poverty, unemployment, loss of cultural identity, and other socio-economic problems among First Nations. For these and other reasons, First Nations are seeking greater autonomy from government control and entrenchment of the right to self-government in the Canadian Constitution.

KEY TERMS

bill, 61

by-law, 66

Cabinet, 60

Cabinet solidarity, 60

executive branch (federal), 59

executive branch (provincial), 64

government bill, 62

judicial branch, 63

legislative branch (federal), 60

legislative branch (provincial), 65

majority government, 56

member of Parliament, 56

minority government, 57

municipal council, 66

party loyalty, 56

private bill, 62

private member's bill, 62

proportional representation, 57

representative government, 55

responsible government, 56

triple E Senate, 61

WEBSITES

Assembly of First Nations: http://www.afn.ca/description-of-the-afn/

City of Ottawa: http://ottawa.ca/en

Elections Canada: http://www.elections.ca/home.aspx

Fair Vote Canada: http://www.fairvote.ca

Federal Court of Appeal: http://cas-cdc-www02.cas-satj.gc.ca/portal/page/portal/fca-caf_eng

Federal Court of Canada: http://cas-cdc-www02.cas-satj.gc.ca/portal/page/portal/fc_cf_en/Index

First Nations Child and Family Caring Society of Canada: https://fncaringsociety.com/news/first-nations-child-and-family-caring-society-canada-would-express-our-heartfelt-appreciation

Government of Canada: https://www.canada.ca/home.html

Government of Ontario: https://www.ontario.ca

Government's Defeat Sets Up Election Call: http://www.cbc.ca/news/politics/government-s-defeat-sets-up-election-call-1.1068749

Governor General of Canada: http://www.gg.ca/index.aspx

Indian Act: http://laws-lois.justice.gc.ca/eng/acts/I-5/

Indigenous and Northern Affairs Canada: http://www.aadnc-aandc.gc.ca/eng/1100100010023/1100100010027

LEGISinfo: http://www.parl.ca/LegisInfo/Home.aspx?Language=E&Mode=1&ParliamentSession=41-1

Municipal Act, Ontario: http://www.mah.gov.on.ca/Page184.aspx

Ontario Ministry of the Attorney General: https://www.attorneygeneral.jus.gov.on.ca/english/

Parliament of Canada: http://www.parl.ca/?Language=E

Senate of Canada: https://sencanada.ca/en/

Supreme Court of Canada: http://www.scc-csc.ca

Tax Court of Canada: http://cas-cdc-www02.cas-satj.gc.ca/portal/page/portal/tcc-cci_Eng/Index

REFERENCE LIST

Access to Information Act, RSC 1985, c A-1

Assembly of First Nations. (n.d.). Retrieved from http://www.afn.ca/about-afn/

Barnes, A., Bédard, M., Hyslop, C., Spano, S., Paré, J.-R., & Robertson, J.R. (2011, September 12). Reforming the Senate of Canada: Frequently asked questions. Library of Parliament. Retrieved from http://www.parl.gc.ca/Content/LOP/ResearchPublications/2011-83-e.pdf

Bélanger, B. (2001). The King–Byng affair. Retrieved from http://faculty.marianopolis.edu/c.belanger/quebechistory/federal/kingbyng.htm

British Columbia votes, 2009. (2009). *CBC News*. Retrieved from http://www.cbc.ca/canada/bcvotes2009/ridings/053/

British North America Act, 1867, 30 & 31 Vict, c 3

Canada Elections Act, 1985, RSC 1985, c E-2, as amended.

Canadian Charter of Rights and Freedoms, Part I of the *Constitution Act, 1982*, being Schedule B to the *Canada Act 1982* (UK), 1982, c 11 [Charter].

Constitution Act, 1982, being Schedule B to the *Canada Act 1982* (UK), 1982, c 11.

Ditchburn, J. (2012, April 23). Five-star hotel not good enough, Bev Oda opts for posh hotel favoured by royalty. *Toronto Star*. Retrieved from https://www.thestar.com/news/canada/2012/04/23/fivestar_hotel_not_good_enough_bev_oda_opts_for_posh_hotel_favoured_by_royalty.html

Doolittle, R. (2017, February 3). Unfounded: Why police dismiss 1 in 5 sexual assault claims as baseless. *The Globe and Mail*. Retrieved from https://www.theglobeandmail.com/news/investigations/unfounded-sexual-assault-canada-main/article33891309/

Elections Canada. (2017, June). Financing for candidates and official agents. Retrieved from http://www.elections.ca/content.aspx?section=pol&dir=can/man/ec20155&document=index&lang=e

Elections Canada. (n.d.). How to become a candidate. Retrieved from http://www.elections.ca/content.aspx?section=pol&dir=can/bck&document=index&lang=e

Fair Vote Canada. (n.d.). Is a "ranked ballot" a voting system? Retrieved from http://www.fairvote.ca/ranked-ballot-is-not-a-voting-system/

Federal Court. (n.d.). Jurisdiction. Retrieved from http://cas-cdc-www02.cas-satj.gc.ca/portal/page/portal/fc_cf_en/Jurisdiction

Final referendum results: Referendum on electoral reform. (2005, May 17). Retrieved from https://web.archive.org/web/20051128012938/http://www.elections.bc.ca:80/elections/ge2005/finalrefresults.htm

Francis, R.D., Jones, R., & Smith, D.B. (2000). *Destinies: Canadian history since Confederation* (4th ed., pp. 8, 82–83). Toronto: Thomson Nelson.

Harper promises bill to elect senators. (2006, September 7). CBC News. Retrieved from http://www.cbc.ca/news/canada/story/2006/09/07/harper-senate.html

Hedley, M.J. (1992). Native peoples in Canada. In K.G. Pryke & W.C. Soderlund (Eds.), *Profiles of Canada*. Toronto: Copp Clark Pitman.

Income Tax Act, RSC 1985, c 1 (5th Supp), as amended.

Indian Act, RSC 1985, c I-5

Legislative Assembly of Ontario. (n.d.). Bills & lawmaking. Retrieved from http://www.ontla.on.ca/web/go2.jsp?Page=/bills/bills_main

Martin urges parliamentary reform, end to "democratic deficit." (2002, October 22). CBC News. Retrieved from http://www.cbc.ca/news/canada/story/2002/10/21/martin_021021.html

McLachlin, B. (2009, May 5). Access to information and protection of privacy in Canadian democracy. Retrieved from http://www.scc-csc.ca/judges-juges/spe-dis/bm-2009-05-05-eng.aspx

Miller, J.R. (2002). Unity/diversity: The Canadian experience from Confederation to the First World War. In R.D. Francis & D.B. Smith (Eds.), *Readings in Canadian history: Post-Confederation* (6th ed., pp. 34–42). Toronto: Thomson Nelson.

Municipal Act, RSO 1990, c M.45.

Municipal Elections Act, 1996, SO 1996, c 32

Muniscope. (n.d.). Municipal election schedule in Canada. Retrieved from https://www.muniscope.ca/research/municipal_facts/Elections/

Ontario Citizens' Assembly of Electoral Reform. (2007, May 15). One ballot, two votes: A new way to vote in Ontario. Retrieved from http://www.citizensassembly.gov.on.ca/assets/One%20Ballot,%20Two%20Votes.pdf

Ontario Ministry of Municipal Affairs and Ministry of Housing (2016). 2016–2018 candidates' guide for Ontario municipal and school board by-elections. Retrieved from http://www.mah.gov.on.ca/Page15082.aspx#nominations1

Ontario Ministry of Municipal Affairs & Ministry of Housing. (n.d.). *Municipal Act*. Retrieved from http://www.mah.gov.on.ca/Page184.aspx

Ontario rejects electoral reform in referendum. (2007, October 10). *CBC News*. Retrieved from http://www.cbc.ca/news/canada/ontario-rejects-electoral-reform-in-referendum-1.632735

Parliament of Canada. (n.d.). Fixed-date elections in Canada. Retrieved from https://lop.parl.ca/ParlInfo/compilations/ProvinceTerritory/ProvincialFixedElections.aspx

Privacy Act, RSC 1985, c P-21

Provincial Offences Act, RSO 1990, c P.33

Rodan, G. (2017, June 1). Unfounded: How police and politicians have responded to The Globe's investigation so far. *The Globe and Mail*. Retrieved from https://www.theglobeandmail.com/news/investigations/unfounded-sexual-assault-the-reaction-from-police-forces-so-far/article33927647/

Russell, P.H. (2002). Provincial rights. In R.D. Francis. & D.B. Smith (Eds.), *Readings in Canadian history: Post-Confederation* (6th ed., pp. 21–33).Toronto: Thomson Nelson.

Smith, M-D. (2016, May 5). Federal government slashes fees for access-to-information requests to strengthen accountability. *National Post*. Retrieved from http://news .nationalpost.com/news/canada/federal-government -slashes-fees-for-access-to-information-requests-to -strengthen-accountability

Tax Court of Canada. (n.d.). About the court. Retrieved from http://cas-cdc-www02.cas-satj.gc.ca/portal/page/portal/tcc -cci_Eng/About

Town of Bradford West Gwillimbury. (1998). Bradford West Gwillimbury community profile, p. 7.

Williamson, P. & Roberts, J. (2004). *First Nations peoples* (2nd ed.). Toronto: Emond Montgomery.

EXERCISES
True or False?

_____ **1.** If a political party does not win at least 169 seats in the House of Commons in an election, it automatically loses.

_____ **2.** Cabinet solidarity refers to the principle of government members agreeing, at least publicly, on given policy matters.

_____ **3.** Under the Constitution, local governments are responsible for such services as roads, police, firefighting, sewers, water, and garbage collection.

_____ **4.** The *Indian Act* and individual treaties govern the relationship between the federal government and First Nations.

_____ **5.** Settling land claims is an important step toward Indigenous self-government because this would give many communities economic gains and, ultimately, make them less dependent on the federal government.

Multiple Choice

1. One major advantage of a proportional representation electoral system is that

   a. it produces "false majorities"

   b. it more accurately reflects voter preferences

   c. it gives 100 percent of political power to the successful candidate

   d. it has been used in Canada since Confederation

   e. it produces the same result as the first-past-the-post system

2. Canada's head of state is

   a. the governor general

   b. the Queen

   c. the prime minister

   d. the lieutenant governor

   e. the Senate

3. The judiciary exists to

   a. make laws

   b. uphold the legitimacy of government

   c. legitimize the law

   d. make constitutional amendments

   e. enforce the principle of the rule of law

4. Key political decisions are made by

   a. the prime minister or premier and Cabinet

   b. political parties

   c. the Senate

   d. the governor general

   e. the Queen

5. A majority government is formed when

   a. one party has more MPs in the House of Commons than any other party

   b. one party's MPs hold a majority of seats in the House of Commons

   c. the official Opposition has a majority of MPs in the House of Commons

   d. the majority of MPs are backbenchers

   e. the majority of MPs are appointed to Cabinet

Short Answer

1. Define "responsible government." How does it differ from "representative government"?

2. One criticism of Canada's political system is that far too much power is vested in the prime minister and Cabinet. What reforms might solve this problem?

3. What factors do you believe the prime minister should consider when choosing Cabinet ministers? What external factors might limit his or her choices?

4. Why has the Senate lost its credibility as an institution? What can be done to repair this image problem?

5. Why are First Nations seeking the right to self-government?

6. How do minority governments differ from majority governments? Which do you prefer, and why?

Politics, Society, and Law Enforcement

5

LEARNING OUTCOMES

After completing this chapter, you should be able to

- describe how the three levels of government cooperate in law enforcement;

- relate the evolution of public law enforcement in Canada to broader socio-economic changes in Canadian society;

- relate the political spectrum model to the major federal political parties;

- describe the major characteristics of Canadian political culture;

- demonstrate how political ideology informs the development of public policy;

- describe some of the major issues currently facing the justice system;

- use information in this chapter to forecast future trends for law enforcement in Canada; and

- analyze the impact of increased police activity on the political process and on democracy.

Introduction

Previous chapters have described how government structure and the political process have evolved in Canada and what this requires of the federal, provincial, and municipal levels of governments. This chapter examines how these roles often overlap and affect one another in the area of public justice. The chapter then looks at political and socio-economic influences on law enforcement and the Canadian justice system. As you will discover, historical changes reveal much about current attitudes toward politics and the manner in which justice is carried out in our country.

It is also important to remember that government activity should properly be viewed as organic in nature. It is a network where decisions in one area have consequences in another. Therefore, as you read, remain aware of these relationships. This will help you to put what you have studied into perspective.

Government Relations

Recall from Chapter 2 that the Fathers of Confederation anticipated a dominant role for the federal government, granting it blanket power over "peace, order, and good government" and the ability to legislate in any areas not specifically mentioned in the Constitution. The provinces were handed what were then considered to be minor areas of responsibility, such as education, health, and welfare. These were considered of little importance because, at the time, government usually did not fund or actively participate in running social programs. Instead, support for these areas was considered the responsibility of the individual, family, or local community and came from private charities and philanthropists. Increasing urbanization and industrialization after the turn of the 20th century and growing public expectations have subsequently enhanced the significance of these provincial areas. The federal and provincial governments are regularly at odds over which has jurisdiction in a particular area, and these increasing squabbles over political turf have come to characterize Canada's political culture.

Ironically, municipal governments are the weakest politically of the three levels of government, even though the public services they provide affect us more directly on a daily basis than either of the other two government levels. Further, even though municipal politics provides the greatest opportunity for citizen participation in government, it attracts little public notice most of the time.

The Constitution provides for the coordination of law enforcement across Canada. The federal government is responsible for creating criminal law, while the provinces are responsible for administering and enforcing its provisions and for creating and administering civil law. Municipal policing services are an extension of this provincial authority. Disagreements over how to approach justice issues can put provincial initiatives at odds with federal ones; similarly, local initiatives can be at odds with provincial ones. The remainder of this chapter will examine some of the political, social, economic, and other influences on law enforcement.

Evolution of Government Services

Canada's population grew dramatically in the years following Confederation, from about 3.6 million to nearly 8.8 million in 1921 (Francis, Jones, & Smith, 2000, p. 133). As Canada moved into the 20th century and cities drew increasing numbers of people to industrial employment, the need for coordinated social services became acute. Existing private agencies lacked the resources and expertise necessary to meet the needs of urban-industrial society, and reformers began calling for government intervention in social services. Education in Ontario had become free, universal, and compulsory in 1871, and by the 1920s public health and social assistance were being regulated. The economic growth of Canada and the shift of the population to urban centres that began around the turn of the century were factors that led the provincial governments to assert themselves more. Provincial concerns about federal domination have existed ever since.

Public demand for government-funded social services considerably enhanced provincial authority in the federal system because the vast majority of these areas fell within their provincial jurisdiction. However, limited provincial taxing capacity made it difficult to fund the ever-increasing costs of providing these services. Matters grew worse during the Great Depression of the 1930s as unemployment and poverty dramatically increased, and federal funds became necessary to meet the added costs of running relief programs. This set the stage for the later pattern of **cost sharing**, where the federal government "topped up" provincial programs in return for setting national standards in that area. During and after the Second World War, the federal government continued to dominate provincial actions by using its **federal spending power** to fund programs in areas outside its constitutional jurisdiction. Taken together, these events had the effect of centralizing power at the federal level because the provinces subsequently became dependent on federal money for social program funding.

In the 1960s, the provinces began to reassert themselves in the Canadian federation, increasingly challenging Ottawa's dominant position. Beginning with Quebec's Quiet Revolution (see Chapter 3) and spreading to other regions such as the West during the 1970s and 1980s, this more confrontational approach to federal–provincial relations has characterized Canadian politics up to the present day. Federal belt-tightening measures have aggravated the problem. As Ottawa has reduced its funding for social programs, provinces have called for more flexibility in the manner and means by which the federal government delivers these services. Similarly, provincial government reductions in transfers to municipal governments have caused municipalities to either cut services or find new ways to fund them. In some communities, cost-cutting has affected the quality of recreation programs, public maintenance, and emergency services as local politicians struggle to control costs while maintaining public services. As you learned in the first chapter, politics is about power and who wields it, and because there are never enough money and resources to satisfy everyone's wish list, politicians are constantly seeking an appropriate balance between the services demanded by citizens and the taxes they are willing to pay in order to fund these services. For example, would you be willing to pay more tax to fund a national daycare program? How about subsidies to help pay for post-secondary education? Better health care for those in the most underserved areas of the country? Depending upon who you are and what your circumstances might be, your priorities may differ from those of other individuals and groups. As the old saying goes, "There is only one taxpayer," so these decisions must be taken very seriously by those whom we elect to make them. The evolution of our justice system exemplifies this situation.

cost sharing
funding of provincial programs that combines federal contributions with provincial funding

federal spending power
the power of the federal government to raise the greatest share of tax revenues

Law Enforcement at the Three Levels of Government

As Canada grew and moved toward a more urban and industrial way of life, new social realities and subsequent public concerns spawned changes in the nature and operation of policing and the justice system in general.

Although jointly overseen by the federal justice and solicitor general departments and provincial attorneys and solicitors general, public law enforcement was for the most part left to individual communities to administer. The larger urban centres, such as Toronto and Montreal, were exceptions to the rule with their formal law enforcement systems. What has resulted from the constitutional division of powers is a sometimes confusing mix: the federal government creates laws governing the behaviour and activities of people and businesses; the provincial governments administer and enforce these laws, with some exceptions, through provincial agencies; and the municipal governments also enforce these laws through local police services, licensing, and so on.

The three levels of government often cooperate to safeguard the public safety of all Canadians. Better communication and coordination have become paramount concerns since the terrorist attacks on the World Trade Center on September 11, 2001. Thus Canadian law enforcement participates in a larger international sphere as a means of combatting threats from abroad. This cooperation provides for consistency and equity in enforcing the laws of Canada, especially in the prosecution of criminal offences. The federal enforcement agencies (described in detail in Chapter 10) work in concert with the various provincial and municipal enforcement services in combined forces operations, a prime example of the three levels of government working together for the public good and sharing costs.

Governments determine the kinds of laws we have and to what degree they are enforced (see "Policy Instruments and Degrees of Regulation" in Chapter 8). Also, each level of government except the municipal level is permitted by the Constitution to raise sufficient funds through taxes to pay for the cost of operating various programs and services. By provincial law, municipal governments can raise money through property taxes and through licence fees and fines.

The same applies to the administration of justice in the provinces. Again, by sharing in the operating costs, the federal government can greatly influence how justice is administered. At present, justices of the Supreme Court of Canada are appointed and paid for by the federal government; lower-court judges are appointed and paid for by the provinces. Other differences in the justice system exist in such areas as correctional services for adult and young offenders and public policy and protection relative to combatting organized crime.

Federal Law Enforcement

As has been observed, the evolution of the justice system in Canada was rather uneven up to Confederation. As the country matured, however, standardization and regulation were implemented to lend stability as the country grew and changed. Accompanying the economic and social changes was a gradual recognition of the importance of public policing to control crime and maintain civil order amid the transitions that were taking place in Canadian society. In 1873, Prime Minister John A. Macdonald, who was doing double duty as justice minister, supervised plans for a national police force "to bring law, order and Canadian authority to the Northwest Territories" (present-day Alberta and Saskatchewan) (Royal Canadian Mounted Police, January 1, 2001). In doing so, Macdonald hoped to guard against American encroachment, maintain friendly relations with the many Indigenous communities, and facilitate an orderly settlement of the region. Known initially as the North-West Mounted Police (NWMP), this national police force was renamed the Royal Canadian Mounted Police (RCMP) in 1920.

During the First and Second World Wars, the NWMP/RCMP conducted border patrols and surveillance of potential security threats. In 1932, it consolidated a number of other government services to form the Marine Section to give Canada a national presence in its territorial waters. The RCMP also helped to create and coordinate a national database, providing resources such as fingerprints, a crime index, firearms registration information, a photo section, and forensic expertise to help police investigators across the country.

Potential internal security threats, exemplified by the Front de libération du Québec (FLQ) Crisis of 1970 in Quebec (in which radical Quebec separatists kidnapped British diplomat James Cross and Quebec labour minister Pierre Laporte and later killed Laporte), led to an expansion of security and intelligence operations. In 1984, these were formally separated from direct RCMP operations with the creation of the Canadian Security and Intelligence Service (CSIS). Today, the RCMP has policing responsibilities in every province and territory, including policing contracts in eight provinces, the three territories, and hundreds of municipalities (Royal Canadian Mounted Police, October 28, 2011). The RCMP is administered by Public Safety Canada. Other enforcement agencies organized and paid for by the federal government include the Immigration and Refugee Board of Canada and Fisheries and Oceans Canada, which are administered by the appropriate ministries responsible for the area of jurisdiction. These agencies generally focus their efforts on their respective related federal laws—for example, the *Immigration Act* (1985) and the federal *Fisheries Act* (1985). Recently, the duties of Canada Border Services Agency (CBSA) officers have been extended to include enforcing *Criminal Code* (1985) driving offences and other federal statutes. Along with other federal enforcement officials, customs officers have been given the powers and protection of peace officers as described in the *Criminal Code*.[1]

It is clear that the policies developed by the federal government greatly influence the kinds of services provided by the provincial governments. Historically, the federal government, because it collects the majority of tax money, has determined the amount of money to transfer to each province for specific purposes. The lion's share is for social programs, particularly in the areas of health care and education, which are both provincial responsibilities. The amount of money transferred to the provinces generally depends on each respective provincial government's adherence to the wishes of the federal government, which is often led by a different political party.

Provincial Law Enforcement

Ontario and Quebec have their own provincial police services. The Ontario police service is administered through the provincial Ministry of Community Safety and Correctional Services, formerly the Ministry of the Solicitor General. Provincial police work through joint forces operations with the RCMP and municipal police services to ensure that major criminal activities, such as drug trafficking, illegal immigration, and counterfeiting, are investigated efficiently and cost-effectively.

The history of provincial policing in Ontario dates back to 1875, when the first full-time paid criminal detective was hired by the attorney general's office. The staff gradually increased, and in 1909 an order-in-council was passed in the provincial legislature officially creating the Ontario Provincial Police (OPP) force (Ontario Provincial Police, n.d.).

The history of the OPP resembles that of the RCMP, most notably in the areas of professionalization and technological innovation. Pioneers in highway patrol, OPP officers used motorcycles, marked cruisers, and, after 1947, radio communication to enforce the province's *Highway Traffic Act* (1990). In fact, by 1956, 75 percent of provincial policing was taken up by this activity (Ontario Provincial Police, n.d.). As with other government services, the OPP expanded greatly during the 1960s and 1970s. As outlined in later chapters, the postwar period in Canada was a time of expansion in government services, including law enforcement. Police forces were able to keep up with technological changes as

---

1   For specific information about the CBSA's mandate, see http://www.cbsa-asfc.gc.ca/agency-agence /menu-eng.html.

they emerged, and governments at all levels seemed ready, willing, and able to underwrite the additional costs. For example, this philosophy enabled the OPP to become the first police force in North America to enforce traffic regulations from the air (Ontario Provincial Police, n.d.).

Provincial governments seem to be intervening more and more in existing federal laws and policies. The federal *Young Offenders Act* (1985),[2] for example, was widely criticized after its inception in 1984, leading eventually to its replacement with the passage of the *Youth Criminal Justice Act*, which came into force on April 1, 2003. Now, young people who commit very serious criminal acts can be tried as adults. Less serious offences, however, may be settled through a number of alternative measures, such as local youth justice committees. For example, Ontario's *Parental Responsibility Act* (2000) imposes a fine of up to $6,000 on parents to pay for property damage or loss caused by their children under 18, unless the parents can prove that the damage or loss was not intentional or that they provided reasonable supervision of their children.

Municipal Law Enforcement

police services board
civilian board that oversees a local police service

Municipal police services are administered by their **police services boards**, which consist of locally elected and appointed civilians. The board oversees the police service and, for example, establishes policies for managing the service, creates guidelines for dealing with public complaints against the police, and approves operating budgets. It does not, however, deal with the day-to-day management of the police, which is done by the police service itself. A board can have as few as three members or as many as seven, depending on the size of the municipality.

Influences on Law Enforcement

Political Parties and the Political Spectrum

right wing
a political attitude or philosophy that favours more individual freedom and less government intervention

left wing
a political attitude or philosophy that favours more government intervention to help achieve social equality

political spectrum
a model that shows political philosophy on a continuum from left wing to right wing

Do you think, like many people, that the only thing distinguishing one political party from another is its name? Although some parties share similar platforms, many observers use the terms **right wing** or **left wing** to describe a party's fundamental philosophy. These terms have their origins in France, after the revolution of 1789, when the new political assembly was shaped like a semicircle. Members who favoured the traditional social hierarchy and economic status quo sat on the right side, while those who supported social equality and the major economic changes this would necessitate sat on the left. Moderate members—ones who favoured a more balanced approach to government—sat in the middle. Over the years, these labels have been attached to broader political ideas, as illustrated in Figure 5.1, commonly referred to as the **political spectrum**.

Today, "right" and "left" are generally associated with degrees of government involvement in the lives of citizens. Supporters of the right, commonly referred to as "conservatives," tend to prefer more individual freedom and less government intervention, particularly in the economy. This group therefore supports measures such as the privatization of government-owned corporations and less government regulation of business in general. Further, they would tend to favour policies such as tax cuts, less social spending, and more emphasis on individual responsibility. This group also tends to support "law-and-order" agendas,

---

2 For information on background and amendments passed by Parliament in 2012, see *Youth Criminal Justice Act* summary and background (n.d.).

Figure 5.1   Political Spectrum

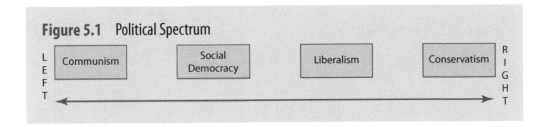

including tougher law enforcement and stiffer penalties for convicted criminals, a topic discussed further in the section "The Politics of Justice: Law Enforcement and the Political Spectrum." Those on the left, usually referred to as "liberals" or "democrats," tend to favour more government intervention, particularly in economic matters, with the aim of achieving greater social equality of citizens and mitigating the effects of an unpredictable economy. It is important to highlight two points here. First, while there are similarities between them, the terms "conservative," "liberal" and "democrat" are not to be confused with formal political party names (i.e., Conservative, Liberal, Democrat). The former refer to political ideologies—general philosophical positions about politics that we all hold—while the latter point to political parties whose specific party platforms may combine several ideological approaches and can adapt to the demands of the electorate they wish to govern.[3]

More recently, many political observers have also argued that these distinctions are too simple and no longer reflect the realities of political values of the 21st century. One way to address this is by adding a vertical axis to the traditional left–right economic divide that incorporates a social scale indicating how much control a government has over the actions of its citizens.[4] Adding this element allows users to chart preferences for whether the state or the individual should have primary responsibility for deciding what citizens can and cannot do. Thus the further up the scale one goes, the more authoritarian the government would be; the further down, the more individual freedom each citizen would have (see Figure 5.2). So, for example, someone who believes that governments should have an active role in promoting equality of opportunity by taxing the wealthy but is also pro-choice and supports same-sex marriage would most likely appear in the lower left quadrant. A person who favours smaller government and tax cuts and supports conservative social values, such as marriage being exclusively for heterosexuals and being pro-life, would probably plot in the upper right quadrant. One's proximity to the centre line of each axis would indicate how strongly he or she feels about each set of political values.

As with any measurement tool, this representation has its limitations. However, it can assist individuals who are unsure of their political preferences with at least an initial baseline from which to begin. Curious? There are several websites that use this model of analysis, which enable you to see where you might be most comfortable, politically speaking. For instance, during the past few provincial and federal elections in Canada, CBC has created a Vote Compass website, which asks users a series of pertinent political questions and graphs their results, indicating which party might best match their political values. Likewise, the British-based website The Political Compass offers a similar survey, although in a much more general format.

---

3 Witness, for example, the federal Liberal Party's campaign promise to use deficit financing to invest in infrastructure versus the NDP's fiscally conservative proposal to balance the budget, during the 2015 election campaign (Political Compass, n.d.).

4 This approach is based on those developed by The Political Compass (n.d.) and CBC's Vote Compass (n.d.) websites.

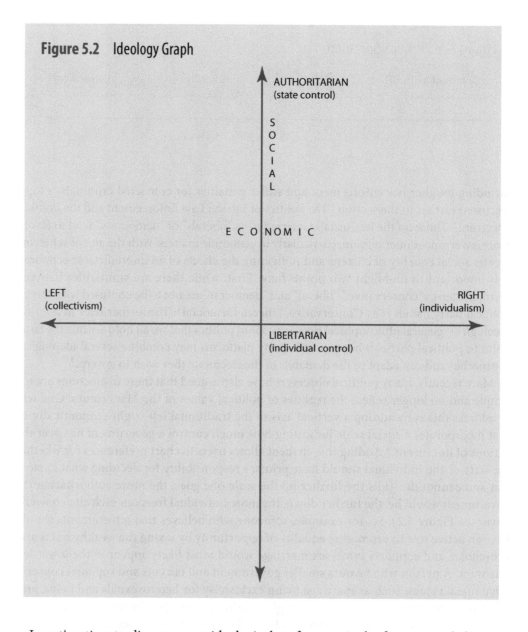

Figure 5.2   Ideology Graph

Investing time to discover your ideological preferences is the first step in helping to determine which political party might best represent you the next time there is an election call. After trying out The Political Compass, you may find that not all of your ideological preferences align with the left or the right. On a variety of issues, you may find yourself all over the political spectrum. Political parties encourage ideological consistency, but they do not always adhere to it, and they, like us, evolve over time. There's nothing wrong with contradiction. In fact, these contradictions often present opportunities for compromise and reaching across the aisle. Can you think of a time when you have changed your mind about a popular issue? What about a time when a political party changed its position? Did you see it as opportunistic or pragmatic, given the circumstances? As you become more aware of federal, provincial, and municipal cooperation and interaction, keep an eye out for how political parties attempt to navigate ideological contradictions.

Figure 5.3 shows where four of Canada's major federal political parties sit in relation to one another on the domestic political spectrum. Notably absent here is the politically left-leaning Bloc Québécois, which only runs candidates in Quebec and, because of its philosophy based on French Canadian cultural nationalism and ethnicity, does not easily

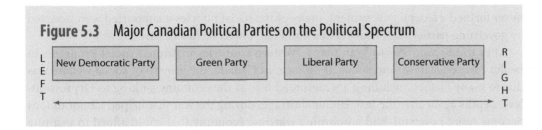

Figure 5.3 Major Canadian Political Parties on the Political Spectrum

fit into this model. When compared to other Western democracies, Canada as a nation sits slightly left of centre, along with other progressive social democracies, such as the Scandinavian countries of Europe.

Political Parties and the History of Canada

Since Confederation, Canadians have witnessed many changes in the political landscape mapping the fortunes of major federal political movements and the parties they often inspired. A historical context not only enables you to recognize some of the political, social, and economic factors that led to their creation, but also helps to explain why, over the years, some parties have shifted their position on the political spectrum.

Only two parties have ever formed the federal government: the (Progressive) Conservative Party and the Liberal Party. Until almost the turn of the 20th century, federal politics was dominated by the Conservatives, created and guided by John A. Macdonald, Canada's first prime minister. Under his tutelage, the party took a pro-business attitude, combining an allegiance to Britain with a deep mistrust of the United States.

Conversely, the Liberals dominated Canadian federal politics during most of the 20th century, having held power for almost 70 of those years.[5] The party had its roots in a loose political coalition of reformers who favoured more socially progressive policies (than did the Conservatives) and freer trade with the United States. Notable among their early leaders was George Brown, publisher of *The Globe* in Toronto. Despite its beginnings around Confederation, the Liberal Party did not really come into its own until Wilfrid Laurier assumed its leadership in 1887. Unlike the Conservatives, the Liberals were more open to relations with the United States and had a strong base of support in Quebec.

Aside from a smattering of protest parties, these two parties dominated the political landscape during Canada's first 60 years. English–French relations proved to be a sore point for both parties during this time. Episodes such as the state execution of Louis Riel in 1885, the Manitoba Schools Question in the early 1890s (over the replacement of a dual Protestant–Catholic school system in Manitoba with a single Protestant one), and the Conscription Crises of the First and Second World Wars created deep divisions between French and English Canada. Neither party seemed able to address this problem to the satisfaction of both sides. The Great Depression of the 1930s, however, temporarily shifted the political focus away from English–French tensions.

During the Great Depression, many people became frustrated with the inability of the established parties to deal with the economic hardships. This eventually led to the creation of a new party in 1932—the Co-operative Commonwealth Federation. This decidedly left-wing party evolved into the New Democratic Party in the early 1960s, and, although it has

---

5 The exceptions were 1911–1921, 1930–1935, 1957–1963, 1979–1980, and 1984–1993 (Colombo, 1998, pp. 122–130).

never formed a federal government, many of the social policies it supported were adopted by governing parties (e.g., Canada Pension Plan, universal health care).

After the Second World War, many Western countries instituted social programs in health care, education, and social assistance. In Canada, the growth of social welfare was due to many factors, including a widespread fear of the economy sinking to Depression-level depths again after the war, labour shortages during the war that helped labour unions become more powerful, and a booming wartime economy that could afford to institute more government services. This general shift to the left of the political spectrum lasted until the 1970s, when the political winds of conservatism began to reappear. Once more, the slow reaction of the existing political parties to this change proved to be the catalyst for the creation in 1987 of the Reform Party, which changed its name in the spring of 2000 to the Canadian Alliance and then merged with the Progressive Conservative Party in 2003 to become the Conservative Party. Created originally as a party supporting Western Canadian concerns, the Conservatives espouse right-wing policies such as cuts to taxes, cuts to social programs, smaller government, and stricter controls on immigration (Wells, 2006).

The 1980s also witnessed the birth of the federal Green Party, which sought to draw attention to environmental issues. By broadening its platform to include such issues as electoral reform and economic sustainability, the party has increased its support among voters, electing its first MP, Green Party leader Elizabeth May, in the federal election of 2011 (Canada Guide, n.d.; Green Party, n.d.).

The first two decades of the 21st century have seen Canadian voters toy with both sides of the political spectrum. After nine years of a Conservative government under Stephen Harper and a brief surge in support for the NDP, which saw it serving as the official Opposition, Liberal leader Justin Trudeau was elected on a socially progressive campaign platform that included investing in infrastructure, electoral reform, and the legalization of marijuana for recreational use. While his government has, for the time being at least,

Jagmeet Singh celebrates with supporters after winning the first ballot in the NDP leadership race to be elected the leader of the federal New Democrats in Toronto on Sunday, October 1, 2017. Leadership conventions provide members of a political party with a chance to voice a variety of opinions and suggest policy ideas to candidates.

abandoned reform of Canada's electoral system, it seems likely that federal government initiatives will continue the trend away from the right-wing emphasis of its Conservative predecessor. Of course, only time will tell, and ultimately it will be up to us as Canadians to decide whether to follow or buck this trend. Stay tuned!

The Politics of Justice: Law Enforcement and the Political Spectrum

Tough on crime.

Law-and-order candidate.

Victims' rights.

Perhaps you have noticed such slogans and similar ones during recent political campaigns in your community. Where do they come from and what informs their message? Most of us would agree that criminal behaviour in Canadian society is indeed an undesirable thing and every attempt should be made to prevent crime and preserve civil order. How a government chooses to go about these tasks reveals a lot about its ideological preferences.

The moral viewpoints of the political party in power have always had a major impact on the kinds of government services provided to Canadians. Each political party has its own views on how Canada should be managed and which government services should be given priority, including those that apply to public safety. For example, in spite of the daily barrage of media reports about rampant crime, the rate of police-reported violent offences has, until 2015, been in steady decline for decades ("Canada's crime index rises," 2016).[6] During this same period, federal corrections was moving away from mega-jails toward smaller institutions and rehabilitation, while some provinces shut down smaller jails, opting for private mega-jails and a "get tough" approach, particularly in the area of young offenders. These different philosophies can manifest themselves at all levels of government and reflect ideological disagreements over how to deal with crime in society. Their implications become clear when we look at where each political party in power sits on the political spectrum.

Right-wing ideology tends to emphasize self-reliance, individual responsibility, and a "survival of the fittest" attitude toward society. Therefore, issues of crime and punishment focus on making individuals accountable for the choices they have made—that is, "Do the crime, do the time." On the other hand, left-wing ideology emphasizes collective responsibility and sees the state as a means through which to overcome inequality and look after those who are less able to look after themselves. Thus left-wing proponents see criminals as products of a social system that prevents them from achieving their potential. In the eyes of the left, it's the system that's at fault. Therefore, they would argue, punishing an individual won't solve the problem. The environment they come from will continue to produce the same criminal behaviour. Socially progressive policies emphasize preventative measures (e.g., providing assistance for disadvantaged families, funding activities for youth) and focus on restorative, rather than punitive, justice policies to help reintegrate offenders back into their communities.

While the reality of governing often tempers a political party's ideological preference, on occasion the Supreme Court is left to make sense of government initiatives that may violate

---

6 For detailed information on overall decline, see Statistics Canada (2017a).

fundamental citizen rights guaranteed under the *Charter of Rights and Freedoms*. A good example of this occurred in 2016 when, in two separate rulings, the court struck down the former Harper government's mandatory minimum crime legislation on the grounds that it interfered with judicial independence (the right of judges to make decisions without political influence) and that the application of such laws represented cruel and unusual punishment (Fine, 2016).

Should governments spend more money on tracking down, prosecuting, and incarcerating criminals, or should they focus on improving the social conditions that lead to criminal acts? Examining costs may provide some insight. In the fiscal year 2015–2016, operating expenditures for policing in Canada totaled $14.2 billion (Alam & Greenland, n.d.).

As has been emphasized throughout this text, public respect for and belief in the rule of law rests in large part on the belief that our system of justice does its utmost to preserve and uphold fundamental rights of citizenship, even if many of us take these rights for granted. The hard reality is that protecting citizens' rights costs money. In 2015–2016, it cost Canadians $4.6 billion to operate the federal adult corrections system (Reitano, 2017). The average cost per day to keep a man in a maximum-security federal prison was $426.98 ($155,848 per year), and for a woman $528.06 ($192,742 per year). In contrast, it costs $47.06 per day ($17,176 per year) to monitor offenders in the community—for example, by applying measures not involving prison time, such as conditional sentencing, electronic supervision, probation, and parole.[7] Research also shows that it can cost seven times more tax dollars to process an offender through the justice system and related government services than to invest in social programs that help at-risk youth. Such programs have been shown to reduce crime and rates of violence.[8]

There is no right or wrong answer here; rather, it is a question of resource allocation. Crime will always be a part of society. The question we as citizens should consider is, What is the most efficient and effective way to mitigate crime and its consequences?

Canadian Political Culture

What does it mean to be Canadian? Beyond the obvious stereotypes of beer, hockey, and cold winters, people often find it difficult to define a national sense, or identity. Although Canada is recognized internationally for the creation of, and participation in, peacekeeping,[9] it also is well respected as a nation that embraces justice and respect in a multicultural context. Several political observers have suggested that we have developed these national character traits through experiences and realities that have forced us to compromise and cooperate in order to accomplish tasks that would prove insurmountable to any one part of the country. This instinctive sensibility about ourselves helps shape our political culture.

political culture
the basic attitudes people have toward one another, the state, and authority

Political culture refers to "the basic attitudes people have toward each other, the state, and authority, that in essence reflect the impact of history on a society's beliefs" (Hauss &

---

7   Figures compiled from personal communication with A. Serin, July 29, 2017. The cost of maintaining an offender is obtained by dividing Correctional Service Canada's overall operating expenses by the annual average number of offenders. That annual cost is then divided by 365 to get the cost per day. Please note that information per security level is not available for women's facilities as those institutions are multi-level and managed as one institution. The authors wish to thank Avely Serin for gathering these statistics.

8   For analysis, see Waller (2006).

9   Due to changing government priorities and uncertain international conditions, Canada's role in this area has, in many respects, evolved from one emphasizing "peacekeeping" to one based on "peacemaking."

Smith, 2000, p. 10). Canadian political culture has been and continues to be influenced by a number of factors. Our political views have been shaped by our history and geography and by the diversity of our population.

Canada evolved from former French and British colonies, all of which were carved from lands once occupied by Indigenous peoples. The mutual agreement and cooperation necessary for Confederation and coexistence between these two dominant linguistic groups have infused Canadian politics with a tendency toward compromise, rather than confrontation, when disagreements appear.

Regionalism

Regional loyalties have always coloured the Canadian political landscape. Within our immense geography are several regions—notably, Atlantic Canada, Quebec, Ontario, the Prairies, British Columbia, and the North—all with differing interests and viewpoints as to how the Canadian political system can and should function. These feelings have even manifested themselves through the formation of formal political parties, such as the Reform Party (absorbed into the Conservative Party) and the Saskatchewan Party in the Western provinces, and the Parti Québécois and Bloc Québécois in Quebec.

Regionalism has been strengthened by economic disparity, some of which dates back to the time of Confederation. For example, over the past 100 years, the residents of such regions as the North, the Atlantic provinces, and the predominantly agricultural Prairie provinces have faced many economic challenges because of an inhospitable climate, a lack of development, unpredictable commodity prices (recall the 2015 crash in oil prices), and other factors. Canadians have thus tended to relocate to areas that promise better opportunities, creating large urban centres whose residents have high expectations for a better life. The majority of immigrants also tend to settle in the major urban centres, where jobs, housing, schools, and other facilities are more plentiful. This concentration in a few major cities poses many challenges and creates social problems, not the least of which is a growing gap between the "haves" and the "have-nots." We see this shift occurring in the lower mainland of British Columbia, in the large cities of Alberta, and in Southern Ontario, which is experiencing a dramatic growth in population. These regions tend to have low unemployment and a high cost of living. They also tend to have growing numbers of homeless people and more complex social problems.

American Influence

Another way many people define "Canadian" is with the glib reply "not American." This being said, they are often hard pressed to explain their statement in any more detail. Yet there is little doubt that Canada's geographic proximity to the United States has had a part in informing Canadian identity. Historically, Canada has adopted both bilateral and multilateral arrangements in its external relations, in an attempt to find a national position that both serves its interests and preserves relations with its powerful neighbour to the south.

"Bilateralism" is a political term referring to a relationship between two powers—in this case, Canada and the United States. We see this in operation when both countries

---

10 For example, it was discovered only recently that the UN's *Universal Declaration of Human Rights* was drafted by Canadian John Humphrey, a McGill University professor (Francis, Jones, & Smith, 2004, p. 354). For a more general synopsis of Canada's position in the early postwar era, see Conrad (2003).

sign agreements to coordinate border security or form commissions to fight pollution in the Great Lakes. "Multilateralism" refers to relations involving more than two powers. Canada has adopted this policy in circumstances where it feels that its interests might be overshadowed by American influence in a particular area. This was the case internationally following the Second World War. Concern about overzealous anti-communist American policies prompted the Canadian government to foster alliances with other nations. Good examples of this approach are found in Canada's contribution as a founding member of the United Nations in 1945 and membership in the North Atlantic Treaty Organization (NATO) in 1949.[10] Because our interests remain closely tied to those of the United States, it is sometimes assumed that we will follow its lead. However, as demonstrated by Canada's refusal to support American military action in Iraq in 2003 and, more recently, the "America First" policies of President Donald Trump's administration, these differences can extend to areas of trade and culture.

The overwhelming barrage of American culture and the United States' close economic relations with Canada have blurred traditional differences between what is considered cultural preservation and what is considered economic protectionism. For example, in 2017, the US Department of Commerce announced that it would impose duties on imports of Canadian softwood lumber products in response to what it sees as unfair financial support for the Canadian industry. The potential for revenue and job losses underscores the critical importance of this relationship to our economy and how quickly circumstances can change.[11]

Multiculturalism

Canada's political culture has developed out of a long tradition of immigration and interrelations between groups over time, from earliest contact between Indigenous people and European explorers to successive waves of new arrivals thereafter and through to today. Our Constitution specifically recognizes two dominant European cultures—French and English—which informs Canada's policy of two official languages, or bilingualism. Although English–French relations still command considerable influence within Canadian politics, Indigenous and other self-identifying cultural groups have come to play a considerable role in the political mix—especially at the community level.[12]

multiculturalism
cultural and racial diversity; in Canada, a constitutionally enshrined policy that recognizes the diversity of our population

Traditional politics has also been influenced tremendously by the *Canadian Charter of Rights and Freedoms* (1985), which enshrines **multiculturalism** as a characteristic of Canadian society that is to be maintained and enhanced. The Charter has permitted citizens and individuals to participate in political decision-making through the courts, forcing politicians to recognize constitutional guarantees in policy matters. Some critics have charged that this change has removed the spirit of compromise that characterized the politics of earlier times (Hauss & Smith, 2000, pp. 63–64). This debate demonstrates the ongoing evolution of political culture in Canada and serves to remind us that although political culture is informed by past events, it cannot be held prisoner by them forever.

Canada's multiculturalism policy aims to promote the full participation of *all* Canadians in our society, tolerance for diversity, and a reduction in prejudice. In spite of this, minorities

---

11   The Conference Board of Canada estimates these measures could cost the lumber industry $1.7 billion annually and result in the loss of 2,200 jobs ("Canadian softwood producers," 2017).

12   For a more thorough analysis of successive waves of immigration to places like Canada, see Saunders (2010).

still struggle for recognition and representation in a number of social areas. For example, of the 338 seats in Parliament, only 88 (26 percent) are held by women. As well, the 2015 election saw 46 (13.6 percent) visible minority candidates elected, as well as 10 Indigenous candidates (Coles, 2015).

First Nations

Chapter 4 introduced some of the history of First Nations' relations with government, including some of the reasons for increased Indigenous activism and desire for self-government. In the past decade, Canadians have witnessed some serious confrontations between First Nations communities and law enforcement agents over land claims, traditional hunting and fishing rights, logging rights, and other issues. The standoff between police and Indigenous protesters in Oka, Quebec over a land claim in 1990 and a similar disagreement in Caledonia, Ontario in 2006 are only two examples.

It is important to remember that although the term "First Nations" encompasses many groups, it does not include the Inuit and the Métis. The Inuit people of the Far North, for example, have a very different lifestyle and cultural traditions from the Plains Indians' bands. Even today, with the growing Indigenous movement to address the social, economic, and other ills that have characterized the lives of many bands since colonial times, there are widely differing views on how to achieve these aims, including whether civil disobedience is justified to make their voices heard.

A substantial shift of responsibility for Indigenous governance, including the administration of reserves and of government-funded services to reserves, is occurring as more and more bands win the legal right to self-government. We have witnessed this in Western Canada in the settling of large land claims and in the creation of Indigenous police services on some reserves (e.g., Dakota-Ojibway Police Service of Brandon, Manitoba; Rama Police Service just outside of Orillia, Ontario).

These are truly historic steps in the fight for Indigenous self-determination, but we must keep in mind that these steps do not solve the serious

This photograph of Canadian Army Private Patrick Cloutier and Mohawk warrior Brad Laroque illustrates the tension that pervaded the land claim dispute at Oka during the summer of 1990.

problems—low life expectancy, lack of basic infrastructure and government services, high unemployment, and low education levels, to name only a few—faced by many of these communities.

What exactly does **self-government** mean for Indigenous peoples? It means that bands are allowed to pursue their own policies rather than government-imposed ones. Instead of reserves being simply places set aside by government for the purpose of controlling people, the reserves become communities that develop, for example, economic activities, services, and infrastructure for the benefit of their residents—just like any other community in Canada. However, note that overall control of reserve policy is still in the hands of the federal government as set down in the Constitution. The right to self-government has yet to be added to the Constitution (although many Indigenous groups have been fighting for such an amendment for years). Despite obstacles, some of which go back almost 400 years, the struggle continues to strive for greater political, economic, social, and cultural independence (Hedley, 1992, p. 88).

Indigenous self-government
greater autonomy of First Nations to pursue their own political, social, cultural, and economic objectives with limited interference from the federal government

In practical terms, self-government will have effects on law enforcement and the justice system. Some of the changes already include Indigenous police services (see below), which have been replacing the RCMP and provincial police services on reserves. Efforts are being made to recruit more people of Indigenous heritage as court workers, paralegals, justices of the peace, legal clinic staff, and so on. These measures are intended to bring elements of Indigenous culture and custom to the justice system and make it more responsive to the needs of offenders from these communities. A new form of alternative justice—the sentencing circle—has been set up on some reserves. Sentencing circles, composed of community members, hear cases affecting people in their community that are considered to be better addressed at the local level than in the mainstream court system. The aim is to heal, rather than punish, the wrong that has been done, and this form of justice usually brings together victim, offender, and family members to discuss and seek appropriate remedies that take into account all points of view. The circle may impose a sentence that includes community service, counselling, or restitution to the victim in some form (Williamson & Roberts, 2007).

FIRST NATIONS POLICING

First Nations policing is a relatively recent innovation in public law enforcement. It has evolved out of a desire on the part of Indigenous communities to police themselves and a growing public understanding of the need for and benefits of a police system that recognizes the unique traits of the many Indigenous cultures. Beginning in the 1970s as a series of joint pilot projects, on-reserve policing has developed into a complex system of operations that can involve individual communities and the federal and provincial levels of government.

In his role as president of the First Nations Chiefs of Police Association, Rama Police Chief John Domm addresses delegates at the 2016 Assembly of First Nations Annual General Meeting in Niagara Falls, Ontario.

In 1991, the federal government passed legislation setting up the legal and bureaucratic framework for self-policing in Indigenous communities across Canada. To date, there are 55 of these police services operating across Canada.[13] The variety of treaties and diversity of communities defy absolute bureaucratic standardization; however, there are some general principles on which all policing agreements are based. Because Indigenous relations fall within federal jurisdiction, it is ultimately the responsibility of the federal solicitor general to work with communities to set up and manage policing services in each one. However, in many instances, provincial governments assist in funding, training, and administration.

Increasingly, Indigenous police services are developing into organizations similar in structure and authority to those in non-native areas. In Northern Ontario, for example, the Rama Police Service is regarded as a regional service similar to those of York, Peel, and South Simcoe–West Gwillimbury. Although not subject to the provincial *Police Services Act*, the force trains its recruits at the Ontario Police College. Fifty-two percent of Rama's funding comes

---

13   For a full list of all police services, including First Nations policing, see Policing in Canada (n.d.).

from the federal government, while the Ontario government makes up the remainder. In 2016–2017, its total budget was $3.1 million. The Rama Police Service currently has 19 uniformed officers and 3 civilian staff.[14]

Special Interest Groups and Citizens' Organizations

In Canada, social movements have tended to be based around "region, workplace, and household" (Adam, 1992, p. 64). For example, French nationalism (and the desire for Quebec separation) is probably the most significant regional movement in Canada. Other important movements include the labour (union) movement, environmentalism, multiculturalism, feminism and women's rights, and the LGBTQ community movement. In recent years, globalism—the interrelationships among cultures and economies around the world—has been gaining momentum. Important political decisions cannot be made without considering their effects on others.

It has been said that "the ideal of democratic governance is to ensure [that] citizens enjoy an ability to participate meaningfully in the decisions that closely affect their common lives as individuals in communities" (Barney, 2002, pp. 262–289). The danger of growing public apathy about politics has previously been discussed. The perception that average citizens simply can't make a difference in politics has spawned a number of initiatives that attempt to reclaim political power. Known collectively as "direct democracy," these activities seek to actively engage voters in holding politicians accountable between elections and provide an avenue for citizen-driven legislation. For example, a recall allows voters who are not happy with their elected representative between elections to hold a vote on whether or not that representative should be allowed to continue to hold office. The vote occurs once a certain percentage (say, 20 percent) of signatures is gathered in that constituency. The referendum and plebiscite provide a means through which people vote directly on a specific issue. Normally, a referendum is considered binding on a government—that is, politicians will follow the wishes expressed by the majority. A plebiscite is understood as providing information and guidance to officials, and the result is not considered binding. Canada's most recent use of a national referendum came in 1992, when Canadians were asked to vote on whether to adopt the constitutional changes contained in the Charlottetown Accord. An initiative allows citizens to present a proposal directly to fellow citizens, who vote to decide whether it will become law. Again, a certain number of signatures must be gathered in order to get the proposal on the ballot.

While proponents of direct democracy argue that it empowers citizens, the concept is not without fault. Critics point out that, in some respects, direct democracy hinders, rather than aids, representative democracy. For example, a recall prevents sitting politicians from making tough but necessary decisions such as tax increases or changes in services. It also undermines the fundamental principle of party loyalty, vital to parliamentary democracy. Referendums, while useful in some circumstances, often artificially polarize debate into a yes/no proposition, overshadowing equally important, but more complex, issues for consideration. Likewise, initiatives can, in effect, "seize the agenda" from an elected legislature by introducing laws that may interfere with larger government policies and directions. In addition, initiatives speak to single issues; thus their objectives may produce unintended consequences that have a negative impact on citizens, hindering them from achieving

---

14 The authors wish to thank Nishnawbe-Aski Police Service's Chief of Police B.W. Luloff for research and support materials. Thanks also to Allan R. Morrison, education officer/special projects coordinator at Windigo First Nations Council. See also the Nishnawbe-Aski Police Service's website: http://www.naps.ca.

15 For further analysis, see Green (2003).

their intended purpose. One example of the ambiguity of direct democracy was evident in the 2003 voters' recall of California Democratic governor Gray Davis, which resulted in the election of movie star and Republican candidate Arnold Schwarzenegger. Davis was recalled because of California's crumbling public services, in spite of the fact that prior citizen initiatives contributed to the state's financial problems.[15]

In a democratic state, politicians are supposed to consider all points of view, but there remains the danger that when some voices become too loud, they drown out other voices or cause them to be ignored altogether. As you have seen throughout the first part of this text, Canada owes much of its enviable quality of life to its tradition of consultation and compromise. It is important to keep this in mind when considering the viability of direct democracy here.

Government Downsizing and Public Opinion

We submit various types of taxes to the three levels of government to pay for the services they provide. Federal and provincial income taxes are based on the income earned by individuals and businesses. Other taxes include the federal goods and services tax (GST), provincial sales tax (PST)—combined in some provinces with the GST and known as the harmonized sales tax (HST)—in all provinces except Alberta and except the three territories, and local property taxes based on an assessment of the municipal property residents own, which is generally determined by the market value. Governments also raise revenue by assessing fees for various licences and permits, including, among others, business, vehicle, hunting, fishing, and firearms. As well, special programs such as employment insurance and the Canada Pension Plan are funded by employer–employee payroll deductions.

During broader periods of economic stability, the cost of government programs is relatively inconsequential and generally escapes public notice, outside of specific political debates. Following the 2008 global economic crisis, Canadians have been forced to address their mounting debts due to government spending and taxation; in turn, governments are still struggling to respond to the crisis by balancing budgets. Interestingly, municipal governments, by provincial law, cannot run deficits (spend more than they collect in taxes). They establish a working budget and then assess the cost against the local ratepayers (taxpayers).

There exists a widespread perception that government waste and inefficiency during the 1970s and 1980s led to large annual deficits and accumulated public debts during this time. Although this was partly the case, there were other factors that led to the fiscal crisis, resulting in government cutbacks and downsizing in the decade that followed. First, the extremely high interest rates of the 1970s and early 1980s (at one point, 21 percent) greatly compounded the charges governments had to pay on the money they borrowed. Second, the burden of taxation shifted from the corporate sector to individual taxpayers. Thus citizens have found themselves shouldering a larger share of the tax burden than was previously the case. As other countries have lowered their corporate tax rates, Canada has been forced to follow suit. Finally, an ideological swing to the political right that began during the 1980s changed public perceptions about the role and purpose of government. The public embraced tax cuts and less government involvement in our lives, resulting in the downsizing and privatization of many public services.[16]

---

16 Alternative views on the issue of government debt and taxation have been explored by several researchers. See, for example, McQuaig (1995).

Policing in Canada has not been immune from these government initiatives to save money. Police budgets are now coming under much more scrutiny than in the past, while police services are expected to maintain service and adapt to increasingly sophisticated criminal activities. The threats of organized crime and Internet fraud require cutting-edge computer technology and surveillance equipment—expensive propositions for cash-strapped agencies.

As an example, despite the falling crime rate, police budgets have increased over the past decade by an average of 41 percent—far in excess of inflation. In Toronto, in spite of City Council's directive to submit a 2017 budget of no more than $978.6 million, Toronto's police service proposed one costing in excess of $1 billion (Toronto Police Accountability Coalition, 2017). Paying for Toronto's police service now accounts for approximately 10 percent of the city's total budget.[17] To put this in perspective, consider that the one extra day (February 29) in 2016 cost the police service—and thus Torontonians—an additional $1 million!

The issue of "blank cheque" funding for police services is often justified with the adage "Crime doesn't take holidays." While this is no doubt true, we, as citizens, have to remember that our tax dollars pay for policing and other services, and bigger budgets in the public sector present politicians with the dilemma of either cutting service in other areas or raising our taxes to cover the additional cost.

At the same time, relatively stable crime rates in Canada have caused some politicians to question the need for yearly increases to police budgets. Statistics show that Canada's overall crime rate has been declining since 2006, with only slight increases in 2015 and 2016.[18]

Some services have begun to consider replacing uniformed officers with civilians in some areas of service—for example, front desks and traffic enforcement. Police unions have resisted such a move, however, arguing that civilians lack police powers that give them public respect and moral suasion. As one police union official put it: "When an officer's directing traffic, he's not just directing traffic. He's also watching for other things" (Morrow, 2011). Booming sales of alarm systems and anti-theft devices, as well as a marked growth in private security (e.g., corporate and private security guards), suggest that Canadians are feeling less, not more, safe. An aging workforce and budget restraints have led to chronic shortages of police officers, accelerated the growth of private law enforcement, and forced large police services to reorganize in an attempt to cut costs and improve efficiency. For example, the OPP has reconfigured its operations from six regionally-based commands to four operations-based ones (Ontario Provincial Police, n.d.). The RCMP has created four regions and eliminated subdivisions, creating geographical districts. While cost savings and efficiency lie at the heart of these initiatives, it is still too early to assess whether they are achieving these goals amid rising security costs overall.

Police Responses to a Changing Society

The influences mentioned have caused policing services to rethink and reorganize the way they do business and to recruit personnel that mirror the people they serve. In addition, **community policing** has become commonplace all across Canada. Community policing is based on a belief that the officer on the street and members of the community can

community policing
approach to policing based on the police and the community working together

---

17   For further analysis of this dilemma, see Morrow, A., (2011), What price for law and order? *The Globe and Mail*, p. A4.

18   Although overall crime rate increased by 1 percent in 2016, it is still 29 percent below what it was in 2006 (Statistics Canada, 2017b).

work together to prevent crime and resolve disputes. This approach emphasizes greater communication between police and residents, more input on local issues from rank-and-file officers and the public, the importance of having a police service that reflects the diversity of the surrounding community, and a more people-oriented approach to policing in general (Aulakh, Boyington, Kazarian, & Roberts, 2017, pp. 141–170).

The Ontario *Police Services Act* (1990) sets out six principles on which police services are based. Note how the spirit of community policing is contained in this declaration of principles.

> Police services shall be provided throughout Ontario in accordance with the following principles:
> 1. The need to ensure the safety and security of all persons and property in Ontario.
> 2. The importance of safeguarding the fundamental rights guaranteed by the *Canadian Charter of Rights and Freedoms* and the *Human Rights Code*.
> 3. The need for co-operation between the providers of police services and the communities they serve.
> 4. The importance of respect for victims of crime and understanding of their needs.
> 5. The need for sensitivity to the pluralistic, multiracial and multicultural character of Ontario society.
> 6. The need to ensure that police forces are representative of the communities they serve.

Following these principles benefits police services, as well as the community, because officers who reflect their community and behave professionally receive more respect and cooperation from the public. Also note that being representative of the community not only means having more officers who share the cultures and ethnicities of community members, but also having more female officers.

Most citizens have a limited understanding of how different policing is in the 21st century from what it was a generation ago. Policing is no longer simply a matter of responding to crimes after they have occurred. Officers are involved in school and community-based programs, such as Crime Stoppers and Neighbourhood Watch, to deter crime, and in victim assistance programs that provide support for victims of crime. In addition, police services have made concerted efforts to be sensitive to, and representative of, the social and ethnic diversity of the citizens in their respective communities. Efforts are ongoing to actively recruit officers from historically underrepresented groups, including people of colour, women, and Indigenous peoples. Police services in large urban centres are attempting to form positive links with community groups representing a wide range of interests in an effort to gain their support. In recent years, the Toronto Police Service has made concerted efforts to reach out to and recruit members from non-white, Indigenous, and LGBTQ communities in an effort to make its members more sensitive to an increasingly diverse population. Along these lines, the service has established an Aboriginal Peacekeeping Unit and a full-time LGBTQ liaison officer, who provides support to LGBTQ officers, as well as doing in-service training and outreach to the larger community (Toronto Police Service, n.d.). The pace of change, combined with the realities of today's policing environment, makes these initiatives more difficult to achieve, as illustrated by a 2016 survey of police services' diversity across the country. In Toronto, for example, recruitment from these groups continues to increase—from roughly 10 percent in 2000 to almost 25 percent in 2016 ("Toronto police force still much whiter," 2016). However, when compared with the general population—more than half of which is non-white—the results are less impressive. Periodic hiring freezes and slow attrition rates inside the service have limited the number of spaces to add new recruits, but the hope is that efforts to move in this direction will make police services more demographically representative of the communities they serve and protect.

Some police officers have expressed concern that politicians are out of touch with the reality of police work. Police want to have greater input and influence in political decisions that affect them. Politicians and members of the public have been slow to acknowledge the greatly increased workload now expected of individual officers. Groups such as the Canadian Association of Chiefs of Police, the Ontario Association of Chiefs of Police, the Ontario Provincial Police Association, and the Ontario Association of Police Officers are making their positions known on a variety of justice-related issues. Through these and other associations, the police are now taking a much more active role by publicly questioning political decisions. However, this political activity has its limitations in a free and democratic society, and some critics say that this greater political activism threatens the integrity of civilian authority over police and the fundamental principles of elected representation.

Get Real!

Change Is Here for the RCMP

As illustrated in the preceding pages, democratic governance requires constant attention to fair and just treatment under the law to all citizens in order to preserve public respect for, and compliance with, those very same laws. Policing provides an interesting example where the justice system itself must seek to strike a balance between the rights of ordinary citizens and those who are sworn to protect them. Recent events confronting the RCMP highlight this challenge.

Sustained failure to achieve pay parity with the majority of police services in Canada and continued understaffing are two of the main concerns that prompted RCMP officers in North Vancouver—and soon after, detachments across the country—to stop wearing their work-issued yellow-striped cargo pants in early 2017 in favour of plain dark pants (Correia, 2017).

Supporters of the campaign were protesting, among a number of items, pay disparity with many municipal forces. For example, first-class RCMP constables working side by side with similarly ranked municipal counterparts in Halifax earned thousands of dollars less annually. The pay discrepancy was even bigger in cities such as Calgary or Vancouver (Booth, 2017). In Ontario, municipal forces and the Ontario Provincial Police continued to widen the pay gap by securing respective increases—often with retroactive corrections for past wage freezes—through collective bargaining agreements. In Ontario, first-class constables' salaries trend toward $100,000 annually (Powell, 2015; "Labour deal," 2017).

So, in April 2017, when Public Safety Canada gave members of the national police force retroactive salary increases but failed to establish pay parity with similar forces, the yellow-stripe campaign was born. Mounties of the rank superintendent and below who had not had a raise since 2014 received only a 1.25 percent raise effective to January 1, 2015, another 1.25 percent raise for January 1, 2016, and a 2.3 percent market adjustment as of April 1, 2016 (LeBlanc, 2015).

Meanwhile, RCMP management were about to head to trial in Moncton that same month. The federal Ministry of Employment, Workforce Development, and Labour's law-enforcement wing had charged the force with four counts of failing to provide patrol officers with adequate skills, equipment, or weaponry when a gunman shot and killed three Mounties in June 2014 (Babstock, 2017). It wasn't the first time officer safety and equipment had been in the spotlight ("RCMP on trial," 2017).

The yellow-stripe protest, which went national only a few weeks after it started on the West Coast, struck a chord with the rank and file, and galvanized unionization efforts.

The National Police Federation (NPF), the largest of a number of associations wanting to unionize the force, reported a surge in membership to more than 10,000 members—a majority of the force (Booth, 2017; Royal Canadian Mounted Police, 2017).

Despite the association movement having a long history dating back to the 1970s, it wasn't until 2015 that Mounties were legally allowed to unionize. In a 6–1 decision in January 2015 (see *Mounted Police Association of Ontario v Canada,* 2012), the Supreme Court of Canada struck down legislation that made it illegal for the RCMP to unionize. At that time, the RCMP was the only police force in Canada without a union. The court ruled the law violated the Charter right to freedom of association and then gave the federal government a year—later adding an extension—to create a new bargaining system for RCMP ("Supreme Court gives Ottawa 4-month extension," 2016).

Collective bargaining will not be the only influence on the future of this police service. The RCMP is but one of several agencies the federal Liberal government has promised to fold into a forthcoming broader national security watchdog, and there is mounting speculation as to whether this will encourage a pivot from the force's current management structure to a civilian oversight board in the style of municipal forces (Harris, 2017).[19]

For all the talk of systemic issues and a broken force over the past few decades, change is finally here for the RCMP. But it is difficult to predict how that change will manifest or how it will balance attempts to bring the force in line with policing standards across Canada while also accounting for the force's unique national role and purview. Do you agree with the strategy adopted by uniformed officers? How might those who disagree with your opinion respond to its message? Given the Supreme Court's decision in favour of Charter rights, should police unions also have the right to limit or curtail their services as part of their collective bargaining powers?

---

19 See also Canada's Minister of Public Safety Ralph Goodale's comments to Chris Hall regarding the prospects of civilian oversight (Goodale, 2017).

CHAPTER SUMMARY

Politics and history have and continue to have a significant role in the development of public law enforcement in Canada. In the country's early years, law enforcement agencies, like other government departments, were limited in both scope and size, due in large part to the sheer size of the country and the contemporary understanding of what constituted effective law enforcement.

As Canada was transformed from a rural-agricultural society into an urban-industrial one, new realities and the resulting new demands imposed themselves on public law enforcement agencies. The arrival of mass communication, more sophisticated transportation networks, and technological innovations has challenged and changed the justice system.

The political spectrum informs the ideologies of the major federal parties in Canada. Each government is influenced by the political and moral views of its elected body, and these views inform the analysis of, and proposed solutions to, social issues. This is especially true in relation to policing services, crime, and the administration of justice. The three levels of government often have interrelated and overlapping roles and responsibilities. We see this particularly in the area of law enforcement. This situation can be beneficial, as in the case of joint efforts to combat crime, but it can also result in government agencies working against, rather than with, one another.

Popular demand for greater government accountability and fiscal restraint has affected police services, resulting in reorganization and fresh dialogue with individuals and groups representing a variety of backgrounds, including First Nations and other cultural groups and citizens' organizations. Part of this new strategy is an attempt to communicate to the public how policing has changed over the years so that the communities being served understand better the realities of the job and the demands being placed on rank-and-file police officers. Deciding how far to push this message is at the centre of current debates, such as the one concerning political activism by police.

KEY TERMS

community policing, 95

cost sharing, 79

federal spending power, 79

Indigenous self-government, 91

left wing, 82

multiculturalism, 90

police services board, 82

political culture, 88

political spectrum, 82

right wing, 82

WEBSITES

Bill C-10 Safe Streets and Communities Act: http://laws-lois.justice.gc.ca/eng/AnnualStatutes/2012_1/

Bloc Québécois: http://www.blocquebecois.org/?accueil

Broadbent Institute: http://www.broadbentinstitute.ca

Canada and International Peace Efforts: http://www.veterans.gc.ca/eng

Canada Border Services Agency: http://www.cbsa-asfc.gc.ca/menu-eng.html

Canadian Forces: http://www.forces.ca

Canadian Pension Plan: http://laws-lois.justice.gc.ca/eng/acts/C-8/

Canadian Security Intelligence Service (CSIS): https://www.csis-scrs.gc.ca

Canadian Taxpayers Federation: http://www.taxpayer.com

Citizenship and Immigration Canada: http://www.cic.gc.ca/english/index.asp

City of Thunder Bay Police Services Board: http://www.thunderbaypolice.ca

Conservative Party of Canada: http://www.conservative.ca

Criminal Code: http://laws-lois.justice.gc.ca/eng/acts/C-46/

David Suzuki Foundation: http://www.davidsuzuki.org

Durham Police Services Board: https://members.drps.ca/internet_explorer/police_service_board/index.asp

Equalization Program: http://www.fin.gc.ca/fedprov/eqp-eng.asp

Fisheries and Oceans Canada: http://www.dfo-mpo.gc.ca/index-eng.htm

Fraser Institute: https://www.fraserinstitute.org

Green Party of Canada: https://www.greenparty.ca/en

Halton Regional Police Service: https://www.haltonpolice.ca

Immigration and Refugee Board of Canada: http://www.irb-cisr.gc.ca/Eng/Pages/index.aspx

Immigration and Refugee Protection Act: http://laws-lois.justice.gc.ca/eng/acts/I-2.5/index.html

Judge Barry Stuart on *Bill C-10*: http://www.cbc.ca/radio/thecurrent

Liberal Party of Canada: http://www.liberal.ca

National Office for Victims: https://www.publicsafety.gc.ca/cnt/cntrng-crm/crrctns/ntnl-ffc-vctms-en.aspx

New Democratic Party of Canada: http://www.ndp.ca

Nishnawbe-Aski Police Service: http://www.naps.ca

Office of the Federal Ombudsman for Victims of Crime: http://www.victimsfirst.gc.ca/serv/wvr-qdv.html

Ontario Crime Stoppers: http://ontariocrimestoppers.ca

Ontario Highway Traffic Act: https://www.ontario.ca/laws/statute/90h08

Ontario Parental Responsibility Act: https://www.ontario.ca/laws/statute/00p04

Ontario Parole Board: http://www.slasto.gov.on.ca/en/opb/Pages/default.aspx

Ontario *Police Services Act*: https://www.ontario.ca/laws/statute/90p15

Ontario Provincial Police (OPP): http://www.opp.ca

Ontario's Ministry of Community Safety and Correctional Services: http://www.mcscs.jus.gov.on.ca/english/default.html

OPP Auxiliary: https://www.opp.ca/index.php?id=115&entryid=56b758c48f94ac9e5828d172

Public Safety Canada: https://www.publicsafety.gc.ca/index-en.aspx

Royal Canadian Mounted Police: http://www.rcmp-grc.gc.ca/index.htm

Sûreté du Québec (Quebec Police Services): https://www.sq.gouv.qc.ca

Toronto Police Service: http://www.torontopolice.on.ca

Toronto Police Services Board: http://www.tpsb.ca

United Nations: http://www.un.org/en/index.html

United Nations Peacekeeping: https://www.un.org/en/peacekeeping/

United Steelworkers Union: https://www.usw.ca

World Trade Organization: https://www.wto.org

Youth Criminal Justice Act: http://laws-lois.justice.gc.ca/eng/acts/Y-1.5/

REFERENCE LIST

Adam, B.D. (1992). Social inequality in Canada. In K.G. Pryke & W.C. Soderlund (Eds.), *Profiles of Canada* (p. 64). Toronto: Copp Clark Pitman.

Alam, S., & Greeland, J. (n.d.). Police resources in Canada. *Juristat*. Retrieved from http://www.statcan.gc.ca/pub/85-002-x/2017001/article/14777-eng.htm

Aulakh, H., Boyington, S., Kazarian, S., & Roberts, J. (2017). *Diversity and Indigenous peoples in Canada* (3rd ed.). Toronto: Emond.

Babstock, C. (2017, July 4). RCMP trial enters final phase this week. *Times & Transcript*. Retrieved from https://www.telegraphjournal.com/times-transcript/story/100252614/

Barney, D. (2002). Quoted in O'Neill, B., Democracy in action: Elections, referendums and citizen power. In R. Dyck (Ed.), *Studying politics: An introduction to political science* (pp. 262–289). Toronto: Thomson Nelson.

Booth, L. (2017, April 12). No discipline for RCMP over yellow stripe protest: Top mountie. *Times & Transcript*. Retrieved from https://www.telegraphjournal.com/times-transcript/story/100158258/rcmp-mounties-pay-yellow-stripe

The Canada Guide (n.d.). Government political parties. Retrieved from http://www.thecanadaguide.com/government/political-parties/

Canada's crime index rises for 1st time in 12 years, lifted by spike in Alberta. (2016, July 20). *CBC News*. Retrieved from http://www.cbc.ca/news/canada/calgary/canada-crime-stats-rate-increase-statistics-canada-severity-index-police-1.3686871

Canadian Charter of Rights and Freedoms, Part I of the Constitution Act, 1982, being Schedule B to the Canada Act 1982 (UK), 1982, c 11 [Charter].

Canadian softwood producers brace for 2nd wave of US lumber duties. (2017, June 25). *CBC News*. Retrieved from http://www.cbc.ca/news/politics/softwood-lumber-duties-1.4177436

Coles, T. (2015, October 20). Women and visible minorities make election gains, *Yahoo! News*. Retrieved from https://ca.news.yahoo.com/blogs/canada-politics/women-and-visible-minorities-make-election-gains-154729934.html

Colombo, J.R. (Ed.). (1998). *1999 Canadian global almanac*. Toronto: Macmillan.

Conrad M., & Finkel, A. (2003). *Canada: A national history*. Toronto: Pearson Education.

Correia, C. RCMP strip their yellow stripes in protest. (2017, April 6). Retrieved from http://www.cbc.ca/news/canada/british-columbia/rcmp-stripe-protest-pay-1.4057952

Criminal Code, RSC 1985, c C-46.

Dobbin, M. (1999). *Ten tax myths*. Toronto: Canadian Centre for Policy Alternatives.

Fine, S. (2016, April 16). The Supreme Court strikes down Tories' tough-on-crime laws. *The Globe and Mail*. Retrieved from https://www.theglobeandmail.com/news/national/supreme-court-strikes-down-tories-tough-on-crime-laws/article29641784/

Fisheries Act, RSC 1985, c F-14.

Francis R.D., Jones, R., & Smith, D.B. (2000). *Destinies: Canadian history since Confederation* (4th ed., p. 133). Toronto: Thomson Nelson.

Francis R.D., Jones, R., & Smith, D.B. (2004). *Destinies: Canadian history since Confederation* (5th ed.). Toronto: Thomson Nelson.

Green Party of Canada (n.d). Platform. Retrieved from https://www.greenparty.ca/en/platform

Green, M. (2003, August 13). A script tailored for a star. *The Globe and Mail*, p. A11.

Goodale, R. (2017, June 24). Interviewed by C. Hall. The Liberal approach to national security. *The House*. Retrieved from http://www.cbc.ca/radio/thehouse/the-liberal-approach-to-national-security-1.4172816

Harris, K. (2017, June 20). Liberals to create "super" national security watchdog as part of anti-terror law overhaul. *CBC News*. Retrieved from http://www.cbc.ca/news/politics/security-terrorism-legislation-1.4168780

Hauss, C., & Smith, W. (2000). *Comparative politics—Domestic responses to global challenges: A Canadian perspective* (3rd ed.). Toronto: Nelson.

Hedley, M.J. (1992). Native peoples in Canada. In K.G. Pryke & W.C. Soderlund (Eds.), *Profiles of Canada* (p. 88). Toronto: Copp Clark Pitman.

Highway Traffic Act, RSO 1990, c H.8.

Human Rights Code, RSO 1990, c H.19.

Immigration Act, RSC 1985, c I-2.

Labour deal sets Ottawa police constables on $100K salary track. (2017, June 12). *CBC News*. Retrieved from http://www.cbc.ca/news/canada/ottawa/ottawa-police-labour-deal-1.4157186

LeBlanc, D. (2015, February 17). RCMP wage review calls for 10-per-cent pay increase to get quality recruits. *The Globe and Mail*. Retrieved from https://www.theglobeandmail.com/news/politics/rcmp-wage-review-calls-for-10-per-cent-pay-increase-to-get-quality-recruits/article23041739/

McQuaig, L. (1995). *Shooting the hippo*. Toronto: Viking/Penguin.

Morrow, A. (2011, January 8). What price for law and order? *The Globe and Mail*, p. A4.

Mounted Police Association of Ontario v Canada, 2012 ONCA 363.

Ontario Provincial Police. (n.d.). Who we are. Retrieved from https://www.opp.ca/index.php?id=123

Parental Responsibility Act, SO 2000, c 4.

Police Services Act, RSO 1990, c P.15.

Policing in Canada. myPolice.ca (n.d). Retrieved from http://mypolice.ca/police_agencies/Canada.html

The Political Compass. (n.d.). Retrieved from https://www.politicalcompass.org/

Powell, B. (2015, March 16). Half of Toronto police workforce earned $100,000 last year. *Toronto Star*. Retrieved from https://www.thestar.com/news/city_hall/2015/03/16/half-of-toronto-police-workforce-earned-100000-last-year.html

RCMP on trial: Stalled salaries, officer safety in focus. (2017, April 23). *The Globe and Mail*. Retrieved from https://www.theglobeandmail.com/news/national/rcmp-court-case-to-highlight-concerns-over-wages-safety/article34794478/

Reitano, J. (2017, October 28). Adult correctional statistics in Canada. *Juristat*. Retrieved from http://www.statcan.gc.ca/pub/85-002-x/2017001/article/14700-eng.htm

Royal Canadian Mounted Police. (2001, January 1). Historical highlights. Retrieved from http://www.rcmp-grc.gc.ca/hist/hh-ps/index-eng.htm

Royal Canadian Mounted Police. (2011, October 28). Contract policing. Retrieved from http://www.rcmp-grc.gc.ca/ccaps-spcca/contract-eng.htm

Royal Canadian Mounted Police. (2017, April 12). Commissioner's broadcast. Retrieved from http://www.rcmp.gc.ca/en/news/2017/12/commissioners-broadcast

Saunders, D. (2010). *Arrival city: The final migration and our next world*. Toronto: Knopf Canada.

Statistics Canada. (2017a). Canada's crime rate: Two decades of decline. Retrieved from http://www.statcan.gc.ca/pub/11-630-x/11-630-x2015001-eng.htm

Statistics Canada. (2017b). Police-reported crime statistics, 2016. Retrieved from http://www.statcan.gc.ca/daily-quotidien/170724/dq170724b-eng.htm

Supreme Court gives Ottawa 4-month extension for rules on RCMP collective bargaining. (2016, January 15). *CBC News*. Retrieved from http://www.cbc.ca/news/politics/rcmp-collective-bargaining-supreme-court-1.3406043

Toronto Police Accountability Coalition. (2017, January 17). *Bulletin 101*. Retrieved from http://mypolice.ca/police_agencies/Canada.html

Toronto police force still much whiter than the city's population. (2016, July 14). *CBC News*. Retrieved from http://www.cbc.ca/news/canada/toronto/toronto-police-diversity-1.3679994

Toronto Police Service. (n.d.). Aboriginal peacekeeping unit. Retrieved from http://www.torontopolice.on.ca/community/aboriginal.php

Vote Compass. (n.d.). CBC. Retrieved from https://votecompass.cbc.ca/

Waller, I. (2006). *Less law, more order: The truth about reducing crime*. Westport: Praeger.

Wells, P. (2006). *Right side up: The fall of Paul Martin and the rise of Stephen Harper's new conservatism*. Toronto: Penguin Random House Canada.

Wiliamson P., & Roberts, J. (2011). *First Nations peoples* (Rev. 2nd ed., Chapter 7). Toronto: Emond.

Young Offenders Act, RSC 1985, c Y-1.

Youth Criminal Justice Act summary and background. (n.d.). Department of Justice. Retrieved from http://www.justice.gc.ca/eng/cj-jp/yj-jj/tools-outils/back-hist.html

Youth Criminal Justice Act, SC 2002, c 1.

EXERCISES

True or False?

_____ 1. Municipal policing services are an extension of provincial authority over the administration and enforcement of criminal law.

_____ 2. Through cost sharing, the federal government can greatly influence how justice is administered in the provinces.

_____ 3. Someone who supports right-wing ideology tends to view crime as a product of a social system that is inherently unequal.

_____ 4. Someone who supports left-wing ideology tends to view crime as an individual choice and therefore an individual responsibility.

_____ 5. The close proximity of the United States has no effect on Canada's political culture.

Multiple Choice

1. Public law enforcement is administered by

   a. the federal government

   b. the provincial governments

   c. the municipal governments

   d. all three levels of government

   e. none of the above

2. "Political culture" refers to

   a. the attitudes of politicians about government

   b. basic attitudes of citizens toward one another, the government, and authority

   c. political views that have been shaped by a country's history and geography

   d. a and b

   e. b and c

3. "Left wing" refers to

   a. a seat on the left side of the House of Commons

   b. a political philosophy that emphasizes tax cuts and smaller government

   c. a political philosophy that emphasizes social welfare and the collective good

   d. a political philosophy that emphasizes individualism and little government intervention

   e. all of the above

4. Only two parties have formed the federal government since Confederation:

   a. New Democratic Party and Progressive Conservative Party

   b. Liberal Party and New Democratic Party

   c. Canadian Alliance and Progressive Conservative Party

   d. (Progressive) Conservative Party and Liberal Party

   e. New Democratic Party and Canadian Alliance

5. Right-wing ideologists tend to believe that

   a. criminals should go to prison

   b. crime is a product of inequalities in the social system

   c. criminals must take responsibility for their actions

   d. a and b

   e. a and c

Short Answer

1. How do social realities affect decisions about what policing services are provided at the federal, provincial, and local levels and the nature of these services?

2. What is Indigenous self-government? What is its purpose?

3. As a city councillor, how would you deal with proposed police budget increases and shortfalls? Explain your answer.

4. How might the principles of cooperation and compromise be employed to overcome current disagreements over the role of police in the political process?

5. Which side of the political spectrum most appeals to you? Why?

6. Choose the federal party you believe you will support in the next election. On what basis do you make this choice? Visit the party's website and see whether it has any information on the subjects you are interested in.

7. Using the framework of the political spectrum, choose three news items and analyze them from a left-wing and a right-wing perspective. How are the solutions to these issues coloured by the respective ideologies?

PART III

Public Administration

A Cog in the Machine: Public Administration and Bureaucracies

6

LEARNING OUTCOMES

After completing this chapter, you should be able to

- define public administration and describe its relation to the political process in Canada;

- explain and compare theoretical concepts of bureaucracy;

- outline the benefits and drawbacks of each concept;

- describe the degree to which each of these concepts has been adopted by private and public bureaucracies;

- outline the differences between public and private enterprise; and

- understand the difficulties that democratic societies face when accommodating competing viewpoints.

Introduction

Prime Minister Promises $1 Million to Each Canadian.

Hold on! Before you drop this text and run off in search of your share of the cash, think for a moment about where exactly you'd be searching for this windfall. The prime minister's residence probably wouldn't be high on your list. You might visit the local federal government building, go online, or phone a federal government office in an attempt to discover how to receive payment. Now the bad news: as far as the authors know, there is no substance to this headline (but we could be wrong). The good news is that, if you reacted to this headline as stated, you have already demonstrated an understanding of the difference between the political and administrative elements of government. Even though the prime minister announces that funding will be made available for all kinds of programs, the actual distribution of these funds or the services they provide is carried out by a vast and complex network of people and institutions referred to collectively as the public service.

Because of the close interaction between politics and public administration, it can be difficult to distinguish between them. Both are responsible for managing the day-to-day operation of government. Similarly, political and administrative bodies attempt to respond to citizens' needs by discussing and developing public policy. However, public administration differs from its political counterpart in several ways. First, we do not directly elect public servants. Instead, they are usually hired in much the same way as any other employee, although, as you will see, some may be appointed by government to sit on a board or carry out a special duty. Second, public administration is, ideally, concerned with how to implement political will rather than with deciding what it is the public actually wants. Thus in the above fantasy, it is the public service that would serve as the vehicle that would give each of us our money. In short, politicians make decisions while public servants implement, or carry out, those decisions.

Theories of Bureaucracy

The model we have just described provides a general explanation of the relationship between politics and public administration, but the ongoing interaction is seldom this simple. The administrative side alone involves thousands of bureaucrats—basically, unelected government officials—intricate layers of communication, and an adherence to rules and regulations for the purposes of evaluation and accountability. This administrative machinery that supports government has been with us for as long as civilization itself. As humans began to congregate in larger and larger groups, structures of government developed; in turn, rulers depended on others to carry out their wishes. It is no surprise then that societies with highly developed bureaucracies were capable of considerable achievements. Though the word has many popular negative connotations, a **bureaucracy** is really just an organizational structure through which governments put their decisions into action. The word is a combination of the French *bureau*, for desk or office, and the Greek *cratie*, for rule. A **bureaucrat** is simply an employee of a bureaucracy—a public servant. Huge bureaucracies existed in ancient China and Egypt, societies whose legacies live with us today in the Great Wall and the pyramids, respectively. Bureaucrats even had an effect on the location of Jesus's birth! Mary and Joseph went to Bethlehem in accordance with Roman policy, which decreed that people must return to their hometowns for taxation purposes. Thus, while they form an integral part of society, public bureaucracies have for the most part gone unnoticed or have been overshadowed by events with which most of us are familiar.

bureaucracy
the organizational structure through which government exercises its power

bureaucrat
public servant

The nature and function of bureaucracies began to interest political thinkers during the 19th century. The field has expanded greatly since then, helped along by the theoretical ideas of several notable figures. These people can be categorized according to three general schools of thought: classic, structuralist, and human relations or humanist. We will deal with each category separately.

Classic Theories of Bureaucracy
Karl Marx (1818 – 1883)

> From each according to his abilities, to each according to his needs. (Marx, 1992, p. 452:5)

Karl Marx is best known for developing the political ideology of communism. In general terms, this way of thinking about society proposed that **capitalism**[1] creates two classes of people: the poorer class, collectively known as the "proletariat," and the wealthier class, which Marx called

Karl Marx

capitalism
an economic system based on private ownership and competition in a free market

the "bourgeoisie." Marx argued that this class division occurs because competition in the free market forces bourgeois employers to exploit their proletariat employees—that is, work them as hard as possible for as little money as possible. Marx observed the terrible working conditions spawned by the Industrial Revolution of the late 1700s through the mid-1800s. This was a time of major economic change as new machinery and technology revolutionized industry. The mainly rural population of Europe and other parts of the world moved to the cities in greater and greater numbers in search of jobs in the new factories. A new—and poverty-stricken—working class developed who worked under sometimes appallingly dangerous conditions, and Marx became convinced that it was just a matter of time before these workers would overthrow their capitalist oppressors, creating a society with no social classes or private ownership.

Marx speculated that eventually there would be no need for government because people would work toward a common good and share equally in resources. As far as Marx was concerned, government was nothing more than a tool of the wealthy classes, which they used to maintain their positions of social and economic privilege. Bureaucracy was merely an extension of this apparatus, a means of legitimating state oppression of the working classes while perpetuating an illusion of fairness, justice, and objectivity. Recall from Chapter 1 that these are all vital elements underpinning public confidence in the rule of law and the political system in which it functions. Marx reasoned that as workers collectively became aware of their situation, conflict would increase between workers and the dominant classes. The latter would respond by resorting to more violence to keep the working classes in line. For example, the police or army might be called on to break up demonstrations or intervene in labour disputes. Thus, for Marx, the civil service was part of a systemic social problem of one class over another, and bureaucracy became more complex as government attempted to deal with class conflict.

Many scholars have attempted to interpret Marxist theory and explain its relevance to current events. Referred to as neo-Marxists, this group argues that the state exists for

---

1 The term "capitalism" refers to an economic system based on private ownership. Individuals or corporations use what they own (land, factories, resources) to produce goods and services, competing with one another in the free market. This means simply that we, as consumers, are free to choose from among these offerings on the basis of such things as price, quality, and reputation.

three major purposes. First, it accumulates and concentrates wealth and power within the wealthy classes. For example, the state may give the rich favourable tax treatment or provide corporations with generous job-creation subsidies. Second, the state serves to legitimize the disadvantaged position of the working classes by pretending that social inequality is simply the result of the natural superiority of the upper classes. In other words, those on top deserve to be there by virtue of the fact that they are there. Finally, the state exists to quash any social unrest that may emerge as a result of worker dissatisfaction with the status quo (Kernaghan & Siegel, 1995, p. 33).

CRITICISM OF MARXIST THEORY

One criticism of Marxist social analysis is that it cannot adequately explain the social mobility that takes place among members of different classes. For example, some people who are born into a disadvantaged class are able to work their way up to a higher class. Marxism also stereotypes people according to their class and therefore cannot accommodate individual differences. In addition, notions of social class today are very different from when Marx first conceived his ideas. Most Canadians like to think of themselves as middle class regardless of whether their income actually meets the definition.

Statistics Canada defines "middle class" according to how incomes are distributed on either side of the median income; however, this equation provides a fairly simplistic overview of the definition. According to the 2016 census, which used income ranges to map out who falls where, the average Canadian household earned $70,336 annually (Statistics Canada, 2017). The gap between the richest and poorest Canadians has remained fairly stable over the past decade, however examining data over a longer period of time reveals that Canada's overall wealth is increasingly concentrated among fewer and fewer households. For example, a 2012 analysis conducted by the Broadbent Institute (n.d.) showed that top 20 percent of Canadians owned 70 percent of the country's wealth, compared with the 6 percent owned by the bottom 50 percent of Canada's population. While there is little likelihood that rigid socio-economic class structures that inspired Marx will re-establish themselves, there is growing concern over what this inequality does to the overall health of a nation. Mounting evidence suggests that societies with large income gaps suffer much higher rates of physical and mental illness, as well as higher crime and incarceration rates (Wilkinson, 2011).

Still, the desire to self-identify as middle class persists, and political parties have exploited and encouraged this self-perception because they can appear to present a broad but targeted platform that will appeal to a critical mass of voters during elections. In the 2015 federal election, for example, the Liberal Party used an income range between $44,700 and $89,400 to describe middle-income households[2] (see Table 6.1).

Nevertheless, Marxist philosophy does provide some insights about how and why public bureaucracies function as they do, particularly when it comes to public law enforcement. Marxist analysis is imbued with a negative view of government, and this has implications for institutions that are charged with preserving public safety and civil order. It casts state armies and police forces as defenders of an unfair and self-serving regime, protecting and preserving the property and entitlements of the dominant classes. Thus, when workers attempt to force any changes on the existing social order, the upper classes can call on these law enforcement agencies to counter the perceived threat. They can also use other

---

2 The range was used to propose a tax cut for the middle class. See Liberal Party of Canada (n.d.).

Table 6.1   Data Tables, 2016 Census After-Tax Income Groups

The median income of a specified group is the amount that divides the income distribution of that group into two halves (i.e., the incomes of half of the units in that group are below the median, while those of the other half are above the median). Median incomes of persons not in families are calculated for all units, whether or not they had income.

After-tax income groups	Canada	
	Year	
	2015	2005
Total – After-tax income	5,313,545	4,307,135
Under $5,000	315,875	282,555
$5,000 to $9,999	257,870	245,195
$10,000 to $14,999	450,115	377,985
$15,000 to $19,999	617,555	587,035
$20,000 to $24,999	637,460	537,530
$25,000 to $29,999	471,530	395,415
$30,000 to $34,999	442,155	382,340
$35,000 to $39,999	404,910	317,705
$40,000 to $44,999	339,115	252,920
$45,000 to $49,999	273,390	205,305
$50,000 to $59,999	398,445	284, 400
$60,000 to $69,999	254,770	173,575
$70,000 to $79,999	161,920	104,410
$80,000 to $89,999	95,680	56,065
$90,000 to $99,999	56,310	31,975
$100,000 and over	136,445	72,730
Median after-tax income ($)	28,959	26,483

Sources: Statistics Canada (2016).

government institutions, such as the legal system, to deal with resistance. As a result, neo-Marxist theory puts little faith in the integrity of law enforcement, viewing it with suspicion and as an institution in need of constant monitoring.

Max Weber (1864–1920)

The state is a relation of men dominating men, a relation supported by means of legitimate (i.e., considered to be legitimate) violence. (Weber, 1992, p. 724)

Max Weber

traditional authority
authority on the basis
of heredity, religion,
or divine right

charismatic authority
authority based on the
unique talents and popular
appeal of an individual

legal authority
authority based on
the rule of law

hierarchy
an organized system of
labour characterized by
a superior–subordinate
relationship

continuity
the long-term or ongoing
nature of a bureaucracy;
continuity means that the
people working within an
organization are full-time
employees who can make a
career out of what they do

impersonality
the objective nature of
jobs and routines in a
bureaucracy, based on
written rules and records

expertise
knowledge of or ability in a
particular area or subject

Max Weber was a German scholar who studied social issues using systematic methods. As you have learned, bureaucracies have existed for as long as human civilization; however, it was Weber who pioneered the study of bureaucratic structure, function, and behaviour. His work remains relevant today because it offers insights into the ways public policy is developed and implemented.

Weber began his study of bureaucracy by relating it to his previous work in the field of political sociology. He identified three sources of authority that can form the basic power structure in a society: traditional authority, charismatic authority, and legal authority. **Traditional authority** refers to the right of someone to rule on the basis of heredity, religion, or divine right (a right sanctioned by a higher spiritual power). A good example of this is the British monarchy, which has claimed legitimacy to rule using all of these criteria at different periods in history. **Charismatic authority** refers to the unique talents and popular appeal that make an individual particularly attractive as a public leader. These attributes may or may not be related specifically to the political arena (witness the election of real estate mogul and reality TV star Donald Trump to the US presidency in 2016); however, the attributes are definitely an asset. **Legal authority** means that authority to govern is legitimated by the rule of law—that is, the laws and regulations that must be obeyed by all members of a society, the rulers as well as those they rule. Thus a queen, president, prime minister, or TV star turned president is subject to the law. It is the law that we trust and hence obey that legitimates the power of our leaders. Weber argued that modern bureaucracies are necessary parts of regimes whose power rests in legal authority (Weber, 1968, pp. 31–38). Because of this, a government can tell us what to do ("men dominating men") and can resort to coercive measures in order to ensure that we comply ("legitimate—i.e., considered to be legitimate—violence").

You can probably think of several examples in which one, some, or all of these sources of authority exist. Pierre Trudeau, for example, came to power in 1968 riding a wave of popularity known as "Trudeaumania." Many observers pointed to a similar phenomenon when his son Justin led the Liberal Party into the 2015 federal election. Still, the reason that these leaders and others like them continue to govern after the hoopla has subsided is because this power is ultimately vested in legal authority.

Weberian theory contends that, by its very nature, legal authority relies on bureaucratic organization to maintain itself. This is not meant to suggest that bureaucracies do not exist in other expressions of political authority; rather, Weber emphasized that legal authority cannot exist without a bureaucracy to support it. He went on to describe what he considered to be the fundamental components of an "ideal bureaucracy," which could then be used to assess the development of systems of organization in the real world. While Weber himself cited eight separate components, more recent interpretations have consolidated these into four main areas: hierarchy, continuity, impersonality, and expertise (Inwood, 1999, pp. 33–35; Gerth & Mills, 1970, p. 178).

In this context, **hierarchy** refers to an organized system of labour where it is clear who reports to whom in a superior–subordinate relationship. **Continuity** means that the people working within the organization are full-time employees and can make a career out of what they do. **Impersonality** means that jobs and routines are based on written rules and records, which guard against favouritism. **Expertise** refers to hiring practices that are based on merit, rather than patronage, and the ability to control and access information and knowledge specific to a particular area. Weber concluded that the more closely an organization approximates these ideals, the more rational and efficient it will be. In short, organizational efficiency occurs when people are hired for what they know rather than for whom they know. And, as these employees work their way up through the ranks, they will develop expertise that can be used to improve the operation of the organization.

CRITICISM OF WEBERIAN THEORY

The major flaw with the Weberian view of bureaucracy is that it attempts to explain this type of human organization by measuring it against an ideal, or perfect, model. Weber asserted that the closer a bureaucracy came to approximating this model, the more efficient it would become. This is often not the case in the real world. In fact, strict adherence to the Weberian model can sometimes result in a very inefficient organization. For example, hierarchy and continuity can deter initiative and produce apathy as workers begin to feel insignificant and underappreciated. Expertise and strict adherence to formal rules can create a work environment that detracts from the organization's overall aims as employees focus on career advancement rather than on collective organizational needs.

Formal rules that are put in place to ensure fair treatment for everyone may paradoxically achieve the opposite effect. For example, in the past many police services required prospective officers to meet certain height and weight requirements. These criteria were seen as objective requirements of the job. However, these standards inadvertently discriminated against certain groups of people. Because the standards reflected the average for white males, women and some cultural minorities faced unintended discrimination if they chose a career in policing. An argument can be made that physical size is important in law enforcement; however, an opposite argument can be made for equality of opportunity for employment. Thus rules that at first appear neutral and non-discriminatory may produce the opposite effect.

These criticisms aside, Weber's analysis does provide insight into organizational behaviour, and, as you will discover later in this chapter, plenty of evidence exists to support his observations.

scientific management management approach based on using resources in ways that maximize productivity and minimize waste

Structuralist Theory of Bureaucracy
Frederick Winslow Taylor (1856–1915)

> No one can be found who will deny that in the case of any single individual the greatest prosperity can exist only when that individual has reached his highest state of efficiency. (Taylor, 1911, p. 11)

Whereas Max Weber was interested in the general aspects of bureaucratic organization, Frederick Winslow Taylor focused on its key elements. Taylor wanted to find out how best to use human and mechanical resources—workers and machines—to maximize productivity and minimize waste. This approach is called **scientific management**.

A mechanical engineer by trade, Taylor began his career on the factory floors of late 19th-century America. These experiences prompted him to consider ways to improve the efficiency of factory work. His observations of the workers led him to draw two conclusions: (1) they were prone to slacking off, and (2) their jobs were inefficiently organized. Taylor argued that a scientific approach could be used to solve both of these problems and the result would benefit both workers and employers. His method involved having a trained observer watch an above-average employee perform his or her task, identify and time each component of that task, and then teach that employee's method to others in similar jobs. This would provide an empirical, objective standard against which employers could

Frederick Winslow Taylor

measure employee productivity. Taylor proposed solving the awkward organization of the jobs themselves by rearranging them so that each worker would be responsible for one or two clearly defined tasks, rather than doing piecework, which was a common practice during his day.[3] As industrialism pervaded society, Taylor gained a considerable following and, in 1911, he published a book entitled *The Principles of Scientific Management* (1911), in which he outlined several theories of organization modelled on his ideas.

Taylor's approach coincided with the emergence of a new group of managerial professionals who supervised the increasingly complex operations of factories and other large businesses. Scientific management transformed skilled work (e.g., shoe-making) previously done by one person or a small group into simple, repetitive tasks done by a team of workers. As a result, productivity and efficiency were greatly improved. This approach became a template for the assembly-line model of production so familiar today. Hence, "scientific managers" were to think of their workers as part of the "company machine" to be used by them in the most efficient way possible and at the least cost.[4]

CRITICISM OF TAYLOR'S SCIENTIFIC MANAGEMENT APPROACH

Taylor's theories of scientific management have drawn criticism for several reasons. First, he asserted that there should be a clear distinction between management and labour. Implicit in this division was an assumption that managers should be responsible for setting standards and making decisions, which would then be carried out by workers. This has been referred to as the "strong back and weak mind" principle by some critics, who also point out that Taylor's approach prevents workers from having any meaningful say in the duties that are expected of them. To be fair, Taylor recognized the importance of cordial labour–management relations, but his ideas suggest that he believed proper results could be achieved only when management dominated the relationship.

Later theorists criticized this approach for its emphasis on strictly material rewards for workers who performed well. This one-dimensional, mechanistic view of workers as mere cogs in the factory machine was certainly not lost on workers themselves. Much of the labour unrest of the early 20th century occurred as a result of attempts to implement principles of scientific management without workers' consent. Thus Taylor's view of labour as but one (expendable) resource in industrial capitalism cannot address the non-economic human aspects of work—such as job satisfaction, morale, and loyalty—as motivating factors that contribute to overall efficiency.

Human Relations Theory of Bureaucracy
George Elton Mayo (1880–1949)

Problems arising from the top-down nature of hierarchical organizations (the approach embraced by Max Weber and Frederick Winslow Taylor) encouraged a search for other theoretical approaches to better understand individual organizational behaviour and find a way to maximize organizational efficiency. Through the work of a variety of individuals in

---

3   "Piecework" refers to a method of employment where workers are paid for the amount they produce rather than for the amount of time they work. For example, the use of this practice in law enforcement might mean that a police officer would be paid according to the number of traffic tickets given or people arrested.

4   For a summary of the application of scientific management and the development of the Canadian economy, see Francis, Jones, & Smith (2000).

business, psychology, and sociology, another perspective emerged, known popularly as **human relations**. This approach recognizes the importance of attending to the personal and social needs of individuals to promote desired outcomes. George Elton Mayo, a professor from Harvard University, was one of several researchers who applied this school of thought to the workplace. He is best known for conducting workplace experiments in 1924 at the Western Electric plant in Hawthorne, near Chicago. Along with two other researchers, Mayo hypothesized that improving workplace conditions (e.g., lighting) would improve worker productivity. Although the original experiments failed to achieve any conclusive results, they did lead to research into what became popularly known as the Hawthorne effect. Simply put, this principle states that workers who feel that they are appreciated and valued by their employers will be more productive.[5]

George Elton Mayo

Mayo believed that modern industrial capitalism had disrupted more traditional forms of human support and interaction, such as family, community, and traditional work environments. These had functioned as informal meeting places for people and had facilitated feelings of identity and belonging. The modern workplace was not conducive to this informal social interaction, which was just as important a motivator as wages and career aspirations. In short, a workplace that is attentive to human needs results in better productivity. This can be achieved, Mayo argued, by involving workers in organizational decisions, teaching managers to be better listeners, and replacing overbearing supervision techniques with a more casual system of two-way communication.

human relations
management approach that recognizes and addresses the personal and social needs of individuals

CRITICISM OF MAYO'S HUMAN RELATIONS APPROACH

The human relations school of management drew criticism because its precepts appeared counterintuitive to the confrontational nature of labour–management relations. How much say should employees have in organizational decisions? What if these decisions run against those proposed by management? How much time and energy would have to be devoted to this exercise, and at what cost to organizational efficiency? For these and other reasons, the human relations approach has enjoyed limited success in the real world, although its influence is evident in many progressive management practices.

Still, there remains little evidence in the Canadian public sector that the human relations approach has been able to entrench itself in employer–employee relations. Many observers believe that during the heyday of organizational humanism from the 1960s to the 1980s, Canadian governments were still characterized by rigid hierarchies and job structures, little employee participation in decision-making, top-down communication, and other elements of scientific management.

Theory Versus Practice: Contributions to Public Law Enforcement

We have just completed a cursory survey of some of the fundamental theories that address the nature and function of bureaucracies, as well as how they can be managed to maximize efficiency and effectiveness. We can also employ these philosophies as analytical tools to

---

5   The experiments are explained in detail in Roethlisberger & Dickson (1964).

study public law enforcement. As you will discover, each perspective contributes in different ways to an overall understanding of why and how the rule of law operates in Canada.

Marxist ideology is considered left wing on the political spectrum. So you might be tempted to conclude that, in keeping with its tradition of active government social intervention, Marxist thought should embrace large, well-funded police and military establishments. Recall, however, that Marxism—and the socialist sensibilities it spawned—harbours a deep mistrust of law enforcement agencies because they are the means by which those in power preserve their privileged positions. Although this reasoning may sound dated, its influence still permeates socialist views of society. Therefore, people on the political left favour a limited role for agents of state force. They prefer to focus public resources on remedying social inequities that they see as the root cause of crime and civil unrest.

This way of looking at events is also used in other political contexts. For example, the pepper-spraying of protesters at the Asia-Pacific Economic Cooperation (APEC) summit in Vancouver in 1997 could be viewed as a use of force (RCMP officers) by the state (Prime Minister's Office) to quash legitimate expression of protest by members of the public (student activists) against perceived human rights violations. Other examples include a variety of what are generally referred to as "anti-globalization" protests (in keeping with the unprecedented World Trade Organization protest in Seattle in late 1999), the extremely controversial uses of force at the 2010 G20 summit in Toronto, and national demonstrations by the "Occupy" movement, which started in late 2011 on Wall Street in New York. Although Marxist analysis has faded somewhat from popular culture, it does offer a useful, if somewhat pessimistic, set of principles with which to judge the actions of politicians and bureaucrats.

Weber's ideas on bureaucracies give us a more rational view of the role of this type of human organization in society. Weber would recognize many of his bureaucratic ideals in today's complex system of public law enforcement. Officer ranking and the intricate reporting and communications networks among police services demonstrate a clear hierarchy, providing opportunities for merit-based promotion in accordance with clearly articulated codes of professional conduct. On the other hand, in spite of possessing all of these traits, the system of law enforcement can fall prey to many of the criticisms associated with the Weberian model. For example, would any of the many chiefs of police in Canada be willing to assert that the bureaucracy under their control is flawless? Again, the gap between theory and practice can at times be large, but there is little doubt that the intricate network of law enforcement in Canada represents a highly developed and modern society, just as Weber claimed.

Scientific management principles have become so much a part of private and public bureaucracies that most of us simply take them for granted. Managers search constantly for ways to improve the way tasks are accomplished given the resources available to them. For example, how should police officers be distributed across a city to maximize efficiency? To be fair to all citizens, officers might be assigned to patrol certain geographic areas, dividing the city into equal sections. But what if some areas have higher rates of crime? What about public education to prevent crime? As you can see, there are many variables at play in any given decision, and they all have implications for people inside and outside the organization. Still, scientific management continues to exert considerable influence. As a police chief, you might consult empirical data such as crime statistics to help you make decisions. You might draw on the experience of other jurisdictions to assess the success of techniques they have adopted to meet local challenges. In short, the essential elements of scientific management have become part of the management of all bureaucracies, including law enforcement.

As previously noted, the school of human relations has not been adopted to any great extent in private or public administration. However, the importance of human resource departments and cooperative, team-based management strategies proves that this approach has not been totally rejected. Many government agencies whose members are exposed to dangerous or traumatizing events now provide crisis counselling and support to employees. Efforts like these suggest that this approach does in fact have benefits for an organization and its workers.

A good example of this is the Employee and Family Assistance Program (EFAP) for the Toronto Police Service. Developed in 1984, the program provides a broad range of services to police officers, staff, and their relatives in areas such as gambling, drug and alcohol addiction, marital and legal counselling, critical incident stress, and lifestyle management.

Get Real!

2014 Moncton Shootings

Chapter 6 has introduced several theoretical concepts that help to explore the nature and function of modern bureaucracies. In practice, they can also be used to explain what may have led to a breakdown in the proper functioning of such complex organizations when they experience a crisis. The following incident provides a tragic example.

On June 4, 2014, three Mounties were killed while another two were seriously injured after a gunman took to the streets of Moncton, New Brunswick to target police. A north-end neighbourhood in the city—which had a population of about 70,000—was locked down for nearly 30 hours before 24-year-old Justin Bourque, dressed in fatigues and carrying two guns including a semi-automatic rifle, was taken into custody.

The news rocked the province and reverberated nationally as the names of the murdered were released: Constable David Ross, Constable Fabrice Gevaudan, and Constable Douglas Larche.

Bourque pleaded guilty to three counts of first-degree murder and two counts of attempted murder. He was sentenced to life in prison, with no chance of parole for 75 years.

In the weeks following the bloodshed, the RCMP and the public began to ask questions, which led then Commissioner Bob Paulson to appoint Alphonse MacNeil—the recently retired assistant RCMP commissioner—to launch an independent review of the circumstances around the shootings, including an analysis of the RCMP response to the incident. Within 90 days, MacNeil made 64 recommendations—one of the findings was that officers did not have carbines and therefore were at a major disadvantage as they were carrying limited range service pistols (Babstock, 2015). He also recommended officers be trained on how to use the body armour they were carrying in their vehicles.

Less than a year later, in May 2015, four labour code charges were laid against the RCMP in relation to the shootings. The charges alleged the force did not adequately equip or train officers to respond to the shooting (Babstock, July 4, 2017). Each charge is indictable, carrying a fine of up to $1 million each and/or a prison term of up to two years.

In May 2016, a defence lawyer entered not-guilty pleas on behalf of the RCMP management. And in April 2017, the months-long trial began. MacNeil was called by the prosecution to testify about his findings. He told the court that on the night of June 4, 2014 there was a lack of direction, lack of leadership, and poor communication. He said Mounties who headed into the hot zone were not aware their colleagues had been shot and killed, that supervisors that night did not have critical incident training, and that a lack of carbines meant Mounties had to get close to the shooter to use their short-range pistols while the gunman could shoot at police from long range (Babstock, May 17, 2017). Other problems included that the Mounties were not wearing body armour that was in their police vehicles—they needed training on how to use it—and that only one backup officer brought one of four available shotguns to the scene.

Mounties who were among the first to respond to scene on June 4 also testified. Constable Darlene Goguen, who was one of the two injured that night, said she was working for the detachment adjacent to Moncton's that day. She was at a gas station when her family called her and asked if she'd heard there was a gunman nearby on the loose. She hadn't and wasn't able to get her radio to connect to the separate radio channel the Moncton detachment used (Babstock, May 10, 2017). Soon after, she received a call on her radio to go help the Moncton detachment.

Moncton court reporter Craig Babstock (May 10, 2017) painted a vivid description of what then occurred and what was said in her testimony:

> When RCMP Constable Darlene Goguen sped up Hildegard Drive in Moncton the evening of June 4, 2014 to help fellow Mounties respond to reports of a gunman, she thought she was heading to a police staging area at the Hildegard fire hall. Instead, she drove into a hail of bullets.

The glass windows to her car shattered. She was hit in the back of the head, had a bullet lodged in her vest, and had metal in her arm and shoulder. She drove away and called her colleagues to tell them they were headed into the shooting zone, not a staging area.

Another Mountie who testified, Constable Andrew Johnstone, told the court that on that day, after he heard officers were shot, he decided he would put body armour on. He said the armour had only been put in RCMP vehicles days before. He had to take the ceramic plates out of plastic packaging and put them in the vest he had never been trained how to use (Babstock, May 10, 2017). He later found out he had put the armour on backward.

Also called to the stand was Bob Paulson, who was commissioner of the RCMP when the shooting occurred. Paulson testified that it was a horrible event but he believed the officers who responded to the shooting had both the proper equipment and training (Babstock, June 15, 2017). Paulson admitted there were improvements that needed to be made to training but said the level of training at the time was acceptable.

Prosecutor Paul Adams asked Paulson if it was acceptable that front-line Mounties that day did not have carbines, and Paulson answered, "It's not acceptable our officers were killed on that day and this murderer acted the way he did, but this process [to deploy carbines to patrol officers] was underway" (Babstock, June 15, 2017). On the day of the shooting, the carbines for the Moncton detachment were at a military base in a city more than an hour away, being used in training. The prosecutor also questioned the commissioner as to why the Moncton detachment didn't have carbines earlier, citing a 2007 internal briefing note to RCMP's top leaders from senior management making the recommendation. Paulson said that while the force knew it had to get them, research into the firearms and training had to be done. He said the RCMP had to be able to make a case to the public to allow officers to carry the lethal weapon (Babstock, June 15, 2017).

On September 29, 2017, Provincial Court Justice Leslie Jackson found the force guilty on one charge—for failing to provide officers with the right use of force equipment and related training ("RCMP failed to provide," 2017). The force was found not guilty on two other charges related to training and supervision failure, and a fourth charge—which had accused the force of failing to ensure health and safety of officers—was stayed.

In a 64-page judgment, Judge Jackson criticized RCMP management who testified for paying "lip service" to the idea that safety of members was a priority to them, arguing that, if it was, the carbine rollout would have been prioritized ("RCMP failed to provide," 2017).

"Front-line officers were left exposed to potential grievous bodily harm and/or death while responding to active shooter events for years, while the carbine rollout limped along, apparently on the assumption that, as the likelihood of such an event was relatively rare, a timely implementation was not required," wrote Judge Jackson ("RCMP failed to provide," 2017).

What theory in this chapter best applies to the case in Moncton? What are the shortcomings of the theory? How can the organization be reformed to better meet the needs of those on the front line?

CHAPTER SUMMARY

Public administration refers to the vast and complex network of people and institutions that is collectively called the public service. Public administration is ideally concerned with how to implement political will rather than with deciding what the public actually wants. The administrative machinery that supports government is called the bureaucracy. Fundamental theories of bureaucratic organization help us to better understand why bureaucracies have become an essential part of all modern societies.

Karl Marx believed that bureaucracies existed to legitimate inequities among social classes, while Max Weber saw them as central to the emergence of modern nation states. Administrative pioneers such as Frederick Winslow Taylor and George Elton Mayo changed the arrangement and management of tasks and people in order to maximize overall productivity. All of these theorists have had an impact on the nature and functions of bureaucracies and on those who are responsible for managing them. Each theory has contributed to a greater understanding of both private and public bureaucracies, although not all have enjoyed the same degree of acceptance in the real world. What is clear is that bureaucracies remain necessary, if often misunderstood, parts of civil society.

Theories of bureaucratic organization can be employed to explain the nature and operation of government agencies, as well as their reaction to spontaneous protests and civil movements. Doing so provides a variety of perspectives to help understand what happened and why and to guide future practices.

KEY TERMS

bureaucracy, 106

bureaucrat, 106

capitalism, 107

charismatic authority, 110

continuity, 110

expertise, 110

hierarchy, 110

human relations, 113

impersonality, 110

legal authority, 110

scientific management, 111

traditional authority, 110

WEBSITES

Montreal Student Protest Calls for Free Tuition: http://www.cbc.ca/news/canada/montreal/montreal-student-protest-calls-for-free-tuition-1.1210184

Quebec Law Students—*Bill 78*: http://www.cbc.ca/radio/asithappens

Quebec Student Protests as Game Changer?: http://www.cbc.ca/player/play/2239430590

REFERENCE LIST

Babstock, C. (2015, January 16). Bourque had "tactical advantage" over responding officers. *Times & Transcript.* Retrieved from https://www.telegraphjournal.com/times-transcript/story/40898094/bourque-had-tactical-advantage

Babstock, C. (2017, May 10). Mountie injured in shooting takes the stand. *Times & Transcript* Retrieved from https://www.telegraphjournal.com/times-transcript/story/100189566/rcmp-carbines-trial-labour-code-june-4-shootings

Babstock, C. (2017, May 17). Shooter had all the tactical advantages on June 4, MacNeil testifies. *Times & Transcript.* Retrieved from https://www.telegraphjournal.com/times-transcript/story/100199321/

Babstock, C. (2017, June 15). Moncton Mounties acted heroically: RCMP boss. *Times & Transcript.* Retrieved from https://www.telegraphjournal.com/times-transcript/story/100233906/rcmp-commissioner-bob-paulson-trial-labour-code

Babstock, C. (2017, July 4). RCMP trial enters final phase this week. *Times & Transcript.* Retrieved from https://www.telegraphjournal.com/daily-gleaner/story/100252614/rcmp-labour-code-trial-carbines-closing-arguments?source=story-latest

Broadbent Institute. (n.d.). The wealth gap: Perceptions and misconceptions in Canada. Retrieved from http://www.broadbentinstitute.ca/the_wealth_gap

Francis, R.D., Jones, R., & Smith, D.B. (2000). *Destinies: Canadian history since Confederation* (4th ed.). Toronto: Thomson Nelson.

Gerth, H.H., & Mills, C.W. (Eds. & Trans.). (1970). *From Max Weber: Essays in sociology.* New York: Alfred A. Knopf.

Inwood, G.J. (1999). *Understanding Canadian public administration: An introduction to theory and practice.* Toronto: Prentice Hall.

Kernaghan, D., & Siegel, D. (1995). *Public Administration in Canada* (3rd ed.). Toronto: Nelson.

Liberal Party of Canada. (n.d.). Our plan to help middle class Canadians. Retrieved from http://www.liberal.ca/help-the-middle-class/

Marx, K. (1992). In *Oxford Dictionary of Quotations* (4th ed., p. 452:5). New York: Oxford University Press.

RCMP failed to provide adequate equipment, training in Moncton shootings, judge says. (2017, September 29). *CBC News*. Retrieved from http://www.cbc.ca/1.4312673

Roethlisberger, F.J., & Dickson, W.J. (1964). *Management and the worker*. Cambridge, MA: Harvard University Press.

Statistics Canada. (2016). 2016 census of population. Catalogue no. 98-400-X2016131. Retrieved from http://www12.statcan.gc.ca/census-recensement/2016/dp-pd/dt-td/Rp-eng.cfm?LANG=E&APATH=3&DETAIL=0&DIM=0&FL=A&FREE=0&GC=0&GID=0&GK=0&GRP=1&PID=110270&PRID=10&PTYPE=109445&S=0&SHOWALL=0&SUB=0&Temporal=2016&THEME=119&VID=0&VNAMEE=&VNAMEF

Statistics Canada. (2017, September 13). Household income in Canada: Key results from the 2016 census. Retrieved from http://www.statcan.gc.ca/daily-quotidien/170913/dq170913a-eng.htm

Taylor, F.W. (1911). *The principles of scientific management.* New York: Harper & Brothers.

Weber, M. (1968). *Economy and society.* New York: Bedminster Press.

Weber, M. (1992). Quotation in A. Partington, *Oxford Dictionary of Quotations* (4th ed., p. 724). New York: Oxford University Press.

Wilkinson, R. (2011, October 24). How economic inequality harms societies. TED Talk. Retrieved from https://www.youtube.com/watch?v=cZ7LzE3u7Bw

EXERCISES

True or False?

_____ 1. Marx believed that government was necessary because it would eventually ensure that everyone would share equally in a country's resources.

_____ 2. A major flaw in Marxist thought is its inability to explain individual differences and the social mobility that takes place among members of different classes.

_____ 3. Traditional authority is authority that is legitimated by the rule of law.

_____ 4. In Weberian bureaucratic theory, "impersonality" refers to the nature of huge corporations that treat their employees like cogs in a machine rather than like people.

_____ 5. The Hawthorne effect contributed to the field of human relations theory.

Multiple Choice

1. Public administration is concerned with

   a. deciding what the public wants

   b. making decisions for politicians

   c. managing government

   d. implementing political will

   e. making decisions for citizens

2. Marxists see law enforcement officers as

   a. authorities whose work is legitimated by the rule of law

   b. agents of the privileged classes who exist to quash social unrest

   c. bureaucrats who are a necessary part of the machinery of government

   d. agents of the working class who exist to quash unrest among the privileged classes

   e. members of the bourgeoisie who hold a privileged position in society

3. According to Weberian theory, the three sources of authority in a society are:

   a. legal authority, bureaucratic authority, and political authority

   b. traditional authority, scientific authority, and charismatic authority

   c. charismatic authority, hierarchical authority, and legal authority

   d. hereditary authority, legal authority, and traditional authority

   e. traditional authority, charismatic authority, and legal authority

4. The following result is inherent in attempting to achieve Weber's ideal bureaucracy:

   a. hierarchy encourages worker initiative

   b. hierarchy deters worker initiative

   c. hierarchy makes workers feel important

   d. hierarchy makes workers feel appreciated

   e. hierarchy makes workers focus on organizational needs

5. Under the scientific management approach,

   a. workers do piecework

   b. employers measure worker productivity against a subjective standard

   c. resources are used in ways that maximize productivity and minimize waste

   d. workers are responsible for only one or two clearly defined tasks

   e. c and d

Short Answer

1. Define what is meant by "public administration," and describe its role in the political process in Canada.

2. What are the central elements of bureaucracy according to the following theorists?

   a. Karl Marx

   b. Max Weber

   c. Frederick Winslow Taylor

   d. George Elton Mayo

3. How might each of the above theorists view public law enforcement?

   a. Karl Marx

   b. Max Weber

   c. Frederick Winslow Taylor

   d. George Elton Mayo

4. Using examples from current events, determine the effect that these theories have had on both the public and private sectors.

5. Which of the theoretical approaches do you believe would be most effective in public law enforcement? Why?

Evolution of Public Administration

7

LEARNING OUTCOMES

After completing this chapter, you should be able to

■ understand the historical conditions that led to the development of public administration as a distinct field of academic study, and describe the evolution of the public service in Canadian history;

■ relate this evolution to broader social, economic, and cultural changes in Canadian history;

■ define and compare the advantages and disadvantages of the Keynesian approach to government policy;

■ define and compare the benefits and drawbacks of neo-conservatism, noting its effect on Canadian public administration;

■ assess the benefits and drawbacks of privatizing the public sector, with examples; and

■ using the example of public-transit debates at Toronto City Council, begin to examine the complex relationship that exists between political and administrative levels of government.

Introduction

Guidelines for bureaucrats: (1) When in charge, ponder; (2) When in trouble, delegate; (3) When in doubt, mumble.

—James H. Boren, American bureaucrat (1992, pp. 136–137)

The above satirical set of instructions for senior civil servants does little to challenge popular perceptions of the civil service. But without these people, our towns, cities, and entire country would grind to a halt.[1] How did our public service wind up with such a tarnished reputation? One can argue that derogatory public attitudes toward politicians and bureaucrats have always existed. To a point, this is certainly the case. However, by examining the growth of the public sector in the context of larger historical events, it soon becomes apparent that recent criticism may have more to do with the larger currents of political culture than with actual ineptitude.

Public Administration as Modern Academic Discipline

Most scholars cite 1887 as a benchmark for the emergence of public administration as an academic discipline. In that year, future American president Woodrow Wilson wrote an essay entitled "The Study of Administration." In his essay, Wilson emphasized that a disciplined, academic study of public administration would result in more accountable and efficient government. Wilson wanted to make a clear distinction between the administrative and political elements of government because he believed that improving the former would correct corruption in the latter. This may seem a little odd given what you already know about the power of elected over non-elected officials in a democracy. Keep in mind, however, that Wilson wrote this paper at a time in American history when the political system of urban "party bosses" and vote buying was in its heyday.[2] As one of the first advocates of reform in this area, Wilson declared that only a professional bureaucracy— one based on formal rules of conduct and with hiring practices based on meritocratic principles—could clean up existing corruption.

politics–administrative dichotomy
theoretical framework that views politics as the decision-making apparatus of government and administration as performing the implementation function

Wilson's ideas also laid the foundation for a theoretical framework known as the **politics–administrative dichotomy**. This framework views politics as the decision-making apparatus of government and administration as the implementation function of government. In other words, politicians should decide *what* to do, and bureaucrats should then figure out the most efficient way to do it. The main problem with this theory, of course, is that it is too simple. As you have learned, politicians and bureaucrats are inextricable parts of an overall process, and neither can claim exclusive ownership of public policy development. But while the concept in its pristine form has come under considerable criticism—for

---

1 A survey done in 1992 ranked public service at the municipal, provincial, and federal levels fifth, seventh, and eighth, respectively, in a study of impressions of service quality among eight private and public sector organizations (Insight Canada Research, 1992, p. 36).

2 This period in American history is referred to as the Progressive Era. It is perhaps most notable for the widespread reform of public services such as health, education, and welfare, particularly in urban areas. See Walters (1978), Wiebe (1967), and Boyer et al. (1990).

example, it assumes that bureaucrats are politically neutral players in the art of government when in fact they are often central in the process of making public policy (as you will see in Chapter 8)—it remains useful in some quarters.

While public administration quickly gained recognition as an academic discipline in the United States, Canadian universities were slower to grant it similar status in the realm of political science. In fact, it wasn't until 1936 that a Canadian university, Dalhousie, offered a degree program in the field. However, public administration became widely accepted in the years following the Second World War, and today at least 18 Canadian universities offer programs in public administration, some at the master's level.[3] Despite this success, in recent times, public administration has been subjected to severe public criticism. To see why this is so, we need to retrace its evolution in the context of Canadian history.

The History of the Public Service in Canada

As you learned earlier, Canada's past reveals a lot about who we are and why our country's political system operates as it does. It is also important to keep in mind that outside events, issues, and trends have influenced the shape and direction of our political culture. The evolution of public administration in Canada can be used to illustrate both of these ideas.

Pre-Confederation

Before Confederation, colonial administration dictated the structure and operation of public service. Even a century after the decisive battle on the Plains of Abraham between the French and English forces in September 1759, the civil and political fabric of Quebec society retained the influences brought from France. Its bureaucracy reflected a hierarchy-based military order, one steeped in patronage appointments doled out (or denied) by local authorities. The British colonies operated on similar principles, with delegates of the Crown rewarding those in the King's favour with government perks and positions. This practice remained commonplace after Confederation, but as Canada settled into nationhood, new challenges and ideas changed the nature and perception of the public service. One aspect of this came from Max Weber's "ideal bureaucracy" model (see Chapter 6), which at that time was gaining popular acceptance in Europe and the United States (Dobuzinskis, 1998, p. 156). Weber's ideal emphasized the importance of hiring people based on their qualifications rather than on who their friends were. Of course, the temptation to reward political allies did not disappear overnight, but as merit-based hiring became standard practice elsewhere, its advantages soon made themselves apparent to Canadian government officials.

The Minimalist State

As you will see below, Confederation heralded changes in the nature and size of Canada's public service. In comparison with today, however, the public service remained very small.[4] This can be partially attributed to beliefs at the time regarding the nature and function of government. These bear a direct relation to classic theories regarding political studies (as discussed in Chapter 1) that explained state legitimacy and public deference

---

3 For a complete listing, see SchoolFinder.com: http://www.schoolfinder.com.

4 During the time of Sir John A. Macdonald, for example, civil servants numbered only about 2,700 (Heintzman, 1997, p. 4).

to authority—how and why people allow government to have power over them. Thus, beyond very simple needs such as security and conflict management, the role of the state in society remained limited. As commerce and industry developed during the 19th century, governments assumed more responsibility for economic matters.

Most people looked to their governments for defence and order and as providers of infrastructure. All of these were ultimately in the interest of business, trade, and commerce, which were assumed to be the real power behind any great nation. While these pursuits required some public administration, they were limited to what were considered essential or minimal services. This approach to government—common to Canada and most other nations at the time—was illustrative of a **minimalist state**. State resources were used in the interest of the business, or capitalist, classes to promote individual wealth and economic growth, while social services such as health and welfare were to be handled by private charities and individual philanthropists.

As the 19th century drew to a close and modern-day Canada began to take shape, the civil service began to grow, not only to keep up with the country's expanding geography but also to meet new demands brought on by the concomitant challenges of urbanization and industrialism. While only 20 percent of Canada's population lived in urban communities of more than 20,000 people in 1867, this figure had increased to almost 50 percent by 1921 (Finkel & Conrad, 1985, pp. 12–19, 285). Employment opportunities were created for such occupations as postal clerks, customs and excise officials, public educators, and public law enforcement personnel. These, as well as a host of other positions, presented alternatives to the traditional work of farming and other resource-based employment. The public service also offered the emerging middle classes opportunities to improve their economic position by moving up through the ranks of the public service, something they were unlikely or unable to achieve in other sectors. In short, the public service promised these people upward social mobility.

As already noted, this expansion in the public service was accompanied by a growing interest in the serious academic study of public administration. Likewise, Frederick Winslow Taylor's scientific management principles (discussed in Chapter 6) were beginning to show up in the public sector in an attempt to find the "one best way" of managing its people and resources to achieve maximum efficiency. In response to challenges such as immigration and the settlement of the West, governments were increasingly forced to adopt Weberian principles of professionalism and hiring based on merit to ensure accountability and effective communication among the many departments, outposts, and employees being organized to carry out increasingly complex tasks.

In 1908, the Canadian government created the Civil Service Commission, marking the drive toward a more professional civil service. It reinforced this trend by passing further reforms in this area in 1918. These laws gave the commission the power to oversee all appointments to the public service, thereby thwarting political interference in hiring practices. As well, candidates now had to compete for positions by writing exams and, once hired, were prohibited from any political activity. A new job classification system was introduced, and, following the First World War, special provision was made to

minimalist state
approach to government in which state resources are used in the interest of the business, or capitalist, classes, to promote individual wealth and economic growth

John Maynard Keynes believed that governments should be actively involved in the support and promotion of the public good.

favour returning soldiers for these positions. During the 1920s, there was little change in government's approach to public administration, but events that would drastically alter the nature, philosophy, and function of both politicians and bureaucrats were on the horizon.

The Keynesian State

Following the Great Depression and the Second World War, there was a major change in the way that government operated. Many events and people contributed to this shift, but it is commonly accepted that no one played a more significant role than British economist John Maynard Keynes. Keynes laid the theoretical groundwork for a conceptual transformation of the role of government from one of limited intervention to one of active intervention.

Keynes first came to prominence for his predictions about the harsh peace terms dictated to Germany after the First World War.[5] The stock market crash of 1929 and the Great Depression that followed provided Keynes with another opportunity to pitch his unorthodox economic views. First, he asserted that traditional **laissez-faire capitalism**, or free-market capitalism, had led to the economic catastrophe of the 1930s; thus the market could not and should not be left unregulated. Rejecting the tradition of minimalist government, Keynes also argued that government was the only entity capable of intervening in economic affairs, because only government had the power and public authority to do so.

Traditional economic remedies such as **protectionism** and **isolationism** seemed incapable of curing the economic misery for most of the 1930s. Although some Keynesian-style approaches were initiated, it wasn't until after the Second World War that they came into common usage.[6] At its heart, Keynesianism argued that government intervention in the economy was necessary to prevent the extreme economic cycles of boom and bust, with a view to reaching full employment. For example, when the economy was slowing down, governments could create temporary employment opportunities and spend money on public works to "prime the pump" of the country's economic engine to stimulate growth. Governments could also lower taxes and interest rates to encourage consumers and businesses to buy goods and make investments, thus further promoting a healthy economy and getting people back to work. Likewise, when the economy was drawing near to full employment and beginning to overheat, governments could alleviate inflationary pressure by raising taxes or interest rates (see Figure 7.1). This cursory explanation greatly simplifies the Keynesian approach, but the widespread adoption of this philosophy in Canada and elsewhere after the Second World War had a dramatic effect on public policy and the civil service.

Accompanying these economic policy shifts was a growing public demand for government services in other areas of Canadian society. Taken together, these forces spurred growth in the public sector. Each new government program required staff, resources, and infrastructure. As Canada's social safety net took shape during the 1950s

laissez-faire capitalism
free-market capitalism with minimal government interference (*laissez-faire* is French for "let act")

protectionism
a policy whereby a state takes specific economic measures to support a domestic business or industry

isolationism
an economic remedy characterized by a refusal to trade with other countries

---

5 Keynes was among the British delegation at the peace negotiations, and he opposed punitive measures against Germany. The ensuing hyperinflation that accompanied the drastic drop in value of the German currency and the rise of the Nazi Party in Germany were seen as proof that he was indeed correct (Keynes, 1920).

6 One of the most widely publicized approaches was that carried out by US President Franklin Roosevelt, whose "New Deal" and its offspring "National Recovery Administration" attempted to influence wages, work hours, and prices (Friedel & Brinkley, 1982, pp. 221–261).

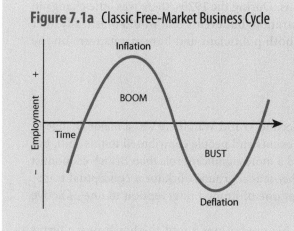

Figure 7.1a Classic Free-Market Business Cycle

Economic Boom
During periods of accelerated economic activity, demand for goods and services creates upward pressure on prices (inflation). As the economy reaches full employment, prices become too high, and demand falls off. As this occurs, the need for labour also decreases, resulting in growing unemployment.

Economic Bust (Recession)
As unemployment rises, demand for goods and services drops, and prices continue to fall (deflation). As the economy sinks into recession, high unemployment causes social upheaval, as individuals struggle to survive (rising crime, family breakup, etc.).

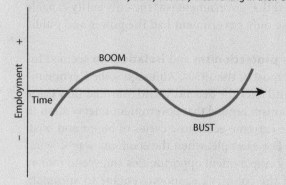

Figure 7.1b Keynesian Business Cycle (Government Intervention)
Keynes and subsequent followers argued that governments could lessen the extremes of the business cycle by actively intervening in their country's economy.

Boom with Government Intervention
1. Higher taxes increase cost of goods and services, thus curbing demand more quickly.
2. Raising interest rates increases cost of borrowing money (car loans, mortgages for homes, etc.), thus slowing consumption.

Bust with Government Intervention
1. Lower taxes and interest rates encourage consumption and investment.
2. "Priming the pump" stimulates economic activity—for example, funding make-work programs or extending cheap loans to aid private enterprise.

and 1960s, the public sector likewise expanded to accommodate the increasing responsibility. Most of the initial recruitment took place through an employment equity program that gave returning war veterans preference in hiring. Although this influx was to triple the size of the public service in Canada, it had little effect on public sector organization and operations. In fact, it wasn't until the baby boom generation entered the workforce in the late 1960s and early 1970s that a substantial transformation occurred. This group produced many university-educated professionals, who saw themselves as more than just tools of policy implementation—they were also instruments of change, and as such should be actively involved in creating and evaluating public policy. These public servants were eager to apply current business strategies and the latest in technical analysis to the practice of government. As their skills became accepted, recognized, and respected, the public service in Canada greatly enhanced its power and influence within the political process.

Some critics feared that bureaucratic influences were threatening the integrity of the political process because unelected technocrats appeared to be supplanting the authority of elected representatives. Democratic principle dictated that politicians be held accountable to their constituents for the policy decisions they made, but how could this happen when these decisions were in reality being made by an unelected bureaucratic elite? This debate was only one among several that contributed to the emergence in the early 1970s of a political philosophy that drew on both new and traditional concepts of governance for its platform. As before, this development would result in dramatic changes in the nature and operation of the public service.

The Neo-Liberal State

The Keynesian approach, often associated with the term "welfare state," came under increasing attack for both theoretical and practical reasons during the 1970s. First, a phenomenon known as **stagflation** cast doubt on the Keynesian economic strategy. Stagflation refers to an economic situation of high unemployment and high inflation at the same time, something that the Keynesian model had determined to be impossible (see Figure 7.1). Second, the public began to lose faith in government's ability to solve social problems and increasingly viewed its activity as invasive, ineffective, and meddlesome. In addition, the media began to scrutinize the actions of government much more aggressively. The widely publicized Watergate scandal in the 1970s, during which US government officials, including then President Richard Nixon, used wiretapping and other undercover means to find damaging evidence against opposition Democrats, highlighted the potential abuse of political power and cast doubt on the integrity of politicians and bureaucrats. Stories of government waste and excess now received sensational media coverage, and governments faced mounting pressure to account for the tax dollars they spent.

Collectively, the general public malaise with government that was characteristic of the mid-1970s led to calls for a return to a more traditional role for government. The ensuing ideological discussion eventually produced a hybrid political philosophy. Known initially as **neo-conservatism** ("neo" meaning new), this ideological shift is now more popularly referred to as neo-liberalism, since, in truth, many of its central tenets draw inspiration from classical liberal economic theory, which emphasizes individual freedom and economic opportunity.[7] Today, most political commentators associate it with laissez-faire capitalism, economic efficiency, and the retreat of government in favour of private initiative. Its proponents criticized the Keynesian approach to government, arguing that government activities should revert to the limited role played during the minimalist era, particularly in social and economic areas. As incoming US President Ronald Reagan (1981) put it in his 1981 inaugural address, "government is not the solution to our problem; government is the problem."

Neo-liberal ideas prompted academics and others to search for new ways of thinking about government's role in society. What resulted became known as the **new public management** (NPM). The general premise of NPM was that government had overextended itself—that is, it was doing too much and had become preoccupied with bureaucratic procedure. As one source put it, government was doing "too much rowing, not enough steering" (Osborne & Gaebler, 1992, pp. 23–24) in its pursuit of the **public good**. In practical terms, this meant shrinking the size and scope of government activity, deregulating various economic sectors, and privatizing the public sector in many jurisdictions.

Neo-liberal government first surfaced in Great Britain under Margaret Thatcher, then in the United States during Ronald Reagan's presidency. In Canada, Prime Minister Brian

stagflation
a situation where an economy experiences high unemployment and high inflation at the same time

neo-conservatism
a conservative political philosophy that argues that government should revert to the limited role it played at the beginning of the 20th century, particularly in social and economic areas

new public management
an approach based on the belief that government has overextended itself by doing too much and becoming preoccupied with bureaucratic procedure

public good
the complex fabric of publicly funded goods and services that contribute to the collective well-being of a state

---

7 For background, see Tucker (2017).

Mulroney's Progressive Conservative government introduced this new approach. The Liberals under Prime Minister Jean Chrétien continued this trend and, as you will see below, prolonged and even accelerated it.

The impact of neo-liberal policies on the Canadian public service over the past three decades has been dramatic. As successive governments have embraced austerity and made economic efficiency a priority, hiring opportunities and practices have been in flux. For example, while full-time permanent employees still made up 86 percent of the federal public service population of 197,250 in 2016, the fastest rate of hiring was among casual and short-term positions (Public Service Commission of Canada, 2015–2016). Critics argue that the growth of precarious employment in this and other sectors can hinder the ability of employees to continue to meet the needs of all Canadians (Mojtehedzadeh & Monsebraaten, 2015).

Table 7.1   Population of the Federal Public Service Canada

Year	Population of the Core Public Administration	Population of Separate Agencies	Combined Population of the Federal Public Service
2000	152,070	59,855	211,925
2001	161,505	62,428	223,933
2002	170,779	66,472	237,251
2003	174,581	68,156	242,737
2004	177,136	67,022	244,158
2005	184,083	59,888	243,971
2006	189,280	60,652	249,932
2007	192,683	61,939	254,622
2008	200,575	62,539	263,114
2009	209,523	64,847	274,370
2010	216,596	66,384	282,980
2011	217,224	65,128	282,352
2012	212,028	66,064	278,092
2013	200,516	62,301	262,817
2014	195,330	61,808	257,138
2015	195,565	61,469	257,034
2016	197,354	61,625	258,979

This table shows the number of people employed specifically by the Government of Canada in core activities, as well as those employed in agencies that help facilitate these activities. Note: For reasons of security, those working in sensitive areas such as the armed forces, RCMP, and CSIS are excluded.

SOURCE: StatCan quarterly demographic estimate (2016).

Private Versus Public Administration: A Tale of Two Prisons

Why don't they run government more like they run a business? You have probably heard someone ask this question, or perhaps you have asked it yourself after hearing yet another media report of alleged government waste and inefficiency. As you have seen in this chapter, government involvement in any part of our lives can be viewed both positively and negatively, and depending on which ideological set of values holds sway at a given time, these public services may be provided or taken away.

Consider the example of two Ontario prisons. In 1997, the Ontario Progressive Conservative government, led by Mike Harris, an unashamedly neo-liberal politician, announced the construction of a pair of "super-jails," one in Penetanguishene, the other in Lindsay. The first prison was privatized and came under the control of an American company; the Lindsay facility remained under provincial control. Controversy seemed to dog the private facility from the start. Unions representing corrections workers opposed the sell-off of their prison, while community residents worried about safety being compromised for the sake of profit. The group Citizens Against Private Prisons (CAPP), composed of business representatives from Penetanguishene and surrounding communities, was especially vocal in lobbying the government to reconsider its decision. They cited increased violence and inmate deaths as evidence of the serious downsides of privatization ("Ontario to take back control," 2006). It would seem that their concerns were well founded: In 2006, the private contract for operating the Penetanguishene jail expired and it was subjected to a comparative performance evaluation by the government. The review concluded that the private prison lagged behind its public counterpart in security and prisoner health care, and had higher repeat offender rates. The Ontario community safety minister (a Liberal as that party had defeated the Progressive Conservatives in 2003) said, "We found that in basically every single area, the outcomes were better in the publicly run facilities." Control of the Penetanguishene super-jail has now been returned to the provincial government, with the transfer costing taxpayers an estimated $4 million ("Ontario to take back control," 2006).

Should this failed experiment in privatization affect future decision-making on how to administer our prison system? Proponents of the public administration facility maintain that the existing prison system is not working either and that privatization can not only reduce overcrowding in public facilities but also lighten the burden on taxpayers. One survey of prisons in the United States found that cost savings could be as high as 20 percent (Segal, 2013). At the same time, critics of this approach point out that introducing a profit motive into corrections leads to poorer inmate conditions and higher rates of recidivism, which result in increased costs to the justice system and, therefore, to taxpayers. With this in mind, what do you think the future of Ontario's prisons should look like? Is there any room for the private sector in public justice? The answers are elusive.

Supporters of private and public administrations continue to argue the merits of their respective sides, and since every case is different, it is difficult to decide which perspective is best. Overall, it is important to keep in mind that while governments and private bureaucracies do many of the same things, their goals are very different. In business, the ultimate aim is economic efficiency: private administrations exist to maximize profit and minimize expense. Government, on the other hand, exists to respond to, maintain, and defend the public good. Its aim is necessarily to benefit all citizens, regardless of their ability to pay for goods or services, and it is accountable to a far greater number of people than is a private enterprise. What we as the public have to ultimately consider is whether society is any better off as a result of privatization. Will promised financial savings contribute to the public good? Should we delegate this kind of power to the private sector? Can a private company be held accountable in the same way as a government? Is the move to privatize based on solid research, or is it a manifestation of right-wing ideology? These are only a few of the many questions that need to be addressed in judging such shifts in public policy.

Today's Public Service

The public service in Canada has very little in common with its 1867 counterpart. Present hiring practices are based on merit rather than patronage, and it is vastly more complex and professional. Employment is handled by the Public Service Commission, an administrative agency reporting to Parliament ensuring "that persons appointed to positions in the federal Public Service meet all of the required job qualifications" (D. Rhéaume, personal communication, June 2004).

The goal, however, remains the same—to serve the public interest. So, who are the people behind the monolithic term "bureaucracy"? How are they organized? Let us begin by noting the difference between the public service of yesterday and today. In 1867, approximately 2,700 people worked for the federal government. Today, the federal government employs almost 260,000 Canadians (approximately 0.72 percent of Canada's population) in a variety of capacities both inside and outside the public sector proper.[8] If you include all levels of government (federal, provincial, territorial, and municipal), this number swells to 3.6 million Canadians—equivalent to 20 percent of the country's workforce (Anderssen, 2015).

Federal public servants work in one of two major occupational categories: "core public administration,"[9] comprised of approximately 70 departments and agencies, paid directly by the Treasury Board; and "separate agencies,"[10] which independently manage job classification, compensation, and employment terms. Each classification denotes certain jobs and pay rates, and these hold true for an employee regardless of the area in which he or she is employed. In addition to general qualifications, other factors such as language, regional interests, and equity affect the hiring process. These determinants reflect a desire on the part of government to respect the **theory of representativeness**. The theory asserts that a representative public service should include employees from all the major ethnic, religious, and socio-economic groups in Canada. In other words, if the public service is to be responsive to the needs of all Canadians, it should represent a cross-section of Canadian society. As noted during the examination of Toronto Police Service recruiting strategies in Chapter 6, police services across Canada want to attract more women and visible minorities to the profession to correct the overrepresentation of white males in their ranks. This aim has been criticized by those who argue that efficiency and effectiveness may be compromised by these initiatives. Should selection favour equally qualified candidates from underrepresented groups? Does one have to be from a certain background to be sensitive to the needs of people of the same background? The issue is complex, and the debate surrounding it will likely continue for some time.

Linguistic and regional representation have played a significant part in shaping who we are as a nation, and this in turn affects the public service. Federal government offices are

theory of representativeness
theory that the public service should represent a cross-section of Canadian society in order to be responsive to the needs of all Canadians

---

8   This figure excludes some employees, such as uniformed RCMP officers and members of the armed forces. For details, see "StatCan quarterly demographic estimate" (2016).

9   For a complete list, see *Financial Administration Act* (Schedule I.1 and Schedule IV).

10   See *Financial Administration Act* (Schedule V).

distributed across Canada to equitably distribute employment opportunities and to provide a local presence for a central government that may be thousands of kilometres away. This manifestation of federal activity demonstrates to citizens that their taxes are, in fact, being used in their area.

The historical importance of the French language and culture in Canada has already been noted, and it is for this reason that the federal government has actively recruited French Canadians to work in the public service. Up to the 1960s, English Canadians constituted the vast majority of federal public servants. Steps were taken to reflect the French presence in Canadian political culture. Through progressive policy action, such as the formation of the Royal Commission on Bilingualism and Biculturalism in the late 1960s and the passage of the *Official Languages Act* in 1969, the federal government succeeded in increasing the number of French Canadians in its public service. They have remained at just under 30 percent of the federal public service for the past decade (Office of the Chief Human Resources Officer, 2017).

Federal public servants won the right to collectively bargain in 1967, long after this right had been granted to workers in the private sector.[11] The unionization of the public sector since then has resulted in some interesting dilemmas for unions and government alike. Unlike in the private sector, where the interests of labour are pitted against profit maximization, collective bargaining in the public sector incorporates the dynamics of political power and the public good. We already know, for example, that governments raise revenues through taxation to fund public services. Therefore, it is the public that ultimately pays for any new expenses incurred as a result of negotiations taking place between government and a public sector union. Beyond this, however, lies a deeper implication. Some observers note that public sector unions may restrict or subvert government policy options by making demands that force their employer to do things it might otherwise reject. For example, a government may wish to give its citizens a tax cut or to cut its deficit and debt, but may be forced to abandon such an endeavour because of the increased wages and benefits it has just negotiated with a union. Further still, the precedent set by one union may serve as the benchmark for all subsequent collective bargaining. For example, a 5 percent wage increase for one police service may be used by other services as their wage demand.

Surveys of Canada's public and private wages suggest that there is an advantage to working in the public sector, both in terms of wages and benefits, although the reason for this disparity varies from region to region and therefore defies simple explanation (Lammam, Pilacios, Ren, & Clemens, 2016). What also emerges from these statistics is that women and minorities tend to benefit most. Findings from a 2015 survey conducted by the Canadian Federation of Independent Business mirrored findings conducted by the Canadian Union of Public Employees, showing that female public sector employees tended to earn about 5 percent more than their counterparts in the private sector, while the reverse was true for males (Canadian Centre for Policy Alternatives, n.d.). As one observer noted, the people benefiting most from this difference were "not fat-cat bureaucrats, but cooks and cleaners and clerks who are getting access to above-the-line poverty wages and sick leave benefits they would have far less access to in the private sector" (Anderssen, 2015). Anti-poverty advocates also make the argument that governments need to maintain a standard of income by forcing private employers to offer similar wages as a bulwark against social inequality. However, as the debate continues, this issue will remain a concern on both sides.

---

11   Trade unions were illegal in Canada before 1872, and afterward governments remained reluctant to grant any meaningful right to bargain collectively (Panitch & Swartz, 1993, p. 17).

Get Real!

Prison Farms

Ideological beliefs can find their way into many aspects of government policy, and, depending on which political party holds power, the focus of attention may change. Consider the example of the former federal Conservative government's move to close prison farms.

In support of its "tough on crime" agenda, the government announced in 2009 that all six prison farms run by Correctional Service Canada (CSC) would close by 2011. Located in Alberta, Saskatchewan, Manitoba, Ontario, and New Brunswick, prison farms, which had operated in Canada since the 1880s, utilized inmates to assist in such tasks as maintenance, feeding cattle, bailing hay, raising hens, harvesting corn, tilling the land, planting crops, and operating milking machinery (Mehta, 2016).

However, a 2008 "strategic review process" initiated by Prime Minister Stephen Harper's governing Conservatives required Correctional Service Canada to re-examine programs it offered to make sure they were "efficient and effective" (Correctional Service Canada, 2017). As a result of the strategic review, a decision was made to shutter the farms since they were deemed too expensive and offenders were not getting employment in agriculture when they were released. The cost of operating the programs was said to be $4 million annually (the farms generated $7.5 million annually in revenues but cost $11.6 million to operate) (Perkel, 2010).

Although proponents of prison farms argued that the facilities served economic and rehabilitative purposes, the federal government had closed all of them by 2011.

The decision affected more than 700 inmates and was met with stiff opposition from area farmers, social justice advocates, opposition political parties, and unions (Mehta, 2016). Organized as the Save Our Farms initiative, advocates pointed out that CSC's analysis was too narrow and ignored several other benefits. For one thing, closing the farm programs eliminated some of the food supply, such as milk and eggs, bound for other correctional institutions that didn't have farms. To compensate for this loss, outside food suppliers would have to be found, resulting in additional costs. In 2010, the year the closures began, Correctional Service Canada had to put out a tender for nearly $1 million to replace some of the milk supply being produced by Kingston's Frontenac Institution ("Government issues prison farm milk tender," 2010).

Save Our Farms spokespeople also argued that job skills learned at the farms were applicable to any industry and supported respect and rehabilitation through caring and compassion for animals (White, 2009). In interviews, prisoners spoke out about the benefits of the farms for their recovery and reconnection with others. As one inmate named Graham stated: "When you've been incarcerated for a long time, you become narrow . . . . You don't talk to people, the guards are the enemy. Then you come here and look after the animals. It opens your heart" (White, 2009).

In keeping with its focus on restorative justice, the federal Liberal government that succeeded the Conservatives announced in 2016 that it would hold consultations to consider reviving the prison farm program. What do you think? If you were asked to provide evidence, what kind of research would best support your assertion?

CHAPTER SUMMARY

The evolution of public administration coincided with the development of a merit-based, professional public service in Canada. The nature and operation of the public service were also affected by socio-economic changes taking place at home and abroad. Before the Second World War, Canada's public service existed within a minimalist state: government activity was limited in scope, so the public service was relatively small.

As the ideas of John Maynard Keynes took hold after the war, government's role expanded greatly as public demand for services increased and state involvement in social services became commonplace. The expansion continued until the early 1970s, when several events contributing to general public dissatisfaction with government resulted in the emergence of a hybrid political philosophy called neo-conservatism. The practice of neo-conservatism in the public sector, called the new public management, has led to a retrenchment of government activity in many areas and the privatization and deregulation of various sectors of the economy. The public service has thus undergone many changes since Confederation. It has evolved into a complex organization employing thousands of people that attempts to reflect a regional and cultural diversity that is uniquely Canadian.

Comparing and contrasting the public and private sectors helps to illustrate what can happen when the rules of private enterprise are applied to public institutions. The results of such policy choices deserve further scrutiny to properly assess both the short- and long-term consequences for society as a whole. As you have seen with the example of prison privatization, the blurring of the line between public and private administration creates challenges in determining who is ultimately accountable to citizens and how problems are to be addressed. Further challenges confront public officials, as politicians and bureaucrats struggle to find creative solutions to common problems.

KEY TERMS

isolationism, 125

laissez-faire capitalism, 125

minimalist state, 124

neo-conservatism, 127

new public management, 127

politics–administrative dichotomy, 122

protectionism, 125

public good, 127

stagflation, 127

theory of representativeness, 130

WEBSITES

Office of the Commissioner of Official Languages: http://www.ocol-clo.gc.ca/html/commissioner_commissaire_e.php

Official Languages Act: http://laws-lois.justice.gc.ca/eng/acts/O-3.01/index.html

Public Service Commission of Canada: https://www.canada.ca/en/public-service-commission.html

TTC chief Gary Webster fired: http://www.cbc.ca/news/canada/toronto/ttc-chief-gary-webster-fired-1.1191677

REFERENCE LIST

Anderssen, E. (2015, March 26). Pay attention private sector: Public sector wages are higher because the gender gap is much smaller. *The Globe and Mail*. Retrieved from https://www.theglobeandmail.com/life/relationships/public-or-private-sector-the-gender-wage-gap-exists-in-both/article23637956/

Boren, J.H. (1992). Quotation in *Oxford Dictionary of Quotations* (4th ed., pp. 136–137). Oxford: Oxford University Press.

Boyer, P.S. et al. (1990). *The enduring vision: A history of the American people*. Lexington, MA: D.C. Heath.

Canadian Centre for Policy Alternatives. (n.d.). Public and private sector pay differences. Retrieved from https://www.policyalternatives.ca/newsroom/updates/public-and-private-sector-pay-differences

Correctional Service Canada. (2017, August 8). Release of results of CSC penitentiary farms public consultation. Retrieved from http://www.csc-scc.gc.ca/consult/index-en.shtml

Dobuzinskis, L. (1998). Public administration. In M. Howlett & D. Laycock (Eds.), *Puzzles of power: An introduction to political science* (2nd ed., p. 156). Toronto: Oxford University Press.

Financial Administration Act, RSC 1985, c F-11, Schedule I.1, Schedule IV, and Schedule V.

Finkel, A., & Conrad, M. with Strong-Boag, V. (1985). *History of the Canadian peoples* (Vol. 2: *1867 to the present*). Toronto: Copp Clark.

Friedel, F., & Brinkley, A. (1982). *America in the twentieth century* (5th ed.). New York: McGraw-Hill.

Government issues prison farm milk tender of $1 million. (2010, May 10). *Kingston This Week*. Retrieved from http://www.kingstonthisweek.com/2010/05/06/government-issues-prison-farm-milk-tender-of-1-million

Heintzman, R. (1997). Introduction: Canada and public administration. In J. Bourgault, M. Demers, & C. Williams (Eds.), *Public administration and public management: Experiences in Canada* (p. 4). Sainte-Foy, QC: Les Publications du Québec.

Insight Canada Research. (1992, Fall). *Perspectives Canada* (Vol. 1, no. 4).

Keynes, J.M. (1920). *The economic consequences of the peace*. New York: Harcourt, Brace and Howe.

Lammam, C., Pilacio, M., Ren, F., & Clemens, J. (2016, December 8). Comparing government and private sector compensation in Canada. Fraser Institute. Retrieved from https://www.fraserinstitute.org/studies/comparing-government-and-private-sector-compensation-in-canada

Mehta, D. (2016, July 10). Ottawa considering reopening prison farms shut down by the Harper government. *CBC News*. Retrieved from http://www.cbc.ca/news/canada/manitoba/reopening-prison-farms-considered-1.3672587

Mojtehedzadeh, S. & Monsebraaten, L. (2015, May 21). Precarious work is now the new norm, United Way report says. *Toronto Star*. Retrieved from https://www.thestar.com/news/gta/2015/05/21/precarious-work-is-now-the-new-norm-united-way-report-says.html

Office of the Chief Human Resources Officer. (2017, March 31). Demographic snapshot of Canada's federal public service: First language. Government of Canada. Retrieved from https://www.canada.ca/en/treasury-board-secretariat/services/innovation/human-resources-statistics/demographic-snapshot-federal-public-service-2016.html#toc2-2-3

Official Languages Act, RSC 1985, c 31 (4th Supp).

Ontario to take back control of private super-jail. (2006, November 10). *CBC News*. Retrieved from http://www.cbc.ca/news/canada/ottawa/story/2006/11/10/private-jail.html

Osborne, D., & Gaebler, T. (1992). *Reinventing government*. Reading, MA: Addison-Wesley.

Panitch, L., & Swartz, D. (1993). *The assault on trade union freedoms: From wage controls to social contract*. Toronto: Garamond Press.

Perkel, C. (2010, May 5). Critics claim closing prison farms would create $1-million milk bill. *The Globe and Mail*. Retrieved from https://www.theglobeandmail.com/news/national/critics-claim-closing-prison-farms-would-create-1-million-milk-bill/article1376319/

Public Service Commission of Canada. (2015–2016). *Annual Report*. Retrieved from https://www.canada.ca/en/public-service-commission/services/publications/public-service-commission-canada-2015-2016-annual-report.html

Reagan, R. (1981, January 20). Inaugural address. Ronald Reagan Presidential Library Archives. Retrieved from https://reaganlibrary.archives.gov/archives/speeches/1981/12081a.htm

SchoolFinder.com. (n.d.). Retrieved from http://www.schoolfinder.com

Segal, G.F. (2003, November 17). Private prisons save money, boost productivity, studies find. Retrieved from http://reason.org/news/show/private-prisons-save-money-boo

StatCan quarterly demographic estimate. (2016, April). Government of Canada. Retrieved from https://www.canada.ca/en/treasury-board-secretariat/services/innovation/human-resources-statistics/population-federal-public-service.html

Tucker, J.A. (2017, May 17). What is "Neoliberalism" anyway? Foundation for Economic Education. Retrieved from https://fee.org/articles/what-is-neoliberalism-anyway/?gclid=EAIaIQobChMIhImHuueV1QIVxbXACh2_VgTAEAAYASAAEgJyOvD_BwE

Walters, R.G. (1978). *American reformers, 1815–1860*. New York: Hill and Wang.

White, N.J. (2009, October 11). A bleak harvest for Canadian inmates. *Toronto Star*. Retrieved from https://www.thestar.com/news/insight/2009/10/11/a_bleak_harvest_for_canadian_inmates.html

Wiebe, R. (1967). *The search for order, 1877–1920*. New York: Hill and Wang.

EXERCISES
True or False?

_____ 1. According to the politics–administrative dichotomy, bureaucrats should decide *what* to do, and politicians should figure out *how* to do it.

_____ 2. In the minimalist state, social services are not considered a responsibility of government.

_____ 3. The Keynesian model offers a solution to stagflation.

_____ 4. Canada's official bilingualism is an example of the theory of representativeness in action.

Multiple Choice

1. The politics–administrative dichotomy views

   a. politics as the implementation function of government

   b. politics as the decision-making apparatus of government

   c. administration as the decision-making apparatus of government

   d. administration as the implementation function of government

   e. b and d

2. The following factor(s) had an impact on the evolution of the Canadian public service:

   a. the urbanization and industrialization of Canada in the late 1800s

   b. events and issues in other countries, such as the United States

   c. growing public demand for government services

   d. theoretical ideas, such as those of Max Weber, Frederick Winslow Taylor, and John Maynard Keynes

   e. all of the above

3. Stagflation is a situation where an economy experiences

   a. high unemployment and low inflation at the same time

   b. low unemployment and high inflation at the same time

   c. low unemployment and low inflation at the same time

   d. high unemployment and high inflation at the same time

   e. no change in unemployment or inflation

4. Neo-conservatism argues that government should

   a. intervene heavily in social and economic areas

   b. have a limited role in social and economic areas

   c. increase the size of the public service

   d. increase the scope of its activity

   e. regulate various economic sectors

5. The theory of representativeness basically holds that

   a. the public service should reflect the ethnic, religious, and socio-economic diversity of Canadian society

   b. the public service can be more responsive to the needs of all Canadians if it represents a cross-section of Canadian society

   c. linguistic and regional representation in the public service is important

   d. a local presence for federal government, in the form of offices across Canada, is desirable

   e. all of the above

Short Answer

1. What is the politics–administrative dichotomy? What is its major shortcoming?

2. Define "minimalist state." What factors led to changing this approach?

3. Explain the major concepts of the Keynesian welfare state. Why did this approach to government come under attack in the 1970s?

4. Explain the theory of representativeness in your own words, and give examples of how the theory is put into action.

5. How is politics involved in public service union collective bargaining? Why do public servants face more challenges in changing their work conditions than their private sector counterparts?

6. Outline the proposed benefits of privatization. What are the potential drawbacks?

The Art of Government: Making Public Policy

8

LEARNING OUTCOMES

After completing this chapter, you should be able to

- define the term "public policy" and describe the process of formulating, implementing, and evaluating it;

- distinguish among a variety of policy instruments and determine why governments choose to use one rather than another in a given situation;

- use recent examples to analyze and assess the changing role of police associations in the public policy process;

- understand the difficulties politicians face in instituting public policy while attempting to satisfy various stakeholders; and

- use examples to explore the reality of public policy development at the provincial and federal levels of government.

Introduction

> What begins as a failure of perception among intellectual specialists finds its fulfilment in policy and action.
>
> —Lionel Trilling (1992, p. 702), literary critic

How often have you heard politicians make promises at election time and then fail to fulfill them once they're elected? During the federal election campaign of 2015, Liberal leader Justin Trudeau promised that if his party won, it would make major changes to Canada's electoral system (see Chapter 4). Likewise, the 2016 American election featured a promise by then-candidate Donald Trump to literally build a wall between the United States and Mexico (and make Mexico pay for the project) (Markon, 2015). Cynics might argue that anything promised by a politician, either in or out of campaign mode, is a lie in the making. Yet, during their tenure in office, politicians and the many public servants who work with them do make good on many of the promises they have made on the campaign trail. However, mainstream media tend not to dwell on these achievements to the same degree. It is easy (and, to a certain extent, occasionally appropriate) to blame individual politicians for making promises that they cannot keep. But it is too shortsighted and simplistic to conclude that the "say one thing, do another" phenomenon is a character flaw exclusive to politicians.

The foregoing raises one of the most puzzling questions about the process that shapes public policy, specifically, why does it appear to most of us that there never seems to be any one definitive answer to problems facing government? This chapter will provide you with at least a partial answer to this question.

What Is Public Policy?

The art of government is based on several key elements, among them leadership, integrity, and the ability to articulate an overall vision that has the support of the population. This requires a great deal of coordination, discussion, debate, planning, and evaluation on the part of officials. The result of this interaction is **public policy**. Defining this term is a challenge, and there are several definitions to choose from.[1] Simply put, however, "public policy is whatever governments choose to do or not to do" (Dye, 1992, p. 1). This statement is intentionally broad. Public policy encompasses the "big picture"; it resists being distilled into a single act or law. In addition, public policy reflects what government does rather than what it says it will do. Statements made by politicians on a particular issue do not always produce policy. Again, however, public policy also reflects what a government chooses *not* to do.

public policy
what government does or does not do

Making Public Policy

There are three fundamental stages to executing almost any exercise: formulation, implementation, and evaluation. The public policy process is no different. However, accomplishing these tasks within an organization as vast and complex as government constitutes a significant challenge for a number of reasons. Let's examine each step to see why this is so.

---

1   For example, see definitions by Aucoin (1979) and Taylor (1987).

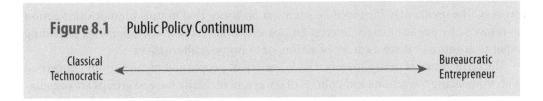

Figure 8.1   Public Policy Continuum

Classical
Technocratic
⟵——————————————————⟶
Bureaucratic
Entrepreneur

Formulation—What Is It We Want to Do?

The two major stakeholders in formulating, implementing, and evaluating public policy are politicians and bureaucrats. The relative power of each of these players can significantly affect the nature and shape of public policy. The theoretical continuum in Figure 8.1 provides a general framework as to where policy originates and the effect this can have on government as a whole.

At one extreme, known as the **classical technocratic** linkage, broad public policy decisions originate with politicians, who then provide bureaucrats with clear direction as to what should be done. This model draws on the Weberian bureaucratic ideal, where structure and communication are hierarchical and instruction is commonly understood and accepted. At the other extreme, the **bureaucratic entrepreneur** approach, bureaucratic experts within government come up with policy ideas and then approach elected officials to obtain the resources and public legitimacy necessary to implement their programs. There are any number of points along this continuum sharing influence between these partners.[2] You may also notice that as one moves toward the bureaucratic entrepreneur end of the continuum, democratic input decreases.

Although simple, this model is useful because it helps illustrate that it is not politicians alone who are responsible for bringing policy ideas to public attention. Take, for example, the Trudeau government's apparent flip-flop on electoral reform. A classical technocratic analysis of this phenomenon might suggest that Liberal politicians were forced to change course because post-election consultation with the public convinced them that there was no logical alternative to the existing "first-past-the-post" system.

If, however, the bureaucratic entrepreneur analysis is employed, the scenario changes. It might be that, although the government began with the best of intentions (a parliamentary committee was struck to study the issue and report back to the House), senior bureaucrats at Elections Canada warned perhaps that it would take too much time to decide upon a particular system and implement it in time for the next scheduled election (October 15, 2019).[3]

Although this example greatly simplifies the reality of the relationship between these two key players, it does shed considerable light on the interdependence of both parties involved. Both politicians and bureaucrats are comprised of a vastly complex organization of individuals and groups, each of which may or may not support policy options as they develop. As you may have already guessed, several other actors also influence the policy-making

classical technocratic
a model of public policy in which decisions originate with politicians, who then provide bureaucrats with clear direction as to what should be done

bureaucratic entrepreneur
a model of public policy in which bureaucratic experts within government come up with policy ideas and then approach elected officials to obtain the resources and public legitimacy necessary to implement their programs

[handwritten margin notes: Classical Technocratic / Bureaucratic Entrepreneur]

---

2   Robert Nakamura and Frank Smallwood (1980, Chapter 7) propose five major types of relationship in *The politics of policy implementation*, New York: St. Martin's Press.

3   Opinions vary as to the actual cause(s) for the change of course. For analysis, see Dutil (2017).

process. The media may focus public attention on issues that in turn prompt some action or response by public officials. Interest groups and lobbyists may also intervene, providing input to advance or deter a course of action, or to propose alternatives.

The term "interest group" covers a wide variety of people and organizations concerned with influencing the actions and policies of government. Many interest groups are organizations with objectives that normally do not involve government but who can become politically active when a proposed or existing public policy affects them. For example, a local historical association whose mandate is to preserve and protect local history might decide to persuade its area politicians to prevent destruction of a heritage building. Other interest groups exist for the express purpose of monitoring and influencing government policy. These are sometimes referred to as "pressure groups."[4] Their primary focus is on how the actions of government affect the issue with which they are concerned. For example, People for Education is a citizen-based organization that monitors the quality of public education in Ontario. It tracks changes to educational policy and funding, releasing periodic reports for discussion and recommending policy initiatives to government.[5]

Although interest groups and pressure groups lobby government for their causes, the term "lobbyist" may be understood as potential "political persuasion for hire"—that is, a lobbyist is a paid professional who provides research, advice, and varying degrees of access to government decisions. The practice of lobbying is not new, nor should it be understood by definition as undesirable. Information supplied by lobbyists can aid politicians and bureaucrats in defining and designing public policy desired by citizens. The danger is that, because there is a degree of self-interest involved, lobbyists may also subvert or distort popular attitudes to achieve their purpose. In an attempt to monitor this situation, both the Ontario and federal governments have enacted legislation requiring lobbyists to register with the Office of the Integrity Commissioner and the Office of the Commissioner of Lobbying of Canada, respectively, but even these agencies capture but a small fraction of this activity.[6]

Implementation—Let's Do It!

Once a policy decision is made, it must be carried out if it is to be of any use. Implementation refers to policy in action. It poses some of the biggest challenges for government, because it is at this stage that intent and consequence often become separated. Increasingly, citizens, interest groups, and the media have been calling on governments to account for discrepancies between policies and subsequent actions and results. Consequently, governments have begun to pay more attention to implementation. Leaving evaluation aside for a moment, let us consider some of the reasons implementation can fail to achieve desired aims.

---

4 The argument for the distinction put forth by some observers is that pressure groups represent a more powerful bloc of influence than do interest groups. See Tindal (2000).

5 For this group's specific mission and publications, see People for Education, retrieved from http:// www.peopleforeducation.com

6 On the role of lobbying as a positive force, see Jackson & Jackson (2000). For a darker summary of lobbying activity, see Tindal (2000). See also Office of the Integrity Commissioner, http://www.oico .on.ca/ and Office of the Commissioner of Lobbying of Canada, https://lobbycanada.gc.ca/eic /site/012.nsf/eng/h_00000.html.

With government as complex as it is, the margin for conscious and unconscious error in the areas of organization, coordination, communication, and time lag can alter the original intent and the ultimate success of a policy decision. Much has been written about these pitfalls and how to avoid them, but their detail is beyond the scope of this text. It may be easier to illustrate the message by using a scenario based on the implementation of a law-and-order promise by an incoming provincial government.

You have just been hired as a police constable in Goodville, a town of about 5,000 in a largely rural area of the province. Having been a diligent student, your knowledge of law and its enforcement extends beyond simple academics to include pertinent issues that affect your job. Scrolling through your online newspaper one morning, you observe that the premier has announced that the province is getting tough on crime. You think this sounds positive, but without specifics, you have no way to judge what this statement means to you and your profession. At the division, other officers and the chief discuss the policy and draw similar conclusions. Should your professional demeanour change? You decide that unless new directives are issued, you will carry on as usual.

A few days later, you are told that the province is drafting a bill to articulate its policy, but the chief confides to staff that politicians are not listening to police chiefs and that she does not support the move. You hear from colleagues in other divisions that their chiefs are opposed as well. Meanwhile, the draft legislation has been criticized as being too costly by the finance department, so changes are being made that will save money but alter the bill's intent. The police chiefs are still unhappy and have recommended other changes to the bill. The media weigh in on the policy, pointing to falling crime rates and questioning the government's actions. After much tinkering and amendment, the bill is passed into law. Your chief declares that she will "interpret" the new legislation for the rank and file, but her perspective on some of its aspects seems at odds with its intent. To complicate matters, the staff and resources required to handle new tasks are being held up in legislative debate. By the time you receive a revised code of conduct, the government has decided not to pursue this matter because health care has become the focus of popular attention thanks to several media stories on the topic. Your chief is happy, but her abrupt retirement a few weeks later results in the appointment of someone who favours the government's abandoned initiative. It's all getting so political that you begin to wonder how anything is accomplished in government.

Before you throw up your hands in frustration, take some comfort in the fact that any large organization faces these challenges every day. But the task of getting things done in the private sector is less complicated than in the public sector. Public accountability and democratic sensibilities add layers of coordination and communication that necessarily encumber efficiency. Often by the time one policy initiative has worked its way through the system, it has changed or has produced an unintended consequence. Governments therefore monitor this process through various stages and techniques of evaluation.

Evaluation—Did It Work?

Evaluation can be conducted during the implementation phase or following its completion—that is, once its outcomes are known. Evaluating the success of a government program isn't as simple as measuring tangibles, such as cost-effectiveness and efficiency, as might be done in the private sector. Because their ultimate goal is to serve the public good, government agencies must look for additional ways to evaluate what they do. Evaluation is all about accountability—demonstrating to interested parties that you are meeting organizational goals in a way that is acceptable to all concerned. In a private company, shareholders tend to focus on profit, so evaluations, whether they are about customer satisfaction or corporate image, ultimately refer back to maintaining or increasing profit. As citizens, we demand accountability from governments because we pay the taxes that enable them to function. But measuring the effectiveness of public sector activity is not simply a matter of a financial cost–benefit analysis. Providing for the public good may mean operating some programs at a loss.

The other challenge facing public service managers is that it is sometimes difficult to identify specific criteria for measurement. How, for example, does one quantify national defence or measure the quality of justice? How would we know that these had improved over time? This problem of intangibility is not unsolvable, nor should it be used to justify abandoning any attempt at public accountability. However, it does highlight some of the challenges of public sector evaluation.

Remember, too, that evaluation costs time and money. For example, hiring or assigning civil servants or outside agencies to audit government programs can add significantly to their cost, meaning less money for the programs themselves, and can divert scarce human resources required to maintain a high quality of service. Thus governments must strike a balance between the need to evaluate their activities and the real costs they will incur as a result.

The success or failure of a policy initiative lies ultimately in the hands of bureaucrats. After all, they are the experts who have supplied much of the information necessary for their political masters to make these critical decisions. Likewise, the ability of public servants to present or withhold certain information in the formulation, implementation, and evaluation stages of the policy process places them at a distinct advantage over their political colleagues. As political scientist Reginald A. Whittaker notes:

> It is the permanent officials who normally have greater access to information resources. Ministers, after all, are also MPs and party politicians who spend much of their time giving speeches, travelling, attending political functions, and engaging in activities quite remote from the business of their ministerial portfolios. In many cases, they have no previous training or experience in the policy fields of their departments, little time to gain such knowledge while there, and a relatively short span in one portfolio before they move on. The bureaucracy, on the other hand, was there before, and will be there long after. (1995, p. 429)

The politics–administrative partnership that Whittaker alludes to can be either creative or debilitating, yet it represents a key element without which government would cease to function. Evaluating government activity is one way of ensuring that both politicians and bureaucrats are acting in a responsible manner. As citizens have demanded more

Cabinet ministers are key players in deciding which policies will dominate a government's agenda. One of the hallmarks of Justin Trudeau's 2015 Cabinet was that women represented 50 percent of its members.

Figure 8.2   Continuum of State Coercion

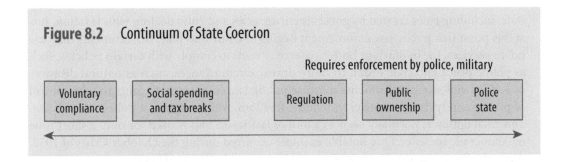

Requires enforcement by police, military

| Voluntary compliance | Social spending and tax breaks | Regulation | Public ownership | Police state |

accountability from government, evaluation has become an important part of public sector programs. Public acceptance of policy decisions is one significant indicator of their success. There are several ways to monitor public compliance with government policy.

Policy Instruments and Degrees of Regulation

Once a policy decision is in place, governments have a range of options to choose from to ensure general compliance. Referred to as **policy instruments**, these are methods employed by governments to achieve their goals. The choice of instrument depends on a number of factors and can range from non-coercive inactive involvement (essentially, letting individuals and businesses regulate themselves) to coercive active involvement, In short, it is a question of the extent to which government wants to intrude into and influence private decisions.

The level of intrusion is best described on a continuum of state coercion (see Figure 8.2). At one end, the state is largely absent from decision making. Individuals may be encouraged to voluntarily comply with a government objective. For example, municipalities might ask citizens to reduce the amount of water they use for conservation reasons. Similarly, groups may be allowed to regulate themselves, such as in the case of the law and medical professions. Actions like these cost very little and may signal relative indifference or reluctance on the part of the state to become involved in a particular area.

Next along the continuum are expenditure instruments, such as social spending (in the form of, for example, welfare, pensions, and private sector assistance) or tax breaks offered to encourage individuals and companies to change their behaviour. For example, a policy to reduce poverty among the elderly might increase social assistance payments to needy senior citizens. Similarly, people may be encouraged to save for their retirement through the creation of tax-sheltered registered retirement savings plans (RRSPs).

After expenditure instruments comes regulation, which is the use of all civil and criminal laws of a

policy instrument
a method employed by governments to ensure compliance with public policy and to achieve their goals

A soldier stands guard outside the Peace Tower on Parliament Hill during the October Crisis of 1970. This event prompted the federal government to invoke the *War Measures Act*, which imposed martial law and greatly limited the freedom of Canadians. (This Act has since been replaced by the more limited *Emergencies Act*.)

state, including rules created by government agencies and rules dealing with taxation. It is at this point that public law enforcement begins to come into play. Governments may use police services, the military, or both to coerce citizens to comply with certain policies, such as public peace and civic order. In more drastic circumstances, such as natural disasters or serious violence, governments may use public law enforcement agents to take control of private enterprises or restrict individual freedom. At its extreme, a police state results. This final option is normally seen as a tool of last resort and is used for only a short time in democratic societies. One notable example occurred during the October Crisis of 1970, sparked by terrorist actions of the Front de libération du Québec (FLQ).

Next along the continuum is public ownership of certain enterprises, which is generally used when a product or service is considered essential for the public good. Thus utilities such as hydro, water, and telephone service are often publicly owned, although we are seeing a trend toward privatization in recent years.

At the far end of the continuum is a police state, which is a state in which democratic rights are taken away or do not exist. Such a state is usually run by a dictator or the army, or is imposed in a time of crisis. Canada witnessed such a measure during the October Crisis, when hundreds of Quebeckers were arrested and detained without being told why and without any evidence that they supported the radical separatists.

Except during crises, it seems logical that policy-makers usually choose the policy instrument that achieves the intended purpose for the least amount of resources, but they must also consider public perceptions. It may be cheaper to simply post speed limits on roads, but hiring police to enforce these limits is much more effective and is a choice of policy instrument that the public generally accepts. However, some experts contend that politicians make these decisions based on expected voter response.[7] Regardless, it should be clear that these choices have tangible consequences for you, both as a citizen and as a professional in the field of law enforcement. This is because there is considerable flexibility within each policy instrument.

This flexibility allows governments to signal the importance of a particular policy in the overall context of their administration. They are restricted in this exercise by legal traditions, social norms, and current public attitudes on the subject. For example, lawmakers may implement a "get tough" policy on speeding by increasing fines for offending motorists. On the other hand, punishing these individuals by sentencing them to life imprisonment would be seen as excessive and could be characterized as cruel and unusual punishment. Remember, too, the added costs to policing, the courts, and the prison system that this decision would have. As conscientious police officers, how might you and your colleagues react if life imprisonment was the penalty? Would you be less vigilant in apprehending speeders? This illustrates the necessity of common sense and prudence on the part of policy-makers in order to secure willing compliance.

---

7 See, for example, Trebilcock, Hartle, Prichard, & Dewees (1982).

Personal Information and the Public Interest

When you give the government personal information in order to receive a student loan, do you expect the government to safeguard that information? How about the personal information you give over to private entities such as the social networking sites you use or the cellphones you purchase? Governments and private corporations are steadily relying on electronic databases to store information, and, as a result, concerns are consistently raised about protecting individual privacy. Should social networking sites be allowed to sell your search history to third-party marketers without your permission? Should government employees in hospitals be allowed to search your medical records for reasons that are not work related?

Canada's Office of the Privacy Commissioner attempts to protect Canadians' privacy by ensuring that the federal government and its agencies, as well as private companies, adhere to the laws that protect our privacy. The office is autonomous in its activity—that is, it operates independently of direct government management—which helps ensure that investigations and audits of government and private corporations can occur without the presence or perceptions of political influence. The commissioner oversees two major pieces of legislation: the *Privacy Act* and the *Personal Information Protection and Electronic Documents Act*.

Canada has established a fairly respectable reputation in this area, thanks to the work of the Privacy Commissioner's office. It has assisted companies and governments in learning from mistakes and preventing them, and strengthening protection of privacy. For example, in July 2015 the office asked a Canadian-based company if it could examine the privacy practices the company had in place following reports of a hack.

The company that was hacked owned dating websites used in more than 50 countries—including one that catered to people seeking discrete affairs. At the time, the hackers had threatened to expose the personal information of the dating service's users unless the company shut down some of its dating websites. Because of the nature of the data breach and the sensitivity of the information, the privacy commissioner, along with the Australian equivalent, felt it was necessary to get involved ("Joint Investigation of Ashley Madison," 2016).

The company did not give into the demands of the hackers, and in August that same year, the hackers published information of 36 million user accounts it claimed to have stolen from the company ("Joint Investigation," 2016).

The investigation by the privacy commissioner looked at the "handling practices that may have affected the likelihood or the impact of the data breach" ("Joint Investigation," 2016). It was found that while the company had a range of information security protections in place, there was no "overarching information security framework" in place to measure how good or bad the company's information security protections were ("Joint Investigation," 2016). The office said organizations responsible for safeguarding personal information need to have security policies in place, staff with privacy and security training, and a risk management strategy.

The company in question agreed to make the necessary changes suggested by the office.

The Office of the Privacy Commissioner has also helped organizations such as Facebook, Google, and Apple to update their corporate practices and privacy policies.[8]

Following a request from the office in 2009, the popular social networking site Facebook agreed to make changes to its site to protect users from having their personal information unwittingly skimmed by outside interests, which were using applications such as games and quizzes to access personal information on profiles without the awareness or consent of those using the site. In response to the office's request—and perhaps due in part to the public attention it generated—Facebook agreed to address the problem. If you use Facebook, you may notice that before you are able to play a game, a box appears asking you to provide consent for the third party to access your information (Mackrael, 2011).

As someone who has chosen a career path related to justice and public law enforcement, why might your privacy be considered particularly important? What kind of personal information would you feel uncomfortable sharing with others? Would your answer be different if the organizations in questions were private rather than public?

---

8 See the website of the Office of the Privacy Commissioner of Canada for updates on all investigations, https://www.priv.gc.ca/en/opc-actions-and-decisions/investigations/

CHAPTER SUMMARY

Public policy refers to the action (and inaction) of government in a particular area of its operation. Public policy is characterized by an ongoing process of formulation, implementation, and evaluation that involves several actors both inside and outside formal government. Ultimately, however, it is the bureaucracy's job to implement the decisions resulting from these complex interactions.

Governments may choose from a variety of options when it comes to ensuring public compliance with particular policies. These can range from symbolic gestures, such as public information campaigns encouraging voluntary changes in behaviour, to rigid enforcement using police and the military. The policy instrument chosen depends on a number of factors, including the importance of the policy, current relevance, and necessity.

Many players other than politicians and bureaucrats influence public policy, which is a reflection of democracy in our society. As the debate concerning sentencing and correctional services policy aptly illustrates, coherent and coordinated policy can still prove elusive.

KEY TERMS

bureaucratic entrepreneur, 139

classical technocratic, 139

policy instruments, 143

public policy, 138

WEBSITES

Drummond Report on Ontario Calls for Cutbacks: http://www.cbc.ca/news/canada/toronto/drummond-report-on-ontario-calls-for-cutbacks-1.1138568

Office of the Commissioner of Lobbying of Canada: https://lobbycanada.gc.ca/eic/site/012.nsf/eng/h_00000.html

Office of the Correctional Investigator: http://www.oci-bec.gc.ca

Office of the Integrity Commissioner (Ontario): http://www.oico.on.ca

Record-High Prison Numbers Sparking Violence: http://www.cbc.ca/news/canada/record-high-prison-numbers-sparking-violence-1.1260764

REFERENCE LIST

Aucoin, P. (1979). Public-policy theory and analysis. In G.B. Doern & P. Aucoin (Eds.), *Public policy in Canada* (p. 2). Toronto: Macmillan.

Dutil, P. (2017). Why Trudeau abandoned electoral reform. In A. Potter, D. Weinstock, & P. Loewen (Eds.), *Literary review of Canada*. McGill-Queen's University Press. Retrieved from http://reviewcanada.ca/magazine/2017/05/why-trudeau-abandoned-electoral-reform/

Dye, T.R. (1992). *Understanding public policy* (5th ed., p. 1). Englewood Cliffs, NJ: Prentice Hall.

Emergencies Act, RSC 1985, c 22 (4th Supp).

Jackson, R.L. & Jackson, D. (2000). *Canadian government in transition* (3rd ed). Toronto: Pearson Education.

Joint investigation of Ashley Madison by the Privacy Commissioner of Canada and the Australian Privacy Commissioner/Acting Australian Information Commissioner. (2016, August 22). Retrieved from https://www.priv.gc.ca/en/opc-actions-and-decisions/investigations/investigations-into-businesses/2016/pipeda-2016-005/

Mackrael, K. (2011, June 21). Privacy watchdog Jennifer Stoddart makes the Web a priority. *The Globe and Mail*. Retrieved from http://www.theglobeandmail.com/technology/tech-news/privacy-watchdog-jennifer-stoddart-makes-the-web-a-priority/article1360485

Markon, J. (2015, July 17). Trump says building a U.S.-Mexico wall is "easy." But is it really? *Washington Post*. Retrieved from https://www.washingtonpost.com/politics/trump-on-the-us-mexico-border-building-a-wall-is-easy/2015/07/16/9a619668-2b0c-11e5-bd33-395c05608059_story.html?utm_term=.cc21d11f5f84

Nakamura, R. & Smallwood, R. (1980). *The politics of policy implementation*. New York: St. Martin's Press.

People for Education. Retrieved from http://www.peopleforeducation.com

Personal Information Protection and Electronic Documents Act, SC 2000, c 5.

Privacy Act, RSC 1985, c P-21.

Smith, M.-D. (2017, February 1). Liberals break electoral reform promise less than a day after signalling collaboration with opposition. *National Post*. Retrieved from http://nationalpost.com/news/politics/liberals-break-electoral-reform-promise-less-than-a-day-after-signalling-collaboration-with-opposition/wcm/9439b2a6-bf5c-4f70-b318-8646a48e1caa

Taylor, M. (1987). *Health insurance and Canadian public policy: The seven decisions that created the Canadian health insurance system and their outcomes*. Kingston, ON: McGill-Queen's University Press.

Tindal, C.R. (2000). *A citizen's guide to government* (2nd ed.). Toronto: McGraw-Hill Ryerson.

Trebilcock, M.J., Hartle, D.G., Prichard, J.R., & Dewees, D.N. (1982). *The choice of governing instrument.* Ottawa: Economic Council of Canada.

Trilling, L. (1992). Quoted in *Oxford Dictionary of Quotations* (4th ed., 702:18). Oxford: Oxford University Press.

Whittaker, R.A. (1995). Politicians and bureaucrats in the policy process. In M.S. Whittington & G. Williams (Eds.), *Canadian politics in the 1990s.* Toronto: Nelson.

EXERCISES
True or False?

_____ 1. The prime minister abandoning electoral reform is an example of public policy.

_____ 2. The relative power of politicians and bureaucrats can have a significant effect on public policy.

_____ 3. At one extreme on the continuum of state coercion, individuals are encouraged to voluntarily comply with a government objective.

_____ 4. Public law enforcement comes into play at the point on the continuum of state coercion where a society becomes a police state.

_____ 5. Debates about policy alternatives among public officials always produce a coherent and coordinated policy response.

Multiple Choice

1. In the classical technocratic approach to shaping public policy
   a. policy decisions originate with politicians
   b. politicians give bureaucrats clear direction on what should be done
   c. structure and communication are hierarchical
   d. instructions are commonly understood and accepted
   e. all of the above

2. Evaluating public policy involves
   a. ensuring that politicians and bureaucrats are acting responsibly
   b. accountability
   c. measuring the effectiveness of public sector activity
   d. demonstrating that goals are being achieved in an acceptable way
   e. all of the above

3. One challenge of evaluating public policy is
   a. the numerous criteria that can be used for measurement
   b. the tangible aspect of results
   c. conducting a simple cost–benefit analysis
   d. focusing on profit
   e. the often unquantifiable nature of outcomes

4. An example of voluntary compliance is
   a. the Chartered Professional Accountants of Canada ensuring that its members follow its guidelines of professional conduct
   b. offering a tax break to anyone who puts money in an RRSP
   c. police enforcement of highway speed limits
   d. requiring a licence to operate a business
   e. requiring citizens to file a tax return

5. Which of the following players influence(s) the policy-making process?
   a. politicians
   b. bureaucrats
   c. citizens
   d. the media
   e. all of the above

Short Answer

1. What is public policy? Who are the key players in the process?

2. Briefly describe the process of public policy formulation, implementation, and evaluation.

3. What external factors can influence the nature of policy implementation? Give examples.

4. Relate the importance of policy evaluation to public accountability. How are the two connected?

5. What is a policy instrument? What factors influence a government's choice of instrument?

The Bureaucratic Machinery: Government Operations

9

LEARNING OUTCOMES

After completing this chapter, you should be able to

- identify and explain the overall purpose of a government department and its role in the Canadian political system;

- identify and compare a variety of other government bodies, including Crown corporations and regulatory agencies, and discuss their role in government operations;

- analyze the nature and function of administrative law in relation to the activities of government; and

- consider the importance of protecting the privacy of Canadians, particularly with reference to those considering a career in law enforcement.

Introduction

Now that you have surveyed the intricacies of the public policy process, the term "machinery of government" no doubt has greater meaning for you. Although this metaphor implies a somewhat negative image, it is useful if you imagine government as a series of organized components, each with a particular purpose, that are connected in some way to the greater whole. For example, the government of Canada is organized through the activity of departments, Crown corporations, and regulatory agencies, all of which make contributions to the public good. This chapter examines the nature and organization of each of these components to further demystify the process of public administration.

Government Departments and What They Do

department
government division responsible for carrying out some aspect of government policy

When the Canadian government decides to undertake a new policy or launch a new program, it must decide what organizational form would best suit the task. One option is to create a **department** (or ministry, at the provincial level). A government department is responsible for carrying out some aspect of government policy—for example, the Department of Health oversees public health and the Department of National Defence protects Canadians through the armed forces and fulfills many international responsibilities.

All departments are statutory bodies—that is, they exist because a law to that effect has been passed in Parliament. At the federal level, the prime minister decides the number and types of departments that are required. There are no formal restrictions, but past practices and current needs guide decision-making in this area. Following the 2015 election, there were 31 federal Cabinet members (including the prime minister), 9 less than the previous Conservative government. As you learned in the first half of this text, the prime minister and the ministers—the heads of the departments—form the Cabinet, where political power is centred and key policy decisions are made.

ministerial responsibility
principle of parliamentary government that makes ministers responsible for the official activities of their departments

Federal Cabinet ministers are almost always chosen from the pool of MPs elected to the House of Commons. This is in deference to the democratic tenet that states that senior representatives of the public interest must be held accountable to the people they serve. In other words, they must be elected. Each minister is responsible for the official activities of his or her department and is answerable to the public for both good and bad actions taken by the department. This fundamental principle of parliamentary government is called **ministerial responsibility**. This concept is similar to the relationship between the coach and players on, say, a hockey team. When the team is doing poorly, it is not the players who accept ultimate responsibility, nor are they the ones who are fired. As head of the organization, the coach assumes responsibility, and hence it is he or she who suffers the consequences. Likewise, even if the minister is personally unaware of departmental wrongdoing, it is the minister who resigns as a symbolic gesture to preserve the public's faith in the political process. This expectation can also be applied to ministers themselves in situations where they have done something that threatens or damages the integrity of the department in which they work or, more generally, the current government as a whole. This is often why members of the Opposition call for the resignation of certain ministers. It is not purely partisan rhetoric or for show, although that does inform the manner in which they call for such resignations.

Traditionally, the principle of ministerial responsibility has carried much weight in Canadian parliamentary affairs. However, recent events have led to speculation that it is losing credibility, both symbolically and in practice. This is because the size and complexity of many government ministries make it virtually impossible for one person to keep track of everything that is happening. Additionally, elections and prime ministerial discretion mean that Cabinet ministers are shuffled in and out of **portfolios** (a term used to describe ministerial duties, including those assigned to a specific department) fairly frequently, in contrast to the private sector.

One real-world example involved federal Minister of National Defence Harjit Sajjan, who was called out for his claim during a speech that he was the military "architect" behind a major joint forces operation in Afghanistan called Operation Medusa in 2006. It turned out that although he had been part of the operation, Sajjan had greatly exaggerated his role in it. Some observers saw the misstep as an "embarrassing exaggeration," viewing it as a minor faux pas in the career of an otherwise upstanding public servant. Others characterized Sajjan's statement as a "blatant lie," which damaged his and the Canadian Force's international reputation, warranting an apology and his immediate resignation. Sajjan did apologize on his Facebook page but refused to resign, and the scandal eventually blew over.[1]

As you can see, there is some justification for re-examining ministerial responsibility. But to simply abandon it would effectively sever the relationship linking the actions of bureaucrats to answer to their political masters and produce a dangerous lack of accountability on the part of the people we elect to represent us. The temptation to abdicate responsibility or shift blame in politics must be kept in check if public faith in the political process is to be preserved.

> **portfolio**
> areas of responsibility or duties of a Cabinet minister, including those related to a department

Deputy Minister

The deputy minister's position marks the point at which political power becomes bureaucratic action. Reporting to the minister (the political head of the department), the deputy minister (DM) is the most senior bureaucrat within that department. Although the minister directs the department, the DM ensures that directions are carried out. As such, the DM acts as the go-between for the minister and the civil servants, conveying departmental policy and voicing employee concerns. As you saw in Chapter 8, communication is ongoing between the political and administrative components of government; thus the role of deputy minister is crucial in the realms of policy advice, dispute resolution, and human relations (the "people management" part of the job).

Deputy ministers are appointed by the prime minister, but they report to and are responsible to the minister of their department. This may seem odd at first, but, given the environment, the justification for this is straightforward. You may have heard the term "Cabinet shuffle," a term used to describe the reassignment of one or more Cabinet ministers in and out of different departments. This can and does happen over the course of a government's mandate and may occur as the result of political expediency (say, when a minister has come under fire for his or her conduct—ministerial responsibility kicking in) or when a prime minister or premier decides his or her government needs rejuvenation—a fresh restart, so to speak. The relative transience of the Cabinet minister in any given portfolio puts departmental stability and continuity at risk (can you imagine having to switch course professors two or three times a semester?). Most DMs are career civil servants who have worked their way up through the ranks and have become experts in their particular area. (Recall Weber's model bureaucracy.) Their consistent presence in the world of political

---

1 For comment, see Pugliese (2017, April 30).

change promotes efficient departmental operation and a reliable source of information and advice for ministers who are new to the job.

As the administrative heads of their respective departments, deputy ministers wield considerable power, some of it in law and some of it in tradition. For example, the *Interpretation Act* (1985), a federal statute relevant to this topic, states:

> 24(2) Words directing or empowering a minister of the Crown to do an act or thing, regardless of whether the act or thing is administrative, legislative or judicial, or otherwise applying to that minister as the holder of the office, include
> (c) his or their deputy

In essence, this allows the minister to delegate a wide range of responsibilities to his or her deputy. DMs are also key players in the development of policy, advising the minister, recommending alternatives, and apprising the minister of expected public responses to and practical limitations of ministerial decisions.

Minister Versus Deputy Minister

Although the minister–deputy minister relationship is characterized by mutual support, it is important to keep in mind the distinction. DMs cannot make regulations, answer to Parliament on behalf of the minister, or sign Cabinet memoranda. These restrictions aside, it is generally accepted that DMs will manage the day-to-day affairs of their departments, including supervising subordinates, tracking budgets, and performing other administrative activities. Although ministers are free to intervene in departmental operations, these are usually left to the DMs. For one thing, Cabinet ministers are usually far too busy with other obligations to become overly involved with departmental affairs.[2] Thus the degree to which ministers and their deputies venture into management and policy matters, respectively, varies according to their personality and preferences, and political necessity. This precarious balance can overwhelm deputy ministers, who often end up being overloaded with both managerial and policy responsibilities.

There are a couple of important aspects characterizing the position of deputy minister. First, it is non-partisan. This means that DMs remain neutral in their duties, favouring neither a particular party nor its ideological beliefs. Rather, they serve the broader public interest of good government. Of course, this is easier said than done because of the politicized nature of policy development and the partisan agenda dictated by individual political parties in power.

Second, the post of deputy minister is insulated from direct public scrutiny by virtue of its relative anonymity. This is appropriate, given that it is the minister—an elected representative—who ultimately must accept responsibility for policy decisions in his or her department. Related to this is the knowledge on the part of DMs that, in return for their frank and honest advice, they will be shielded from public attention. Thus one rarely hears of a particular deputy minister or other senior bureaucrat in relation to government policy matters.

Classification of Departments

Given the diversity of government departments at the provincial and federal levels, it is sometimes difficult to grasp how the departments interact with one another to coordinate

---

2 Among the external duties of a typical Cabinet minister are collective Cabinet and party duties, constituency work, attendance in the House of Commons, and representation of Canadian interests abroad.

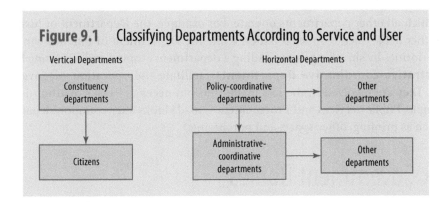

Figure 9.1 Classifying Departments According to Service and User

Vertical Departments | Horizontal Departments

Constituency departments → Citizens

Policy-coordinative departments → Other departments

Administrative-coordinative departments → Other departments

and effectively carry out government policy. Political scientists use various categories to shed light on the inner workings and overall operation of the bureaucratic machinery.[3] Using these classification systems, we can develop a short series of questions to see where a department fits into the big picture.

Us or Them?

Who is the primary beneficiary of the service being provided? Departments exist either to help citizens directly or to assist other government departments. Those that provide services directly to citizens are called **constituency departments** and are considered "vertical" because they hand down services to citizens (see Figure 9.1). These types of public services are the most visible and accessible to the public. For example, Public Safety Canada oversees a range of interrelated programs, including cybersecurity, border integrity and enforcement, policing, corrections, and emergency management (Public Safety Canada, n.d.). Likewise, Employment and Social Development Canada offers a wide range of services across Canada, including job search assistance, access to employment insurance and other benefits, business and tax advice, and travel and health information (Employment and Social Development Canada, n.d.). Because they are universal in scope (available to all residents), these departments employ many people and have large budgets.

constituency department department that provides services directly to citizens

policy-coordinative department department that coordinates policy across government

Follow Them or Lead Them?

Departments that serve other departments are considered "horizontal" because they provide services within and through other departments. They can fall into one of two categories depending on whether they coordinate overall policy or facilitate it. Departments that coordinate policy across government are called **policy-coordinative departments** or central agencies. They set the broad regulation and policy framework

Service Ontario is one example of a collection of "vertical" or "constituency" departments, which provide public services directly to Ontarians.

---

3 For specific approaches, see Hodgetts (1973) and Doern (1974).

under which all other departments operate. For example, the Department of Justice may advise other departments on legal issues, while the Department of Finance can express federal priorities by shrinking or expanding a department's capital and operating budgets. **Administrative-coordinative departments** facilitate the operation of government services. They are involved in the less glamorous but necessary tasks of administration. For example, Public Services and Procurement Canada looks after common departmental needs such as printing, office space, and purchasing.[4]

administrative-coordinative department
department that facilitates the operation of government services

Other Government Bodies

Departments represent one means by which public policy is developed, implemented, and enforced. Accordingly, circumstances may lead decision-makers to choose other types of agencies to achieve these ends. Following are an examination of some of the alternatives common to the practice of public administration in Canada: regulatory agencies and Crown corporations.

Regulatory Agencies

Regulatory agencies defy a simple definition because they can vary so widely in size, authority, and scope. Traditionally, they were used to regulate the private sector (marketing, competition, pricing, and so on), but more recently they have also become involved in areas of social regulation (workplace safety, culture, and environmental protection).

In spite of their differences, regulatory agencies share some common characteristics in how and why they carry out their function. They can be viewed as extensions of a ministry in the sense that each is ultimately answerable to a minister. Unlike ministries, however, regulatory agencies are insulated from direct political influence and therefore demonstrate to the public that official decisions are fair and based on objective criteria. Thus these agencies are a means through which governments can influence a particular sector without undermining public confidence.

delegated legislation
legislation handed down from a parent department that grants a regulatory agency political powers

The legislation that creates regulatory agencies sets out the general rules by which they must operate. Some agencies are granted powers of **delegated legislation**, which means that they have the ability to set and enforce regulations. In effect, political powers are handed down from the parent department, allowing an agency to make specific decisions that have the force of law.

Some agencies are empowered to grant licences or investigate incidents within their jurisdiction. For example, in Canada, communication-related industries are subject to rules enforced by the Canadian Radio-television and Telecommunications Commission (CRTC). The commission has the power to grant, review, and revoke broadcast licences, as well as set fees for some services, such as telephone and Internet access (Canadian Radio-television and Telecommunications Commission, n.d.). Given the influence of broadcast media on public opinion, it is easy to see why this power should not remain under the direct control of the governing political party.

deregulation
reducing or eliminating bureaucratic processes that may hinder private enterprise and limit economic growth

As discussed in Chapter 7, neo-liberal ideology favours a limited role for government. This includes eliminating bureaucratic oversight in the form of government regulation of the private sector. The idea is to do away with bureaucratic processes that may hinder private enterprise and limit economic growth. Commonly referred to as **deregulation**,

---

4 This department also oversees security requirements for organizations wishing to bid on Government of Canada contracts (Public Services and Procurement Canada, n.d.).

the approach seems logical and has struck a chord with many people who view government regulation as overbearing and excessive. However, critics argue that in the rush to deregulate, short-term economic gains may be far outweighed by long-term costs. For example, there is evidence to show that Britain's deregulation of the cattle industry in the 1980s led to the outbreak of "mad cow" disease in the late 1990s because beef producers were no longer subject to strict health standards.[5] Closer to home, a five-year-long 40 percent budget reduction at the Ontario Ministry of the Environment coupled with deregulation and downloading of water quality inspection were cited as factors contributing to the outbreak of *E. coli* bacteria in the town of Walkerton's water supply in 2000.[6]

While incidents such as these are relatively rare, they demonstrate what can happen when the long-term consequences of deregulation are negated or ignored. As citizens, we need to ensure that our politicians do not compromise public health and safety for the sake of short-term fiscal savings or hollow ideological victories aimed at their core base of supporters.

Crown Corporations

It is perhaps easiest to think of most Crown corporations as publicly owned businesses operating in the private sector and serving a public purpose. Like regulatory agencies, they are overseen by a ministry and are ultimately responsible to Parliament. Their distinctness arises from their corporate form and function. Crown corporations operate like any large private sector business, but because of their public accountability and legislated mandate, profit is often a secondary objective. There are currently 47 federal Crown corporations encompassing a wide range of policy areas—Canada Post, VIA Rail, and the Royal Canadian Mint, for example—and governments have particular reasons for choosing this form of organization to facilitate public policy.[7]

Why choose a Crown corporation to facilitate government policy? There are two basic rationales: economic and nationalistic. As you learned in Chapter 2, Canada was born out of several diverse regional interests. Reconciling and accommodating these interests with overarching national goals has become part and parcel of the Canadian political process. Crown corporations provide the federal government with a vehicle to redistribute national resources and encourage public infrastructure. There are also instances where provinces have used the Crown corporation models for similar purposes. For reasons of brevity and relevance, this discussion limits itself to the federal level. A Crown corporation can be

---

5 The chain of events is explained in *Consequences: The private side of Britain* (Richards, 2006), a video documentary exploring the consequences of privatization under former British Prime Minister Margaret Thatcher.

6 The budget cuts resulted in one-third of Ministry staff—many of whom were inspectors—being let go. The resulting lack of expertise and provincial testing has been cited as two of the potential causes of the tragedy. See Talaga et al. (2000) and James (2000). For more background, see "Walkerton tragedy" (2000, June 12).

7 Each Crown corporation may include dozens of subsidiaries. See Stastna (2014, April 1). For a list of major crown corporations and the ministries responsible for their oversight, see Treasury Board of Canada Secretariat (2009, April 6).

created in an area of the economy where private business refuses to operate, either because it is considered unprofitable or deemed too complex. By creating a Crown corporation to address a necessary public need, governments not only stimulate the local economy but create jobs and provide services or goods to an area that might otherwise go without. For example, Marine Atlantic provides ferry services that connect Newfoundland and Labrador with Nova Scotia and the rest of Canada. In addition, a corporation's presence in a community contributes to a sense of Canadian identity by connecting the area to a larger federal infrastructure. The creation of the Canadian National Railway Company in 1922 helped the country knit together a haphazard patchwork of nearly 200 separate smaller companies to give Canada a common, reliable network of transportation.

Another familiar illustration of the Crown corporation as "nation builder" can be found in the Canadian Broadcasting Corporation (CBC). When created in 1936, its aim was to foster communication among and through the various regions of Canada through a network of radio—and later television—stations. The CBC's nationwide access requires staff throughout Canada, including regions such as the Far North, where private broadcasting would be unprofitable. The CBC is also an example of how the Canadian government has used a Crown corporation to offer a distinctly Canadian alternative viewpoint to a media landscape overwhelmingly dominated by American corporate networks and media outlets.

The Canadian Broadcasting Corporation is a Crown corporation that was created in 1936 to establish a cross-county Canadian presence on radio and promote a sense of national identity.

The Crown corporation may also be chosen to put it at "arm's length" from possible political meddling, as noted in the previous section, although, ironically, this may make it vulnerable to misuse by political officials. For example, in the early 2000s, Crown corporations Canada Post and VIA Rail were both used to funnel federal sponsorship money to Quebec advertising firms as part of a larger sponsorship scandal, forcing the federal government to introduce new legislation preventing such actions in future.[8]

By the same token, Crown corporations provide government with insight into the nature and current status of private sector actors engaged in similar activities. For example, in the midst of the oil price shock of the early 1970s, the federal government created Petro-Canada to establish a Canadian presence in the overwhelmingly foreign-owned energy sector.

One of the major drawbacks of choosing a Crown corporation as a policy vehicle is that, unlike private business, the corporation is ultimately answerable to political masters who, in turn, must account for that corporation's management decisions. For example, when Canada Post announced in late 2013 that it was planning to phase out urban door-to-door mail delivery, public outcry was immediate and intense. Citing falling mail volume, senior Canada Post officials warned of ballooning debt and unsustainable administrative inefficiencies, pointing out that, to date, the move to community mailboxes had saved the corporation $80 million (Roman, 2017; Canada Post, 2013). However, many groups, including those advocating for seniors and

---

8   The so-called "sponsorship scandal" resulted in the passage of the *Federal Accountability Act* in 2006. It involved "highly irregular and questionable" payments to advertising firms by Public Works, through Canada Post and VIA Rail, for commissions and other suspect charges. For a summary of the auditor general's report, see Delacourt (2004).

the disabled, countered that door-to-door service was essential and that Canada Post could offset declining revenue from mail delivery by focusing more on parcel delivery and online banking initiatives. The federal Liberals (and NDP) vowed to restore door-to-door service during the 2015 election but, once in power, proved reluctant to do so.[9] As this example illustrates, the public accountability of Crown corporations can complicate the seemingly straightforward business environment in which they operate.

The relatively recent ascendance of neo-liberalism (see Chapter 7) has led some governments to reconsider the utility of Crown corporations in their present form. As these ideas emerged in the 1980s, several Western governments—notably Margaret Thatcher's in Britain—began selling off public assets to private interests. Inspired by these initiatives, Canadian Prime Minister Brian Mulroney oversaw the privatization of many iconic Crown corporations, such as Air Canada (1988) and Petro-Canada (1991). In Ontario, Premier Mike Harris sold off Highway 407 to private interests in 1999, and in 2015, Premier Kathleen Wynne announced plans to partially privatize Hydro One, the province's electrical transmission utility. In both instances, supporters pointed to the financial benefits resulting from the moves. In the former, the province received $3.1 billion; in the latter case, more than $9 billion ("Highway 407 sold," 1999; Canadian Press, 2017). While financial windfalls such as these are an attractive incentive to cash-strapped governments, we must keep in mind that they represent one-time payouts and that ongoing revenues will no longer flow back into government coffers to help offset the costs of other services they provide. Further, simply privatizing Crown corporations for financial reasons not only ignores the historical context of the Canadian experience, but also assumes that private enterprise will assume the public interest for which Crown corporations were originally intended.

Administrative Law

So far, this chapter has been dedicated to outlining the structure and form of political and bureaucratic institutions and their role within the machinery of government. This section briefly surveys the legal parameters governing public institutions, with reference to protection and fair treatment of citizens.

Imagine for a moment that you are a police officer on highway patrol. You clock a car going twice the speed limit. You pull over the vehicle, walk up to the driver's window, and ask for a driver's licence, registration, and insurance. The driver willingly complies, handing over all of the requested documents. Now consider the same scenario, except that this time your request for the three items is met with silence and suspicious gestures by the driver. Are your thoughts and responses different in this set of circumstances?

The second scenario can help to illustrate the concept of **discretionary power**—that is, the interpretive flexibility granted to a police officer as a government employee (in this case, an agent of public law enforcement) to act within a given setting. In the second scenario, you might decide that the driver is mentally unstable, doesn't like the police, or is having a bad day. This, in turn, influences how you will deal with this citizen. There is a procedure police officers must follow in roadside situations such as this one, but it would be virtually impossible for lawmakers to write down all of the potential variations. Thus the government delegates authority and responsibility to civil servants, who then interpret and abide by the set of rules handed down to them. This delegation is limited or controlled

discretionary power interpretive flexibility granted to some government employees to act within a given setting

---

9 The Liberals promised a decision on the matter by spring 2017 but moved the deadline to December (Roman, 2017).

administrative law
body of legislation that details the rules civil servants must follow in doing their jobs

by principles of **administrative law**. This body of legislation (usually drafted by bureaucratic experts in a particular field) details such things as safety standards, applications for immigration, licensing requirements, and the process for appeals. These are the bureaucratic "rules of the game" to be followed by civil servants in their professional dealings with the public and with other government departments.

Although less visible than constitutional law, administrative law is bound by the same precepts and can be challenged in the court system. Laws can be ruled *ultra vires* (unconstitutional) if the Supreme Court of Canada finds that they in some way violate citizens' rights under the *Canadian Charter of Rights and Freedoms* (1985). For example, a directive from the provincial police instructing officers to stop all expensive sports cars and search drivers for drugs is a clear violation of the Charter rights of protection against freedom from discrimination and unreasonable search and seizure.

Principles of administrative law also preserve public faith in the rule of law by protecting citizens from unfair or arbitrary treatment by government agencies. In effect, administrative law helps to ensure that what politicians (as representatives of the people) intend ends up being implemented by bureaucrats in a just and equitable manner. The courts, through the process of judicial review, ensure this fairness. For example, a judge may rule that a regulatory agency has exceeded its authority by creating and enforcing rules that are outside its mandate or that go beyond the authority granted by its creators.

More directly, administrative law ensures that citizens affected by bureaucratic decisions have the right to due process and an appeal. This may include the right to represent themselves at relevant proceedings, the right to legal counsel and cross-examination, the right to be notified of hearing dates, and the disclosure of evidence held by the government body. In short, administrative law builds on the basic framework of constitutional law to ensure that governments and their delegates adhere to the rule of law in their day-to-day contact with the citizens they represent. When there is a dispute in this interaction, administrative law provides the protocol and forum necessary to resolve it.

Get Real!

Part 1 of an Interview with Howard Sapers

Howard Sapers was appointed independent advisor on corrections reform by the Government of Ontario in January 2017 to review the use of segregation of individuals in the province's facilities while also completing a report with an overview of corrections and recommendations for improvements.

In the fall of 2016, the Government of Ontario initiated a review of its corrections system following a series of incidents at provincial facilities, including the extended segregation of Adam Capay, a young Indigenous man awaiting a criminal trial in a Thunder Bay jail. For much of his incarceration, Capay had been confined in an acrylic cell with light constantly shining down on him (White, 2016).

Prior to Sapers's appointment as independent advisor, he had served as Canada's correctional investigator since 2004. In that position, he was responsible for providing in-dependent oversight of the Correctional Service of Canada and acting as ombudsman for federally sentenced offenders.

In an interview, Sapers explained the similarities and differences between both positions and their impact on the public service (personal communication, July 7, 2017):

> I was contacted initially [by the province] just to review the use of segregation in Government of Ontario corrections. My view about segregation is that when segregation is overused it's really a symptom of other problems in the correctional system. So, I agreed to do the review on segregation only if it led to a more fulsome review.
>
> I was appointed to be an independent advisor through order-in-council, which means I'm outside of the public service and report to the minister and the government directly on the areas that I think need to be reformed. The first report on segregation was delivered in May [2017], and I'm in the process of completing my second report now, which covers a number of other operational areas.
>
> The Correctional Investigator of Canada is a statutory ombudsman for federally sentenced offenders, and I was the official oversight body for the Correctional Service of Canada (CSC). In that capacity, I had the statutory authority to access all records, places, people, [and] documents, and review every decision, act, or omission of the CSC based either on complaints from sentenced offenders and their families or on my own motion. It was very broad authority; it was statutory and very independent and [I] reported to Parliament through the Minister of Public Safety.
>
> What I'm most proud of is that, during my tenure [as Correctional Investigator of Canada], the people that worked in my office resolved probably something in the neighborhood of a quarter million complaints. I mean, we would get 20,000 [calls] on our toll-free [phone] line a year. I was there for 12 years, so that's 240,000 times the telephone in my office was answered by my intake staff, who then began to resolve those concerns. And over those years, there were thousands of investigations and thousands of people had their issues resolved. Sometimes not the way they wanted them resolved because sometimes we would get a complaint and we would determine that it wasn't founded, that the CSC had done everything fairly and appropriately and there would be no remedy. But many other times we would find that there was an opportunity to rethink a decision, to reinterpret a policy, to change an action. I'm very proud of the volume of work done by such a small but dedicated staff. When I started in the office there were about 22 staff, [and] when I left the office there were 36.
>
> In the role that I'm in now . . . I am not an ombudsman; in fact, I do not deal with individual circumstances. I'm looking at systemic issues; I'm looking at legislative reform; I'm looking at staff issues. With the Correctional Investigator of Canada, my mandate did not include staff of the Correctional Service of Canada—they had their own oversight mechanisms. What I've been asked to look at in Ontario is all four corners of corrections: everything that has to do with the operations of corrections. It's not complaints-driven; it is to help Ontario build a transformation agenda and modernize their correctional practices.

CHAPTER SUMMARY

Government has been described as machine-like in its operation, and it sometimes feels as if we, as citizens, are nothing more than numbers to the huge bureaucracy. The structure of bureaucracy in its various forms—departments, regulatory agencies, and Crown corporations—carries out government operations. A government department is responsible for carrying out some aspect of government policy, and the minister of a department is answerable to the public for all actions taken by the department, under the principle of ministerial responsibility. The deputy minister plays a critical role in any department, acting as the link between political and administrative power in the operations of government.

Departments are categorized according to whom they serve and their purpose in the bureaucratic hierarchy. Constituency departments deal directly with citizens, while policy-coordinative and administrative-coordinative departments carry out functions among other government departments and agencies. Regulatory agencies and Crown corporations serve different purposes, and they are two non-ministry bodies used by federal and provincial governments in certain circumstances to achieve policy goals.

Administrative law facilitates government activity. Part of its function is to ensure that government officials respect the rights of citizens and that disputes between the two groups are resolved in a just and equitable manner. Finally, although Canada enjoys a positive international reputation when it comes to protecting the privacy of its citizens, we must remain vigilant as more data become available to both public and private organizations.

KEY TERMS

administrative-coordinative department, 154

administrative law, 158

constituency department, 153

delegated legislation, 154

department, 150

deregulation, 154

discretionary power, 157

ministerial responsibility, 150

policy-coordinative department, 153

portfolio, 151

WEBSITES

Canada Post: https://www.canadapost.ca/cpo/mc/languages witcher.jsf

Canadian Broadcasting Corporation: http://www.cbc.radio -canada.ca/en/explore/who-we-are-what-we-do/

Canadian Radio-television and Telecommunications Commission (CRTC): http://www.crtc.gc.ca/eng/home -accueil.htm

Department of Finance Canada: http://www.fin.gc.ca/fin-eng.asp

Department of Justice: http://www.justice.gc.ca/eng/index.html

Employment and Social Development Canada: https://www .canada.ca/en/employment-social-development.html

Health Canada: https://www.canada.ca/en/health-canada.html

National Defence and the Canadian Armed Forces: http://www .forces.gc.ca/en/index.page

Office of the Privacy Commissioner of Canada: https://www .priv.gc.ca/en/

Privacy Act: https://www.priv.gc.ca/en/privacy-topics/privacy -laws-in-canada/the-privacy-act/

Public Safety Canada: https://www.publicsafety.gc.ca/index -en.aspx

Public Services and Procurement Canada: http://www.tpsgc -pwgsc.gc.ca/comm/index-eng.html

REFERENCE LIST

Canada Post to phase out urban mail delivery. (2013, December 11). *CBC News.* Retrieved from http://www .cbc.ca/news/canada/ottawa/canada-post-to-phase-out -urban-home-mail-delivery-1.2459618

Canadian Charter of Rights and Freedoms, Part I of the *Constitution Act, 1982,* being Schedule B to the *Canada Act 1982* (UK), 1982, c 11.

Canadian Press. (2017, May 8). Ontario about to shed more Hydro One shares, could net more than $3 billion. *CBC News.* Retrieved from http://www.cbc.ca/news/canada /toronto/ontario-hydro-one-shares-sale-1.4105569

Canadian Radio-television and Telecommunications Commission (CRTC) (n.d.). Retrieved from http://www .crtc.gc.ca/eng/home -accueil.htm

Delacourt, S. et al. (2004, February 11). Your money, their friends. *Toronto Star,* p. A1.

Doern, G.B. (1974). Horizontal and vertical portfolios in government. In G.B. Doern & V.S. Wilson (Eds.), *Issues in Canadian public policy* (pp. 310–329). Toronto: Macmillan.

Employment and Social Development Canada. (n.d.). Retrieved from https://www.canada.ca/en/employment-social -development.html

Federal Accountability Act, SC 2006, c 9.

Highway 407 sold. (1999, August 14). *CBC News*. Retrieved from http://www.cbc.ca/news/canada/highway-407 -sold-1.191438

Hodgetts, J.E. (1973). *The Canadian public service: A physiology of government* (chap. 5). Toronto: University of Toronto Press.

Interpretation Act, RSC 1985, c I-21, as amended.

James, R. (2000, May 26). When the people you know don't tell you about the water. *Toronto Star*, p. A8.

Public Safety Canada. (n.d.). Retrieved from https://www.public safety.gc.ca/index-en.aspx

Public Services and Procurement Canada. (n.d.) Retrieved from http://www.tpsgc-pwgsc.gc.ca/comm/index-eng.html

Pugliese, D. (2017, April 30). Should Defence Minister Harjit Sajjan resign for his Op Medusa claims? *Ottawa Citizen*. Retrieved from http://ottawacitizen.com/news/national /defence-watch/should-defence-minister-harjit-sajjan -resign-for-his-op-medusa-claims

Richards, G. (Director). (2006). *Consequences: The private side of Britain* [Motion picture]. Toronto: Indignant Eye Productions.

Roman, K. (2017, July 19). Deadline for decision on Canada Post delivery missed as Liberals ponder way forward. *CBC News*. Retrieved from http://www.cbc.ca/news/politics/deadline -for-decision-on-canada-post-home-delivery-missed-as -liberals-ponder-way-forward-1.4213021

Stastna, K. (2014, April 1). What are Crown corporations and why do they exist? *CBC News*. Retrieved from http://www .cbc.ca/news/canada/what-are-crown-corporations-and -why-do-they-exist-1.1135699

Talaga, T., et al. (2000, May 26). Police probe *E. coli* crisis. *Toronto Star*, p. A1.

Treasury Board of Canada Secretariat. (2009, April 6). Crown Corporations—Links. Retrieved from https://www.tbs-sct.gc .ca/gov-gouv/rc-cr/links-liens-eng.asp

Walkterton tragedy. (2000, June 12). *Maclean's*. Retrieved from http://www.thecanadianencyclopedia.ca/en/article /walkerton-water-crisis-follow-up/

White, P. (2016, November 8). Ontario appoints Howard Sapers as corrections adviser. *The Globe and Mail*. Retrieved from https://www.theglobeandmail.com/news /national/howard-sapers-to-lead-ontario-segregation -review/article32724886/

EXERCISES
True or False?

____ **1.** A deputy minister is a politician.

____ **2.** Deputy ministers get their positions by belonging to the same political party as the government.

____ **3.** Administrative-coordinative departments provide services directly to Canadians.

____ **4.** Some government agencies have the authority to make specific decisions that have the force of law.

____ **5.** A police officer who stops a motorist for speeding and proceeds to search the car because the motorist is behaving suspiciously is using discretionary power.

Multiple Choice

1. The number of federal government departments is set by

   a. legislation

   b. the prime minister

   c. the House of Commons

   d. custom and tradition

   e. the Senate

2. The principle of ministerial responsibility means that

   a. a department is responsible for its official activities

   b. the prime minister is responsible for the official activities of a department

   c. MPs are responsible for the official activities of a department

   d. Parliament is responsible for the official activities of a department

   e. the minister of a department is responsible for the official activities of that department

3. The deputy minister is

   a. the most senior bureaucrat in the department

   b. the head of the department

   c. appointed by the prime minister

   d. a and b

   e. a and c

4. A constituency department

   a. serves other departments

   b. coordinates overall policy

   c. facilitates the operation of government services

   d. provides services directly to citizens

   e. all of the above

5. Crown corporations are

   a. privately owned businesses operating in the private sector and serving a private purpose

   b. privately owned businesses operating in the public sector and serving a private purpose

   c. publicly owned businesses operating in the public sector and serving a public purpose

   d. publicly owned businesses operating in the private sector and serving a public purpose

   e. publicly owned businesses operating in the private sector and serving a private purpose

Short Answer

1. Define and explain the purpose of a government department. What is its role in the Canadian political system?

2. Outline the roles and responsibilities of a minister and deputy minister. How do they interact with each other? Design an organizational chart showing the structure of a typical department.

3. What is a Crown corporation? How does it differ from a regulatory agency? Why do governments choose these forms rather than the departmental model?

4. What is administrative law? Explain its role in the bureaucratic process.

Public Law Enforcement: Politics and Public Administration in Action

10

LEARNING OUTCOMES

After completing this chapter, you should be able to

■ describe the functions of key government departments and their roles in the context of government and public law enforcement; and

■ outline the general structure of a number of law enforcement agencies and how they are held publicly accountable.

Introduction

Having established some of the fundamental principles of public administration and its relation to the political process in Canada, it is now time to see "where the rubber meets the road." This chapter outlines how government attempts to apply political and administrative ideals to the reality of public law enforcement. The situation is complicated by the inconsistent and arbitrary use of official names and titles to describe government bodies and the people who work in them.[1] Which departments do what, to whom, for whom, and with what consequences? As you will see, it is often a challenge to reconcile cherished democratic principles with the cut and thrust of everyday law enforcement.

Federal Agencies

Department of Justice Canada

The Department of Justice Canada—known to many familiar with its operations as "DOJ"—has the primary responsibility for criminal justice policy at the federal level.[2] It serves a dual purpose: to advise the federal government on legal matters and to watch over the administration of justice in areas of federal jurisdiction. The department's responsibility to the federal government is referred to as the **attorney general function**, which means that it safeguards the legal interests of the federal government in any situation where the government has jurisdiction. As you know from the discussion of federal and provincial powers in Chapter 2, the division of powers between the federal and provincial levels of government set out in Canada's Constitution restricts the department's ability to act in some areas. Further, the Department of Justice Canada provides legal advice to other federal government departments and agencies, and may represent their legal position in matters of regulation and litigation. The Department of Justice Canada also prosecutes "violations of all federal legislation, other than the *Criminal Code*, in the provinces and violations of all federal legislation, including the *Criminal Code*, in the territories" (Ferguson, 1999, pp. 43:1–43:2).

> **attorney general function**
> the function of the federal Department of Justice Canada to safeguard the legal interests of the federal government

The second major responsibility of the Department of Justice Canada is carried out through the **minister of justice function**. This relates to the more familiar duties of a ministry, such as creating, implementing, and evaluating relevant policy, and overseeing the overall operation of the department. In the case of the Department of Justice Canada, this refers to monitoring federal legislation, directives, and regulations to ensure that they do not violate citizens' Charter rights and, in general, to considering "issues related to a fair and equitable justice system" (Ferguson, 1999, p. 43:2).

> **minister of justice function**
> the function of the federal Department of Justice Canada to monitor federal legislation, directives, and regulations and to consider other justice-related issues

As part of its mandate, the Department of Justice Canada fulfills other responsibilities. It drafts and oversees the implementation of legislation in areas of criminal, family, and youth law, and it advises the federal government in such diverse policy areas as recognition of and reconciliation with Canada's Indigenous peoples, human trafficking, medically-assisted dying, and the legalization and regulation of cannabis products (Department of Justice Canada, 2017a).

---

1   For example, the words "ministry" and "department" may have the same meaning, while "commission" is used to describe agencies of varying size, function, and importance, making categorization by name alone virtually meaningless. Organizing agencies according to function is a better alternative.

2   In addition to the public agencies discussed, many professional, voluntary, and non-profit agencies exist that also contribute in various ways to the maintenance of justice in Canada. Because these organizations are not recognized as official government bodies, they are not dealt with in this section. The summaries of agency duties and responsibilities are drawn from the official ministry websites.

The original act that enabled the Department of Justice Canada to carry out its dual mandate was created in 1868, but the process of remaining relevant and responsive to Canadians is an ongoing one. Most recently, efforts are underway to modernize the *Criminal Code* and to remove obsolete offences (e.g., "challenging someone to a duel") and redundant provisions that are needlessly specific and can be addressed through other *Criminal Code* provisions (e.g., "impersonating someone in a university exam") (Government of Canada, 2017a).

The department has also developed new policies to address such issues as high-technology crime, organized crime, human rights violations, and advances in investigative science and technology (e.g., the implications of improved DNA testing). Increased international threats and concerns about domestic safety have also influenced departmental operations. Following the terrorist attacks on the World Trade Center on September 11, 2001, the department assumed new responsibilities, including shared operational oversight of several government agencies. For example, the department was instrumental in developing legislative reforms to the *Criminal Code* that enhance the power of justice officials to pursue and prosecute those suspected of engaging in terrorism, while preserving rights enshrined in the Charter. One of the ways in which the department strives to maintain this delicate balance is through its partnership with Public Safety Canada in the management of the Cross-Cultural Roundtable on Security, which was created to facilitate discussion among leaders of various communities on relevant issues (Department of Justice Canada, 2016; Public Safety Canada, 2017a).

Overall, the Department of Justice Canada is responsible for over 45 statutes and areas of federal law. It employs more than 5,000 people, over half of whom are lawyers. Dozens of lawyers work in regional offices throughout the country to ensure equitable representation for all Canadians. The annual budget for the department in 2017–2018 was approximately $1 billion (Department of Justice Canada, 2017b).

A justice minister performs a unique role in the federal Cabinet: he or she not only proffers political advice on legislative matters, but also offers legal advice. The distinction is important because it is not unusual for one to be at odds with the other. For example, a justice minister may express the opinion that gun control legislation is an unwise political move because it is difficult to enforce and is unpopular in certain areas, but at the same time the minister may advise the Cabinet that such legislation is well within the federal government's right to act.[3]

Many people are frustrated when they hear government officials say that they refuse to give their views on a hot political issue because it is before the courts. This is not simply a convenient excuse to avoid controversy, although it is often perceived that way. The refusal to comment is based on the legal principle known as **subjudicial rule**, which strictly prohibits government officials from commenting on an issue that is before the courts. The rationale behind the principle is that because government officials are closer to the process than other citizens, their opinions might be perceived as tainting the judicial process and thus may undermine public faith in that process. So the next time you are tempted to react cynically to "No comment," consider why the official has responded this way before judging his or her motives.

subjudicial rule
a rule that prohibits government officials from commenting on an issue that is before the courts

Office of the Commissioner for Federal Judicial Affairs

In addition to the duties outlined above, the justice minister oversees the Office of the Commissioner for Federal Judicial Affairs. This body facilitates the operation of an independent judiciary—that is, it looks after judges' salaries, support, and training. The

---

3   Despite a constitutional challenge from a majority of the provinces, the Supreme Court ruled in favour of the federal government on this subject on June 15, 2000 (Lexum, 2017).

Office of the Commissioner acts as a guarantor of judicial independence by distancing judges and their work from direct political interference by the minister of justice. In 2017, the commission's 80-member staff was responsible for providing services to approximately 1,100 active judges, as well as 850 retired judges and their survivors. Its budget for 2017–2018 was about $570 million (Officer of the Commissioner for Federal Judicial Affairs, 2017).

Public Safety Canada

Public Safety Canada (PSC) fulfills several functions in its mandate to manage the broad domains of justice and public safety in Canada. Formerly known as the Department of the Solicitor General and Corrections and later as Public Safety and Emergency Preparedness Canada, this ministry saw its mandate significantly enhanced in December 2003. It now provides a coordinated government response in four major areas: national security, border strategies, countering crime, and emergency management (Public Safety Canada, 2017c). In its entirety, PSC employs 52,000 people and has an annual departmental budget of approximately $1 billion (Public Safety Canada, 2017c).

Within these four broad categories, PSC oversees many areas of federal justice and law enforcement. National security refers to strategic coordination of areas such as counter-terrorism, protection of critical infrastructure, transportation security, and cybersecurity. Border strategies encompass activities related to customs, immigration, and cross-border law enforcement and crime detection and prevention (Public Safety Canada, 2015a). Countering crime strategies coordinate government action in policing, corrections, and crime prevention, with a specific focus in areas of child sexual exploitation, human trafficking and smuggling of humans, illicit drugs, and gun crime (Public Safety Canada, 2017b). Emergency management monitors and coordinates disaster preparation, as well as mitigation, response, and recovery from disasters, both natural and otherwise (Public Safety Canada, 2016).

This overarching coordination brings PSC into contact with numerous other government agencies, including Correctional Service Canada (CSC), the Parole Board of Canada (PBC), the Canadian Security Intelligence Service (CSIS), the Integrated Threat Assessment Centre, the Royal Canadian Mounted Police (RCMP), and the Canada Border Services Agency (CBSA).

Correctional Service Canada

Correctional Service Canada (CSC) runs the federal prison system. The 2017–2018 budget for CSC was $2.4 billion (Correctional Service Canada, 2017). CSC's operations are divided geographically into five regions: Atlantic, Quebec, Ontario, Prairies, and Pacific. It is headed by a Correctional Service commissioner who, in turn, reports to the minister of Public Safety Canada.

CSC manages institutions of various security levels across Canada and is responsible for the custody and control of offenders serving sentences of two years or longer. It also supervises offenders who have been conditionally released—on day parole, full parole, or statutory release—to serve the last third of their sentence in the community.[4]

---

4 For current spending estimates and personnel, see Correctional Services Canada (2017). For more information on the organization and its programs, see Correctional Service Canada, http://www.csc-scc.gc.ca/text/index-eng.shtml.

OVERSIGHT

Because part of CSC's mandate involves severely limiting individual freedom, it is critical to ensure that the overwhelming power this affords to those who care for inmates is not exercised improperly, either through neglect or intentional abuse. The agency charged with this watchdog function at the federal level is the Office of the Correctional Investigator. As detailed in Part III of the *Corrections and Conditional Release Act*, the office is "to conduct investigations into the problems of offenders related to decisions, recommendations, acts or omissions of the Commissioner (of Corrections) or any person under the control and management of, or performing services for, or on behalf of, the Commissioner that affect offenders either individually or as a group" (Office of the Correctional Investigator, 2013). In this role, it provides "independent, informed and objective opinions on the fairness of the action taken so as to counter balance the relative strength of public institutions against that of individuals" (Office of the Correctional Investigator, 2013). The office has full discretion to independently investigate complaints from inmates, with the requirement that information gathered be used only with reference to a particular investigation and respect federal privacy legislation.

Parole Board of Canada

The Parole Board of Canada (PBC) also falls within the Public Safety Canada portfolio. To ensure that its decisions are made—and are seen to be made—free of direct political influence, it operates at arm's length—that is, it exercises exclusive authority over the parole and conditional release of federal offenders. It also performs this function for provincial inmates in all provinces except Quebec, Ontario, and British Columbia, which operate their own parole boards.

The PBC decides whether to release (or, in some cases, pardon) individuals who have applied for parole, basing its decisions on such factors as prisoner records and risk assessment. In doing so, the PBC works closely with CSC and the RCMP to share information and coordinate the supervision of successful applicants once they have re-entered Canadian society. The board may also decide whether to hold a prisoner in custody until he or she has served a full sentence. This is known as "detention during the period of statutory release." The PBC comprises fewer than 60 full-time and even fewer part-time regional board members, who are each appointed by the governor general on the advice of the Cabinet. The broader department consists of approximately 500 public sector employees. Its annual budget for 2017–2018 was $46 million (Parole Board of Canada, 2016; Government of Canada, 2017d).

Canadian Security Intelligence Service

The Canadian Security Intelligence Service (CSIS) was established in 1984 after a government royal commission determined that national security—formerly included within the jurisdiction of the RCMP—should come under a distinct legislated framework of democratic control and be subject to more direct civilian accountability. As stated in its mandate,

> The Service's role is to investigate activities suspected of constituting threats to the security of Canada, and to report on these to the Government of Canada. CSIS may also take measures to reduce threats to the security of Canada in accordance with well-defined legal requirements and Ministerial Direction. (Canadian Security Intelligence Service, 2017a)

The agency's budget, which has increased greatly since 2001, totals approximately $577 million for the 2017–2018 fiscal year (Government of Canada, 2017b).

The Canadian Security Intelligence Service works with several other domestic and international agencies to investigate activities that may pose a threat to Canada's national security.

The serious nature of CSIS operations—some that may risk bringing it into conflict with the *Charter of Rights and Freedoms*—necessitates a framework of legal checks and balances to govern its activities. The *Canadian Security Intelligence Service Act* outlines the agency's powers and oversight by Public Safety Canada, "confers specific powers and imposes constraints, and sets the framework for democratic control and accountability for Canada's security intelligence service" (Canadian Security Intelligence Service, 2014c). Other legislation that helps to guide agency activities includes the *Immigration and Refugee Protection Act*, the *Anti-terrorism Act*, the *Security of Information Act*, and the *Public Safety Act*.

Increased public concern over Canada's national security, particularly since the 9/11 attacks on the United States, has led to the agency's adoption of several new roles in order to continue to meet its original mandate. Major areas of concern now include international and domestic terrorism, the proliferation of weapons of mass destruction, espionage and foreign interference, cybersecurity, and critical infrastructure protection. To achieve its mandate, CSIS pursues the following: intelligence collection and analysis, intelligence sharing, security screening, academic outreach, and public communication.

- Intelligence Collection—gathers information domestically and abroad about activities that "may constitute a threat to the security of Canada" (Canadian Security Intelligence Service, 2014b) and forwards this to other government agencies.

- Intelligence Analysis—vets information gathered by subject experts to assess quality and usefulness, and "produces reports on emerging trends and issues that could affect the security of Canada and that provide context to specific threats and their security implications" (Canadian Security Intelligence Service, 2014b).

- Intelligence Sharing—shares intelligence domestically and internationally, among government agencies, particularly with respect to threat assessments, which measure the "scope and immediacy of a variety of threats posed by individuals and groups in Canada and abroad" (Canadian Security Intelligence Service, 2017c).

- Security Screening—provides information to prevent non-Canadians identified as a potential threat from gaining entry and "acquiring status in the country" or "from gaining access to classified or sensitive government information, assets, sites or major events" (Canadian Security Intelligence Service, 2017b); also provides screening for government employees having access to sensitive information or infrastructure (e.g., airports, nuclear facilities), as well as Canadians and foreigners working in partnership in domestic and/or international organizations (e.g., North Atlantic Treaty Association [NATO], United Nations [UN]).[5] If requested, security assessments are also provided to provincial governments and police services.

- Academic Outreach—promotes study and discussion of issues affecting Canadian security, through ongoing consultation with "networks of experts from various disciplines and sectors, including government, think-tanks, research institutes, universities, private business and non-governmental organizations (NGOs) in Canada and abroad" (Canadian Security Intelligence Service, 2016). CSIS also participates in and sponsors forums (conferences, roundtables) examining specific issues and emerging global trends.

- Public Communication—liaises with public and private organizations to protect Canadian interests against foreign economic espionage; conducts public outreach, providing information to Canadian government, universities, community groups, and the media regarding CSIS's role, activities, and reports. This includes the Cross-Cultural Roundtable on Security, "a forum aimed at engaging Canadians in a long-term dialogue on national security matters, recognizing that Canada is a diverse and pluralistic society. The Roundtable provides a forum to discuss emerging trends and developments stemming from national security matters and serves to inform policy-makers" (Canadian Security Intelligence Service, 2014d).

OVERSIGHT

The minister of public safety is responsible to Parliament for CSIS and its overall direction and is, in turn, kept abreast of specific implementation of ministry directives by the deputy minister of PSC. The director of CSIS is accountable to the minister for management and control of the agency, issuing periodic reports on specific issues and ensuring standards of accountability are being respected and achieved.

Two monitoring bodies help to guide this process: the Security Intelligence Review Committee (SIRC) and the Federal Court. The SIRC reviews and investigates complaints made against CSIS, including those made by individuals who have been denied security clearance, as well as immigration applications rejected on security or criminal grounds. The Federal Court has the exclusive authority to issue warrants authorizing "intrusive investigation techniques" (Canadian Security Intelligence Service, 2014a), such as wiretaps and cellphone monitoring. In the agency's own words:

Before such an authorization can be made, CSIS must provide solid justification for the proposed use of these techniques in an affidavit, which is reviewed by a senior

---

5   For further details, see Canadian Security Intelligence Service (2017b).

CSIS committee chaired by the Director and comprised of representatives from the Department of Justice, and Public Safety Canada. If the committee endorses the intrusive technique, the affidavit is submitted to the Minister of Public Safety Canada for approval. If the Minister gives approval, the affidavit is then submitted to the Federal Court, which must issue a warrant before CSIS can proceed with the intrusive investigative technique. (Canadian Security Intelligence Service, 2014a)

In addition, through publications such as PSC's *Annual Statement on National Security* and *CSIS Public Report,* the agency strives to "provide Canadians with an assessment of the current security intelligence environment and detail the government's efforts to ensure national security" (Canadian Security Intelligence Service, 2014a).

Integrated Terrorism Assessment Centre

Operating in partnership with the CSIS, the Integrated Terrorism Assessment Centre (ITAC) brings together expertise from numerous other justice-related government agencies under the Public Safety Canada portfolio "to help prevent and reduce the effects of terrorist incidents on Canadians and Canadian interests, both at home and abroad" (Integrated Terrorism Assessment Centre, 2014). Its members also work with departments such as the Canada Revenue Agency, Global Affairs, and Transport Canada to gather and analyze information concerning possible terrorist attacks, trends, and capabilities; produce threat assessment reports; and circulate these reports among partner agencies. Because its operations fall within the CSIS mandate, the ITAC is subject to oversight by the SIRC (Integrated Terrorism Assessment Centre, 2014).

Royal Canadian Mounted Police

The Royal Canadian Mounted Police (RCMP) operates under the control and direction of Public Safety Canada and plays a primary role in both federal and provincial law enforcement. As outlined in its authorizing legislation, the service's mandate encompasses a wide variety of justice-related activities, including "preventing and investigating crime; maintaining peace and order; enforcing laws; contributing to national security; ensuring the safety of state officials, visiting dignitaries and foreign missions; and providing vital operational support services to other police and law enforcement agencies within Canada and abroad" (Royal Canadian Mounted Police, 2017b). In addition to its national responsibilities, the RCMP performs provincial policing functions in all provinces except Ontario and Quebec, and provides policing services to more than 180 municipalities and more than 600 Indigenous communities (Royal Canadian Mounted Police, 2017b). The service is organized geographically into 15 regions, roughly approximating provincial and territorial boundaries, employing 29,188 people, more than 11,731 of whom are constables.[6] Its 2017–2018 annual budget is approximately $3.4 billion (Royal Canadian Mounted Police, 2017c, d).

Specific areas of responsibility include the following:

- Federal and International Operations Directorate—"provides policing, law enforcement, investigative and preventative services to the federal government, its departments and agencies and to Canadians" (Royal Canadian Mounted Police, 2007).

---

6 Figures as of December 1, 2016. See Royal Canadian Mounted Police (2017b).

- National Security Criminal Investigations Program—monitors Canada's national security, with a particular emphasis on countering terrorism threats, through measures such as "protective policing, border integrity, critical infrastructure protection, marine security, air carrier protection, [and] critical incident management " (Royal Canadian Mounted Police, 2016b).

The RCMP is also responsible for the operation and oversight of what are classified collectively as "specialized policing services." These include the following:

- Canadian Firearms Program (CFP)—monitors sales, licensing, registration, and safety training of firearms in Canada.
- Canadian Police College (CPC)—provides advanced education and training to law enforcement officers in specialized areas such as "investigative techniques, technological crime, forensic identification, explosives disposal/investigations, police executive development and professional development for Aboriginal policing" (Canadian Police College, n.d.).
- Criminal Intelligence Service Canada (CISC)—provides specialized intelligence and expertise to combat organized crime, manages the national criminal intelligence databank, and liaises with national and provincial law enforcement agencies to monitor criminal activity and share information (Criminal Intelligence Service Canada, 2014).
- Forensic Science and Identification Services (FSIS)—provides scientific expertise to police, including forensic science services and crime scene forensic identification, and oversees fingerprint, criminal record, and national DNA databanks (Royal Canadian Mounted Police, 2017a).
- Canadian Police Information Centre (CPIC)—national police service database documenting crime and criminals. It facilitates communication between criminal justice and police agencies across Canada and abroad. The database can be accessed by citizens to verify whether a bicycle or a vehicle for sale has been reported stolen (Canadian Police Information Centre, 2017).
- National Sex Offender Registry—maintains a databank of information for police services related to convicted sex offenders (Royal Canadian Mounted Police, 2016c).
- National Child Exploitation Coordination Centre (NCECC)—specializes in identification of children at risk and child victims, investigation of and assistance in prosecution of sexual offenders, and provision of training, education, and research for police services (Royal Canadian Mounted Police, 2013).

OVERSIGHT

Given these broad and potentially intrusive powers, the RCMP is held accountable to the public for its actions in two specific ways: the Civilian Review and Complaints Commission for the RCMP and the RCMP External Review Committee.

Civilian Review and Complaints Commission for the RCMP

With a mission to "enhance the accountability of the RCMP by providing civilian review of RCMP activities and member conduct" (Civilian Review and Complaints Commission, 2017) the commission investigates public complaints made against the RCMP. The commission also has the authority to initiate investigations of RCMP behaviour if and when it determines that it is in the public interest to do so. Once these investigations are complete, the commission issues a report and can make recommendations for changes.

After the RCMP commissioner has tabled a response, a final report is issued, including the commission's recommendations and the police service's rationale for taking/not taking action. A copy of the findings is sent to those directly involved, as well as to the minister of public safety and the justice minister in the province where the complaint originated (Civilian Review and Complaints Commission, 2015).

RCMP External Review Committee

The External Review Committee (ERC) is an independent tribunal that reviews appeals from RCMP members with regard to RCMP management, including dismissal, demotion, or fines for contravention of the RCMP's *Code of Conduct*; harassment complaint investigation; discharge or demotion for being absent from duty; and stoppage of pay and allowance when suspended from duty. Once the ERC has issued its report, the RCMP commissioner may accept or reject its findings but must give reasons for not following the ERC's recommendations (RCMP External Review Committee, 2016).

Canada Border Services Agency

With responsibilities for administering more than 90 domestic laws, regulations, and international agreements governing trade and travel, the Canada Border Services Agency (CBSA) scrutinizes the movement of people, plants, animals, and goods across Canada's borders. One of its main duties involves screening visitors and immigrants, and it has the power to investigate and detain individuals, conduct hearings, and carry out deportations, if necessary. The CBSA's other major area of concern is ensuring safe and efficient international trade and commerce—that is, cross-border shipping and the transport of goods. The agency operates from 1,200 domestic and 39 international locations, including land border crossings, marine ports, rail sites, and international airports. Approximately 6,500 of its 14,000 employees are uniformed CBSA officers (Canada Border Services Agency, 2016). Its annual operating budget for 2017–2018 was $1.7 billion (Canada Border Services Agency, 2017).

Department of National Defence

As the department responsible for civilian oversight of Canada's military, the Department of National Defence (DND) serves two major functions. First, it directs the activities of the Canadian Armed Forces (including the army, navy, and air force), which protect Canada from outside military threats and provide assistance in times of natural disasters and other domestic crises. Second, the department works closely with Global Affairs Canada to fulfill Canada's international obligations in the areas of peacekeeping and disaster relief abroad, and as a member of NATO (Government of Canada, 2017c). The department's planned annual budget for 2017–2018 is approximately $18 billion (National Defence, 2017). The defence minister has ultimate authority over the armed forces even though it is not he or she who actually plans or executes military manoeuvres. Maintaining civilian authority over the military represents another hallmark of democratic government, demonstrating to citizens that the coercive power of the state is accountable.

The Canadian Armed Forces are managed by the chief of the defence staff, who works alongside a deputy minister. In this way, overall goals of the department are coordinated with those of the Canadian Armed Forces. As with all departments, below these key players is a complex bureaucracy of individuals who coordinate and carry out the many aspects of DND policy, whether these involve marshalling equipment for duty overseas or assisting residents of British Columbia to fight the wildfires of 2017.

While civilian oversight of police services and other public safety agencies has become a normal part of administrative structure and public expectation in Canada, Parliament has thus far proven reluctant to share its traditionally exclusive purview of the Canadian Armed Forces with an independent civilian regulatory body. Parliament did establish the little-known Military Police Complaints Commission of Canada (MPCC) in 1999 as a belated response to the "Somalia Affair" in 1993 (in which members of the now disbanded Canadian Airborne Regiment murdered two Somalis during a UN mission), the subsequent attempt by the DND to cover it up, and the results of the ensuing public inquiry in 1997 (Military Police Complaints Commission, 2013). The Somalia Affair is widely considered to have directly fed Canadian ambivalence to the DND budget cuts and the military more generally ("1994: Somalia inquiry,"1994; Fisher, Wilson-Smith, & Demont, 2003; "Somalia affair: The paper chase," 1996; "Somalia debacle a high-level cover-up," 1997). While the MPCC is an independent civilian oversight body, it continues to report directly to Parliament through the minister of national defence and lacks the independence and authority that are integral to civilian oversight bodies. The political will to remedy this situation still appears to be lacking. Prime Minister Stephen Harper's government, for example, came under fire in 2015 for lacking the will and the funding to empower a truly independent DND watchdog following revelations of a navy officer who was spying for Russia in 2013 (Brewster, 2015; "Canada's dysfunctional military spending," 2015).

Provincial Agencies

The various provinces and territories have a variety of structural approaches, making it difficult to describe each one in detail in this chapter. There are many similarities among them, so, in the interest of brevity, the following sections describe the ministries, agencies, and boards that make up the law enforcement system in Ontario.[7]

Ministry of the Attorney General

In many respects, the attorney general can also be thought of as the provincial minister of justice.[8] He or she provides expert legal advice to the government and has overall responsibility for the administration of justice in the province. The statutory responsibilities of the attorney general are outlined in section 5 of the *Ministry of the Attorney General Act* and involve five broad responsibilities: chief law officer, criminal prosecutions, legislative responsibilities, civil litigation, and administration of the provincial court system. Collectively, these duties help to maintain public trust in, and respect for, the rule of law. Thus the attorney general ensures that any actions taken by those in government are both legally and constitutionally valid.

As chief law officer, the minister provides legal advice to the Cabinet specifically and to the bureaucracy and legislature more generally. By doing so, he or she assures citizens that actions undertaken by public officials have been vetted and conform with the law and our Constitution. Ministry stewardship of criminal prosecutions emanates from powers granted by the Constitution, assigning administration of the federal *Criminal Code* and non-federal judicial affairs to provincial jurisdiction (see Chapter 2). Because the public's faith in the justice system is of paramount concern, great care must be taken to demonstrate

---

7   In addition to the public agencies discussed, many professional, voluntary, and non-profit agencies exist that also contribute in various ways to the maintenance of justice in Ontario. Because these organizations are not recognized as official government bodies, they are not dealt with here.

8   In fact, the federal minister of justice also holds the title of federal attorney general, although this term is rarely used.

that the rights and responsibilities of all involved—those accused, victims, and government officials—are respected. Therefore,

> individual criminal prosecutions must be undertaken—and seen to be undertaken—on strictly objective and legal criteria, free of any political considerations. Whether to initiate or stay a criminal proceeding is not an issue of government policy. This responsibility has been characterized as a matter of the Attorney General acting as the Queen's Attorney—not as a Minister of the government of the day. (Ontario Ministry of the Attorney General, 2015b)

Another interesting part of this process is that it is not the attorney general who decides whether to prosecute criminal offences. These decisions are left to the many Crown attorneys who, in turn, do not begin this consideration until police have laid charges. Once again, basic principles of justice underlie this process.

Legislative responsibilities of the ministry involve similar principles of justice and encompass two broad concepts. First, the ministry ensures that proposed legislation conforms with principles of natural justice and civil rights. Second, it advises on the constitutionality and legality of what is being proposed. Thus ministry officials not only advise their respective governments in a number of legal and legislative areas, but also scrutinize proposed legislation from other government ministries to ensure that it is legal, constitutional, and in conformance with accepted principles of justice.[9] Civil litigation powers extend beyond acting on behalf of the government and its agencies in civil cases to include matters of public interest, such as Charter challenges and other matters where the public interest is at stake (Ontario Ministry of the Attorney General, 2015b). Finally, the ministry oversees the administration of the provincial courts. A key part of this role involves protecting judicial independence and liaising with judges within the system so that the public can see that their decisions are being made freely and fairly, without political interference (Ontario Ministry of the Attorney General, 2015b). This function is managed at arm's length by the Ontario Judicial Council, which operates in a manner similar to that of the Office of the Commissioner for Federal Judicial Affairs, described earlier.

As with the Department of Justice Canada, there is a difference between policy advice and legal advice given by a minister in this portfolio. The first is a matter of opinion while the second is a matter of law. The principle of subjudicial rule also applies in cases of criminal and civil law.

Other Affiliated Boards, Agencies, and Commissions of the Attorney General

In keeping with its mandate to preside over all justice-related activity in the province, the ministry is also responsible for a number of boards, agencies, and commissions. Note how each contributes to the ministry's overall mandate.[10]

---

9 Because of the sensitive nature of this decision-making process, these considerations are delegated to the Office of Legislative Counsel to avoid allegations of political interference.

10 The summary of agency duties and responsibilities is drawn from Ontario Ministry of the Attorney General (2017b).

Oversight of Policing

SPECIAL INVESTIGATIONS UNIT

Since 1990, municipal, regional, and provincial police forces in Ontario have been subject to an independent watchdog agency known as the Special Investigations Unit (SIU). Created under provisions of Part VII of Ontario's *Police Services Act*, the SIU reports to the attorney general and looks into "circumstances involving police and civilians that have resulted in serious injury, death or sexual assault" (Special Investigations Unit, 2016).

The Special Investigations Unit (SIU) examines circumstances involving police and civilians that have resulted in serious injury, death, or allegations of sexual assault. Here police meet with an SIU investigator.

Before the SIU's creation, investigations were done in-house—that is, within the police service whose members were involved in the incident or by another police service. This caused public concerns about integrity and objectivity, which eventually led to the creation of the SIU.

Initially, the SIU met with resistance from some in the policing community, partly because it supplanted the traditional authority of the police to police themselves and also because the police feared that external oversight might fail to take into account many of the realities that they faced in carrying out their duties. The SIU represented a new form of police oversight. Relations remained cool during most of the 1990s. However, following substantial funding increases and gradual implementation of recommendations outlined in a report released in 1997, trust in the process improved substantially. As the report's author, George Adams (2003, p. 9), noted: "Through the SIU, the Province seeks to protect the fundamental human rights of all its citizens by ensuring that those charged with enforcing the laws and advancing public safety remain accountable should they violate those rights."[11]

---

11   Known as the Adams report, the study sought to identify and remedy problems that had hindered relations between the SIU and police. Adams conducted a five-year follow-up report in 2003 (Adams, 2003).

Following the example of Ontario, the provinces of British Columbia, Alberta, Manitoba, Quebec, and Nova Scotia have created similar forms of police oversight. The SIU's jurisdiction covers 53 police services across Ontario, representing 26,148 officers. In 2016, the SIU opened 327 investigations. Its annual budget for 2016–2017 was approximately $9.27 million (Special Investigations Unit, 2016–2017).

OFFICE OF THE INDEPENDENT POLICE REVIEW DIRECTOR

The Office of the Independent Police Review Director (OIPRD) is the civilian oversight agency charged with independently overseeing all complaints made against police in Ontario. It deals with issues of police conduct, whether they pertain to an individual member or the service he or she represents. "Conduct complaints are about how a police officer behaves. Policies of a police department are the rules and standards that guide an officer in delivering police services. Services are how effectively and efficiently a particular department performs its duties" (Office of the Independent Police Review Director, 2014). As part of its mandate, the OIPRD also identifies systemic or ongoing issues related to public complaints, provides education to the public and police regarding the public complaints process, and has jurisdiction over all municipal, regional, and Ontario's provincial police service. Excluded from its jurisdiction are RCMP officers, Toronto Transit Commission (TTC) special constables, GO Transit police, First Nations police officers, court officers, campus police, provincial offences officers, and special constables, whose conduct is monitored by other bodies (Office of the Independent Police Review Director, 2014).

ONTARIO CIVILIAN POLICE COMMISSION

Included as part of the Safety, Licencing Appeals and Standards Tribunals Ontario (see below), the Ontario Civilian Police Commission (OCPC) is an independent, quasi-judicial agency overseeing the conduct of police services and municipal police service board members. Its duties include monitoring the adequacy and effectiveness of policing services; hearing appeals of police disciplinary decisions; adjudicating disputes between municipal councils and police service boards involving budget disputes; conducting hearings concerning the creation, abolition, reduction, modification, or amalgamation of police services; monitoring and investigating the conduct of police officers, chiefs of police, and police service boards; and being able to determine the status of police service members. In Ontario, police services and police service boards are accountable to the OCPC, which ultimately reports to the Ministry of the Attorney General (Safety, Licensing Appeals and Standards Tribunals Ontario, n.d.).

Other Agencies Reporting to the Attorney General

There are several other agencies that report to the attorney general:

- Alcohol and Gaming Commission of Ontario—regulates alcohol, gaming, and horse racing in the province (Alcohol and Gaming Commission of Ontario, n.d.).
- Social Justice Tribunals Ontario—a collection of boards and tribunals overseeing appeals and dispute resolution in a broad range of issues. Included are the following:
  - Child and Family Services Review Board (CFSRB)—"conducts reviews and hearings on a number of matters that affect children, youth and families in Ontario" (Child and Family Services Review Board, n.d.), including adoption, foster care, and appeals of student expulsion by a school board.

- Custody Review Board (CRB)—"hears applications and makes recommendations on the placement of young people in custody or detention" (Custody Review Board, n.d.).
- Criminal Injuries Compensation Board—"assesses and awards financial compensation for victims and family members of deceased victims of violent crimes committed in Ontario" (Criminal Injuries Compensation Board, n.d.).
- Human Rights Tribunal of Ontario—adjudicates claims of discrimination and harassment filed under the *Human Rights Code* (Human Rights Tribunal of Ontario, n.d.).
- Landlord and Tenant Board—adjudicates disputes between landlords and tenants, and provides information to both parties regarding rights and responsibilities under the *Residential Tenancies Act* (Landlord and Tenant Board, n.d.).
- Ontario Special Education Tribunals (English Public and Separate Schools, French Public and Separate Schools)—"hear appeals from parents, legal guardians or adult students who disagree with a school board's decision about the identification or placement of students with exceptional learning needs under the *Education Act* and its regulations" (Ontario Special Education Tribunals, n.d.).
- Social Benefits Tribunal—"hears appeals from people who disagree with a decision that affects the amount of, or their eligibility for, social assistance under the *Ontario Works Act* or the *Ontario Disability Support Program Act*" (Social Benefits Tribunal, n.d.).
- Environment and Land Tribunals—a group of five agencies adjudicating applications, appeals, and other disputes in such areas as land use planning, environmental and heritage protection, property assessment, and land valuation. The five agencies include the Assessment Review Board, Board of Negotiation, Conservation Review Board, Environmental Review Tribunal, and Ontario Municipal Board (Environment and Land Tribunals, n.d.).
- Human Rights Legal Support Centre—provides legal services to individuals wishing to pursue human rights complaints, including "assistance in filing applications at the Human Rights Tribunal of Ontario and legal representation at mediations and hearings" (Human Rights Legal Support Centre, n.d.).
- Legal Aid Ontario—promotes equitable access to justice by providing legal aid services to low-income Ontarians (Legal Aid Ontario, n.d.).
- Office for Victims of Crime—provides advice to the ministry on victims' issues, including standards of victim service, use of the Victims Fund, education, and prevention of re-victimization (Ontario Ministry of the Attorney General, 2015a).
- Office of the Public Guardian and Trustee—acts on behalf of mentally incapable people, oversees the public's interest in charities, searches for heirs of deceased persons whose estates it administers, invests perpetual care funds, and monitors issues arising from the dissolution of corporations (Ontario Ministry of the Attorney General, 2016).
- Office of the Children's Lawyer—acts for children under the age of 18 involved in certain aspects of the justice system, including disputes over custody, access, child protection proceedings, and inheritance (Ontario Ministry of the Attorney General, 2017a).

- Safety, Licensing Appeals and Standards Tribunals Ontario—comprised of five adjudicative tribunals covering a wide variety of licensing and standards. These include the Animal Care Review Board, Fire Safety Commission, Licence Appeal Tribunal, Ontario Parole Board, and Ontario Civilian Police Commission (see above).

Ministry of Community Safety and Correctional Services

Because of its multi-faceted mandate and presence in virtually every community, the Ministry of Community Safety and Correctional Services (MCSCS) is the largest operational ministry in Ontario. Like its federal counterpart, this ministry's mandate was at one time captured under the title of solicitor general. However, in April 2002, the duties and title of its minister changed. Administratively, the ministry's responsibilities fall into three broad categories: policing services, correctional services, and public safety and security.[12]

Policing Services

This branch of the MCSCS monitors the quality of public policing and the private security industry in Ontario. It sets out professional training standards and inspection requirements and provides support to all police services, including the Ontario Provincial Police (OPP), as well as to municipal police service boards and other municipal organizations involved in policing. It also operates Criminal Intelligence Service Ontario (CISO) and is involved in a number of community safety and crime prevention initiatives.

ONTARIO PROVINCIAL POLICE

The OPP provides a variety of policing services in contract, non-contract, and Indigenous communities throughout the province.[13] It is one of only two provincial police organizations, the other being the Sûreté du Québec (SQ) or Québec Provincial Police (QPP). As noted earlier, the RCMP is under contract with all other provinces to fulfill this function. From its 160 detachment and satellite locations, OPP members provide policing services to 320 municipalities and 19 Indigenous communities throughout Ontario, with more than 6,200 uniformed officers, 800 auxiliary officers, and 3,100 civilian employees (Ontario Provincial Police, n.d.b, 2016b).[14] The OPP's total annual budget in 2016 was approximately $1.12 billion (Ontario Provincial Police, n.d.a). The service is divided into four senior command areas: Traffic Safety and Operational Support, Investigations and Organized Crime, Field Operations, and Corporate Services.

Traffic Safety and Operational Support

This command is composed of front-line and specialized unit officers, as well as members specializing in information and technology. It has four distinct units:

- Highway Safety Division—focuses mainly on traffic and safety on highways, trails, and waterways (Ontario Provincial Police, 2017c).

---

12 Information about all MCSCS agencies and operations is available from the Ministry of Community Safety and Correctional Services at http://www.mcscs.jus.gov.on.ca.

13 Summarized from the OPP website at http://www.opp.ca.

14 For information about policing in Indigenous communities, see Indigenous Policing Bureau (n.d.).

- Field Support Bureau—oversees Aboriginal Critical Incident Response, Offender Transportation Program, Emergency Management Unit, Specialized Response Teams, and Aviation Services (Ontario Provincial Police, 2017c).

- Security Bureau—supports assessment and management of physical and cybersecurity risks. Specialized sections include the Chief Security Office, Dignitary Protection and investigation Section, Justice Officials Protection and Investigations Section, Queen's Park Detachment, General Headquarters Detachment, and Security Services Section (Ontario Provincial Police, 2017c).

- Communications and Technology Services Bureau—protects the OPP's communication networks by facilitating "the provision of secure computing technology and communication capabilities, network connectivity, data management, and support for the organization" (Ontario Provincial Police, 2017c).

Investigations and Organized Crime

This branch of senior command investigates, analyzes, and supports efforts to combat organized criminal activity by focusing expertise in a number of areas:

- Investigation and Support Bureau—coordinates major multi-jurisdictional investigations requiring technical expertise in areas such as behavioural science, forensic identification, and electronic crime (Ontario Provincial Police, 2017b).

- Organized Crime Enforcement Bureau—seeks to disrupt and suppress organized crime by conducting long-term, specialized investigations and sharing findings with other justice organizations (Ontario Provincial Police, 2017b).

- Provincial Operations Intelligence Bureau—monitors activities of persons or groups suspected of engaging in criminal activity (Ontario Provincial Police, 2017b).

- Investigation and Enforcement Bureau—works with Alcohol and Gaming Commission of Ontario to "to ensure the gaming, alcohol and lottery industries are conducted honestly and are free from criminal elements and activity" (Ontario Provincial Police, 2017b).

- Chief Firearms Office—administers regulations and licensing provisions of the *Firearms Act* (Ontario Provincial Police, 2017b).

- Project Support Centre—supports front-line officers in the preparation, review, and tracking of project reports (Ontario Provincial Police, 2017b).

- Professional Standards Bureau—responds to internal and external complaints and criminal allegations made against uniformed and civilian OPP members. Although part of the OPP, this bureau collaborates with other police oversight agencies, including the Special Investigations Unit and the Office of the Independent Police Review Director (see above).

Field Operations

This command coordinates front-line operations, organized into five regional headquarters located in London, North Bay, Orillia, Smiths Falls, and Thunder Bay. It also manages the Aboriginal Policing Bureau, which works with Indigenous communities to coordinate police services. The command also includes Community Safety Services (including responsibility for the management of the Auxiliary Policing Program), which provides "expertise to the OPP in the areas of crime prevention, community safety and well-being planning, risk analysis and mitigation" (Ontario Provincial Police, 2016b).

Corporate Services

Corporate Services handles several bureaucratic functions necessary to the operation of the OPP. These include the Career Development Bureau, specializing in recruitment; the Fleet Supply and Weapons Service Bureau, which manages all OPP equipment requirements; the Municipal Policing Bureau, managing all contract and non-contract municipal policing; and, finally, the Business Management Bureau, which controls financial oversight and policy development (Ontario Provincial Police, 2016a).

Oversight

As mentioned earlier, several independent agencies oversee OPP accountability, including the Special Investigations Unit, the Office of the Independent Police Review Director, and the Ontario Civilian Police Commission. In conjunction with these agencies, the OPP's Professional Standards Bureau manages internal complaints and allegations of misconduct by members.

Other Agencies Included in Policing Services

CRIMINAL INTELLIGENCE SERVICE ONTARIO

Created in 1966, Criminal Intelligence Service Ontario (CISO) is an independent justice agency that "brings together police services and provincial and federal government agencies to identify and tackle organized crime across the province" (Criminal Intelligence Service Canada, 2014). To do this, it provides training and shares intelligence among a network of similar agencies in each province across the country affiliated with Criminal Intelligence Services Canada (see above under "Royal Canadian Mounted Police").

ONTARIO POLICE ARBITRATION COMMISSION

The Ontario Police Arbitration Commission (OPAC) provides a formal administrative framework within which police associations and their employers negotiate collective agreements. It maintains a roster of arbitrators, sets fees for their services, and makes the necessary administrative arrangements for negotiations to occur. OPAC also sponsors research and is responsible for publishing information on agreements, decisions, and awards (OPAC, 2015).

ONTARIO POLICE COLLEGE

The Ontario Police College provides training for police and civilian members working in policing in Ontario (Ontario Ministry of Community Safety and Correctional Services, 2017a).

PRIVATE SECURITY AND INVESTIGATIVE SERVICES

Private Security and Investigative Services oversee licensing, registration, and professional standards for all private security operations (Ontario Ministry of Community Safety and Correctional Services, 2017b).

ONTARIO SEX OFFENDER REGISTRY

The Ontario Sex Offender Registry provides a non-public database available to police services in the investigation of sex-related crimes. It is also used for tracking sex offenders in the community (Ontario Ministry of Community Safety and Correctional Services, 2016d).

Correctional Services

Correctional Services manages the custody of adult offenders serving sentences of imprisonment or conditional sentences of fewer than two years and terms of probation up to three years. The agency also supervises those who have been granted parole by the Ontario Parole Board and handles individuals awaiting transfer to a federal correctional facility to serve sentences that exceed two years. As with its federal counterpart, provincial corrections manages a series of programs designed to help rehabilitate offenders and prepare them for reintegration into society.

Correctional Services currently maintains 26 facilities for adult offenders, including jails and detention and corrections centres, as well as probation and parole offices. Responsibility for young offenders aged 12–17 was transferred to the Ontario Ministry of Children and Youth Services in April 2004.

Public Safety and Security

Public safety and security in Ontario is covered by a variety of agencies. These include the Centre of Forensic Sciences, the Office of the Chief Coroner, the Office of the Fire Marshal, and Emergency Management Ontario (EMO).

Centre of Forensic Sciences (CFS)—"conducts scientific investigations in cases involving injury or death for crimes against persons or property" (Ontario Ministry of Community Safety and Correctional Services, 2016b). Specific areas of expertise include toxicology, firearms and tool marks, biology, chemistry, and document analysis.

OFFICE OF THE CHIEF CORONER/ONTARIO FORENSIC PATHOLOGY SERVICE

Although distinct, these two agencies work together to ensure that all human deaths are reported and, if necessary, investigated. Individually, or jointly with its partner agency, the Office of the Chief Coroner supervises the province's coroners, who attempt to determine the identity of someone who has died and how, when, where, and by what means he or she died. Its sister agency "provides medicolegal autopsy services for public death investigations under the legal authority of a coroner" (Ontario Ministry of Community Safety and Correctional Services, 2016a).

OFFICE OF THE FIRE MARSHAL

The Office of the Fire Marshal (OFM) is responsible for administering Ontario's *Fire Code* and the *Fire Protection and Prevention Act*. Although it is independent of municipal fire services, the OFM assists them by providing leadership in fire safety, prevention, and protection. As well, the OFM monitors municipal fire departments to ensure that all are providing adequate levels of fire prevention and protection in their respective jurisdictions. The OFM also advises provincial officials on proper standards and professional training. The OFM has investigative responsibilities for fires involving deaths or serious injury; suspicious fires, including those caused by explosions or arson; and fires resulting in losses in excess of $500,000. It also provides expert testimony in criminal prosecutions and coroners' inquests (Ontario Ministry of Community Safety and Correctional Services, 2016c).

EMERGENCY MANAGEMENT ONTARIO

Created in 1980, Emergency Management Ontario (EMO) coordinates the development and maintenance of emergency management programs, particularly those emphasizing prevention and preparation for such events. Because all municipalities and provincial ministries are required to have an emergency management program, EMO's main mission is to provide information and training in the development of these strategies by offering expertise and assistance in developing these programs. Large-scale emergencies beyond the capacity of such measures are handled by the province and, if required, the federal government.

Get Real!

Howard Sapers was appointed as the independent advisor on corrections reform for Ontario in 2017. He previously served as the correctional investigator of Canada from 2004 to 2016.

Part 2 of an Interview with Howard Sapers

By now, you are probably well aware that the field of corrections involves more than prisons, guards, and inmates. Due to the complex and interconnected infrastructure of justice (i.e., courts, police, supervision), the network of people involved in this infrastructure must remain aware of how each part affects the other, keeping in mind that all citizens—unaffected, incarcerated, or victimized—expect to be treated justly and equitably before the law. As the head of corrections oversight agencies at both the federal and provincial levels, Howard Sapers (personal communication, July 7, 2017) has insights to share regarding the need for this position in modern democracies; why we, as citizens, need to remain well informed about what occurs inside these systems; and how to preserve public trust in them and those who work for them.

IMPORTANCE OF OVERSIGHT ROLES

Criminal justice generally, and corrections more specifically, is probably one of the areas of public administration that is most susceptible to abuse because it operates so much behind closed doors. It's very specialized so you've got that combination of there being very little [public] access and very little [public] knowledge. And so that, in and of itself, requires a heightened degree of vigilance and surveillance over how that art of public administration is operating.

This is not specific to Ontario or even to Canada. Modern and mature corrections systems around the world have independent oversight. In fact, it's considered to be a key component to a fair and just system of corrections that you have some independent oversight mechanism and usually a combination of them.

There are different models of oversight and there are benefits to each of them, but they're not all the same.

Independent legislative statutory [offices/officers such as an ombudsman]—that's one thing. It's very public, it's very transparent, and that's very important. It's also very important to have internal checks and balances—have internal controls, to have internal review mechanisms, to have internal audit processes. Just as it's important to have external accountability so the public can maintain confidence, it's also very important for the organization itself to maintain confidence in what it's doing.

Then you have the independent ones such as the role I'm in now, which really has a foot in both camps: we're committed to transparency [and] all the work that I do will be in the public domain . . . all the reports that I generate will be available publicly. But there's also very much an internal component. I have tremendous access to all the decision-makers up and down the decision-making chain. I have access to all the working papers and documents, statistics, and all those resources are at my disposable.

[And part of my job includes] trying to address some things in real time . . . the government is committed to tabling a new *Corrections Act* for Ontario. So, I am very much involved in the discussions with the people that are drafting that legislation.

CHALLENGES OF BEING IN A CORRECTIONAL OVERSIGHT POSITION

The task is daunting. First of all, you have to acknowledge [you are tackling] large issues that are very interdependent on other parts of public administration—corrections doesn't operate in a vacuum. Corrections operates as part of the criminal justice system, the criminal justice system operates as part of the broader social services systems, and then you have jurisdictional issues between the federal and provincial and territorial governments. It's actually a very complex environment. It's like squeezing a balloon: if you change the way the courts operate, you're going to have an impact on corrections, and if you change the way corrections operates, you're going to have an impact on, let's say, community and public health.

Another challenge is these are big risk-averse systems. The public demands that these systems be risk averse [because] they want to have confidence in their criminal justice and their corrections systems, and so change comes slowly. You have to be both patient and optimistic in this work, [and] that's a challenge sometimes because the need for change is quite dramatic in many areas. For example, new population demographics in this country . . . are beginning to be very apparent inside jails and prisons. We have more visible minorities, we have more multicultural, multi-ethnic groups inside our jails, [and] we have more older offenders . . . more people becoming ill with age-related frailties. All of these population demographics, which we see in the greater community, also manifest inside our jails. We have to make sure our jails are keeping pace with those changes.

And, on a philosophical level, I think you have to recognize that jails are not the healthiest [or] safest environments for the men and women that are incarcerated or for the men and women that work there. Knowing that these are environments which create health problems within staff and create hopelessness within those that are incarcerated, it's a very negative ethos and so you have to overcome that. You know sometimes I describe my jobs as trying to make jail "less worse." We're talking about an environment that is taking away the most precious thing: it's taking away people's autonomy and liberty. You have to recognize that that's what we're talking about, and you have to recognize the limitations of how much you can improve on that.

MAKING DECISIONS OR RECOMMENDATIONS THAT MAY BE UNPOPULAR

I don't think that anybody that's really worried about being popular and well-loved by any government should take on one of these roles. Everybody has an opinion about corrections and criminal justice, but very few of those opinions are very well informed. [Corrections is] not largely understood; there's not a lot of good [public] knowledge out there about what it's really like to run a jail, or to supervise somebody on parole, or to be a probation officer, or to run a halfway house.

I've had the privilege of having roles that have allowed me to try to bring more accountability, more transparency, and better outcomes [to corrections] . . . but sometimes that means delivering very tough and unpopular messages, and so be it. If you're not prepared to do that, then you can't do that job.

CHAPTER SUMMARY

This chapter has given you an opportunity to apply your knowledge of the structure and process of politics and public administration in relation to public law enforcement. Examining the respective powers of federal institutions such as the Department of Justice, Public Safety Canada, and the Department of National Defence demonstrates how each contributes to the overall system of justice and law enforcement at the federal level. The various watchdog agencies illustrate how these federal government institutions attempt to ensure fairness, accountability, and sensitivity to public concerns.

The federal bodies have their counterparts in provincial institutions such as the Ministry of the Attorney General, the Ministry of Community Safety and Correctional Services, and the many agencies and boards that have been put in place to monitor the activities of key actors within the government in general and the justice system in particular.

Even so, overlapping jurisdictions can sometimes lead to conflict among these agencies and cause problems that hinder the operation of our justice system.

KEY TERMS

attorney general function, 164

minister of justice function, 164

subjudicial rule, 165

WEBSITES

Alberta Justice and Solicitor General: https://justice.alberta.ca/Pages/home.aspx

An Act to Amend the Criminal Code and Firearms Act: http://laws-lois.justice.gc.ca/eng/AnnualStatutes/2012_6/

British Colombia Ministry of Justice: http://www2.gov.bc.ca/gov/content/governments/organizational-structure/ministries-organizations/ministries/justice-attorney-general

Canadian Border Services Agency: http://www.cbsa-asfc.gc.ca/menu-eng.html

Canadian Charter of Rights and Freedoms: http://laws-lois.justice.gc.ca/eng/Const/Const_index.html

Canadian Firearms Centre: http://www.rcmp-grc.gc.ca/cfp-pcaf/index-eng.htm

Canadian Security Intelligence Service: https://www.csis.gc.ca/index-en.php

Canadian Security Intelligence Service Act: http://laws-lois.justice.gc.ca/eng/acts/C-23/

Centre of Forensic Sciences: http://www.mcscs.jus.gov.on.ca/english/centre_forensic/CFS_intro.html

Coroners Act: https://www.ontario.ca/laws/statute/90c37

Correctional Service Canada: http://www.csc-scc.gc.ca/index-eng.shtml

Criminal Code: http://laws-lois.justice.gc.ca/eng/acts/C-46/

Criminal Injuries Compensation Board: http://www.sjto.gov.on.ca/cicb/

Criminal Intelligence Service Ontario: http://www.mcscs.jus.gov.on.ca/english/police_serv/CISO/crim_int_serv.html

Department of Justice Canada: http://www.justice.gc.ca/eng/index.html

Emergency Management Ontario: https://www.emergencymanagementontario.ca/english/home.html

Firearms Act: http://laws-lois.justice.gc.ca/eng/acts/F-11.6/

Fire Protection and Prevention Act: https://www.ontario.ca/laws/regulation/r07213

Global Affairs Canada: http://www.international.gc.ca/international/index.aspx?view=d&lang=eng

Human Rights Code (for Ontario): https://www.ontario.ca/laws/statute/90h19

Human Rights Tribunal of Ontario: http://www.sjto.gov.on.ca/hrto/

Justice Québec: http://www.justice.gouv.qc.ca/english/accueil.asp

"'Kettling' police tactic controversial everywhere it was used": https://www.thestar.com/news/gta/g20/2010/06/29/kettling_police_tactic_controversial_everywhere_it_was_used.html

Law Commission of Ontario: http://www.lco-cdo.org

Legal Aid Ontario: http://www.legalaid.on.ca/en/

Manitoba Ministry of Justice: http://www.gov.mb.ca/justice/

Ministry of the Attorney General Act: https://www.ontario.ca/laws/statute/90m17

National Defence and the Canadian Armed Forces: http://www.forces.gc.ca/en/index.page

Newfoundland and Labrador Department of Justice: http://www.justice.gov.nl.ca/just/

Northwest Territories Justice: https://www.justice.gov.nt.ca/en/

Nova Scotia Department of Justice: https://novascotia.ca/just/

Nunavut Department of Justice: http://www.gov.nu.ca/justice

Office for Victims of Crime: https://www.attorneygeneral.jus
.gov.on.ca/english/ovss/ovs.php

Office of the Chief Coroner: http://www.mcscs.jus.gov.on
.ca/english/DeathInvestigations/office_coroner/Chief
CoronerforOntario/OCC_chief.html

Office of the Children's Lawyer: https://www.attorneygeneral
.jus.gov.on.ca/english/family/ocl/

Office of the Commissioner for Federal Judicial Affairs: http://
www.fja-cmf.gc.ca/home-accueil/index-eng.html

Office of the Fire Marshal: http://www.mcscs.jus.gov.on
.ca/english/FireMarshal/OFMLanding/OFM_main
.html

Office of the Public Guardian and Trustee: https://www
.attorneygeneral.jus.gov.on.ca/english/family/pgt/

Ontario Assessment Review Board: http://elto.gov.on.ca
/tribunals/arb/about-the-arb/

Ontario Civilian Commission on Police Services: http://www
.slasto.gov.on.ca/en/ocpc/Pages/default.aspx

Ontario Human Rights Commission: http://www.ohrc.on.ca/en

Ontario Ministry of Community Safety and Correctional
Services: http://www.mcscs.jus.gov.on.ca

Ontario Ministry of the Attorney General: https://www.attorney
general.jus.gov.on.ca/english/

Ontario Municipal Board: http://elto.gov.on.ca/tribunals/omb
/about-the-omb/

Ontario Police Arbitration Commission: http://policearbitration
.on.ca

Ontario Provincial Police: http://www.opp.ca

Parole Board of Canada: https://www.canada.ca/en/parole
-board.html

Police Services Act (Ontario): https://www.ontario.ca/laws
/statute/90p15

Prince Edward Island Department of Justice and Public Safety:
http://www.gov.pe.ca/jps/index.php3

Public Safety Canada: https://www.publicsafety.gc.ca/index-en
.aspx

Royal Canadian Mounted Police: http://www.rcmp-grc.gc.ca/en

Royal Canadian Mounted Police Act: http://laws-lois.justice.gc.ca
/eng/acts/R-10/

Saskatchewan Ministry of Justice: http://www.saskatchewan.ca
/residents/justice-crime-and-the-law

Special Investigations Unit (for Ontario): https://www.siu.on.ca
/en/index.php

"Toronto police swear off G20 kettling tactic": https://www
.thestar.com/news/gta/2011/06/22/exclusive_toronto_police
_swear_off_g20_kettling_tactic.html

Victims' Bill of Rights (Ontario): https://www.ontario.ca/laws
/statute/95v06

Yukon Department of Justice: http://www.justice.gov.yk.ca

REFERENCE LIST

1994 Somalia inquiry to investigate Canadian military scandal.
(1994, November 17). *CBC Digital Archives*. Retrieved
from http://www.cbc.ca/archives/entry/1994-somalia
-inquiry-to-investigate-canadian-military-scandal

Adams, G. (2003). Review report on the Special Investigations
Unit reforms prepared for the attorney general of Ontario
by the Honourable George W. Adams, QC. Retrieved from
http://www.attorneygeneral.jus.gov.on.ca/english/about
/pubs/adams/adamsreport.pdf

Alcohol and Gaming Commission of Ontario. (n.d.). What we do.
Retrieved from https://www.agco.ca/

Anti-terrorism Act, SC 2001, c 41.

Brewster, M. (2015, January 18). More stringent oversight
of military intelligence at DND in limbo. *CBC News*.
Retrieved from http://www.cbc.ca/news/politics/more
-stringent-oversight-of-military-intelligence-at-dnd
-in-limbo-1.2917120

Canada Border Services Agency. (2016). About the CBSA: What
we do. Retrieved from http://www.cbsa-asfc.gc.ca/agency
-agence/what-quoi-eng.html

Canada Border Services Agency. (2017). *Quarterly financial
report for the quarter ended June 30, 2017*. Retrieved from
http://www.cbsa-asfc.gc.ca/agency-agence/reports
-rapports/fs-ef/2017/qfr-rft-q1-eng.html

Canada's dysfunctional military spending caused by brain
drain and budget cuts, report finds. (2015, January 24).
National Post. Retrieved from http://nationalpost.com/news
/politics/canadas-dystfunctional-military-spending-caused
-by-brain-drain-and-budget-cuts-report-finds

Canadian Police College. (n.d.). Retrieved from http://www.cpc
.gc.ca/en#

Canadian Police Information Centre. (2017). Retrieved from
http://www.cpic-cipc.ca/index-eng.htm

Canadian Security Intelligence Service Act (Re), 2008 FC 300.

Canadian Security Intelligence Service. (2014a). Accountability
and review. Retrieved from https://www.csis-scrs.gc.ca/bts
/ccntblt-en.php

Canadian Security Intelligence Service. (2014b). Intelligence
collection and analysis. Retrieved from https://www.csis-scrs
.gc.ca/bts/ntllgnc-en.php

Canadian Security Intelligence Service. (2014c). Legislation.
Retrieved from https://www.csis-scrs.gc.ca/bts/lgsltn
-en.php

Canadian Security Intelligence Service. (2014d). Sharing information with the public. Retrieved from https://www.csis-scrs.gc.ca/bts/shrngpblc-en.php

Canadian Security Intelligence Service. (2016). Academic outreach. Retrieved from https://www.csis-scrs.gc.ca/bts/cdmctrch-en.php

Canadian Security Intelligence Service. (2017a). Role of CSIS. Retrieved from https://www.csis-scrs.gc.ca/bts/role-en.php

Canadian Security Intelligence Service. (2017b). The security screening program. Retrieved from https://www.csis-scrs.gc.ca/scrtscrnng/index-en.php#bm01

Canadian Security Intelligence Service. (2017c). Sharing intelligence. Retrieved from https://www.csis-scrs.gc.ca/bts/shrng-en.php

Child and Family Services Review Board. (n.d.). What we do. Social Justice Tribunals Ontario. Retrieved from http://www.sjto.gov.on.ca/cfsrb/what-we-do/

Civilian Review and Complaints Commission for the RCMP. (2015). Complaint and review process. Retrieved from https://www.crcc-ccetp.gc.ca/en/complaint-and-review-process

Civilian Review and Complaints Commission for the RCMP. (2017). About us. Retrieved from https://www.crcc-ccetp.gc.ca/en/about-us

Correctional Service Canada. (2017). Quarterly financial report for the quarter ended June 30, 2017. Retrieved from http://www.csc-scc.gc.ca/reporting/007005-1000-2017-2018-01-eng.shtml

Corrections and Conditional Release Act, SC 1992, c 20.

Criminal Code, RSC 1985, c C-46.

Criminal Injuries Compensation Board. (n.d.). What we do. Social Justice Tribunals Ontario. Retrieved from http://www.sjto.gov.on.ca/cicb/what-we-do/

Criminal Intelligence Service Canada. (2014). About us. Retrieved from http://www.cisc.gc.ca/about-ausujet/index-eng.htm

Custody Review Board. (n.d.). What we do. Social Justice Tribunals Ontario. Retrieved from http://www.sjto.gov.on.ca/crb/about-us/

Department of Justice Canada. (2016). Department of Justice and its role in national security. Retrieved from http://www.justice.gc.ca/eng/cj-jp/ns-sn/role.html

Department of Justice Canada. (2017a). Justice accomplishments: Highlights of 2016. Retrieved from http://www.justice.gc.ca/eng/abt-apd/accom-real.html

Department of Justice Canada. (2017b). Quarterly financial report for the quarter ended June 30, 2017. Retrieved from http://www.justice.gc.ca/eng/rp-pr/cp-pm/qfr-rft/2017_q1/index.html

Education Act, RSO 1990, c E.2.

Environment and Land Tribunals Ontario. (n.d.). About ELTO. Retrieved from http://elto.gov.on.ca/about-elto/

Ferguson, M. (Ed.). (1999). *Federal guidebook: A guide to the Canadian federal government and its decision-makers, 1999–2000.* Perth, ON: J-K Carruthers.

Fire Code, O Reg 213/07.

Fire Protection and Prevention Act, 1997, SO 1997, c 4.

Firearms Act, SC 1995, c 39.

Fisher, L., Wilson-Smith, A., Demont, J. (2003, March 17). Somalia inquiry's damning report. *Historica Canada.* Retrieved from http://www.thecanadianencyclopedia.ca/en/article/somalia-inquirys-damning-report/

Government of Canada. (2017a). Cleaning up the *Criminal Code,* clarifying and strengthening sexual assault law, and respecting the Charter. Retrieved from https://www.canada.ca/en/department-justice/news/2017/06/cleaning_up_the_criminalcodeclarifyingandstrengtheningsexualassa.html

Government of Canada. (2017b). Government expenditure plan and main estimates (Parts I and II). 2017–18 estimates. Retrieved from https://www.canada.ca/en/treasury-board-secretariat/services/planned-government-spending/government-expenditure-plan-main-estimates/2017-18-estimates.html

Government of Canada. (2017c). International peace and security. Retrieved from http://international.gc.ca/world-monde/issues_development-enjeux_developpement/peace_security-paix_securite/index.aspx?lang=eng

Government of Canada. (2017d). Quarterly financial report for the quarter ended June 30, 2017. Retrieved from https://www.canada.ca/en/parole-board/corporate/transparency/reporting-to-canadians/quarterly-financial-report/2017/june.html

Human Rights Code, RSBC 1996, c 210.

Human Rights Legal Support Centre. (n.d.). Welcome. Retrieved from http://www.hrlsc.on.ca/en/home

Human Rights Tribunal of Ontario. (n.d.). What we do. Social Justice Tribunals Ontario. Retrieved from http://www.sjto.gov.on.ca/hrto/what-we-do/

Immigration and Refugee Protection Act, SC 2001, c 27.

Indigenous Policing Bureau. (n.d.). Retrieved from http://www.opp.ca/index.php?id=115&entryid=56b7838d8f94ace85c28d172#sec0

Integrated Terrorism Assessment Centre. (2014). About ITAC. Retrieved from http://www.itac.gc.ca/bt/index-en.php

Landlord and Tenant Board. (n.d.). What we do. Social Justice Tribunals Ontario. Retrieved from http://www.sjto.gov.on.ca/ltb/what-we-do/

Legal Aid Ontario. (n.d.). About Legal Aid Ontario. Retrieved from http://www.legalaid.on.ca/en/about/default.asp

Lexum. (2017). Supreme Court judgments: Reference re *Firearms Act* (Can.). Retrieved from https://scc-csc.lexum.com/scc-csc/scc-csc/en/item/1794/index.do

Military Police Complaints Commission of Canada. (2013). About us. Retrieved from http://www.mpcc-cppm.gc.ca/01/100/100-eng.aspx

Ministry of the Attorney General Act, RSO 1990, c M.17.

National Defence and the Canadian Armed Forces. (2017). Quarterly financial report for the quarter ended June 30, 2017. Retrieved from http://www.forces.gc.ca/en/about-reports-pubs-quarterly-financial/june-30-2017.page

Office of the Commissioner for Federal Judicial Affairs Canada. (2017). Quarterly financial report for the quarter ended June 30, 2017. Retrieved from http://www.fja.gc.ca/publications/qfr-rft/index-eng.html

Office of the Correctional Investigator. (2013). Roles and responsibilities. Retrieved from http://www.oci-bec.gc.ca/cnt/roles-eng.aspx

Office of the Independent Police Review Director. (2014). About the OIPRD. Retrieved from http://www.oiprd.on.ca/EN/About Us/Pages/AboutUs.aspx

Ontario Disability Support Program Act, 1997, SO 1997, c 25, Schedule B.

Ontario Ministry of the Attorney General. (2015a). Office for Victims of Crime. Retrieved from https://www.attorneygeneral.jus.gov.on.ca/english/ovss/ovs.php

Ontario Ministry of the Attorney General. (2015b). Roles and responsibilities of the attorney general. Retrieved from https://www.attorneygeneral.jus.gov.on.ca/english/about/ag/agrole.php

Ontario Ministry of the Attorney General. (2016). The role of the Office of the Public Guardian. Retrieved from https://www.attorneygeneral.jus.gov.on.ca/english/family/pgt/overview.php

Ontario Ministry of the Attorney General. (2017a). The Office of the Children's Lawyer. Retrieved from https://www.attorneygeneral.jus.gov.on.ca/english/family/ocl/

Ontario Ministry of the Attorney General. (2017b). What we do. Retrieved from http://www.attorneygeneral.jus.gov.on.ca/english/about/default.asp

Ontario Ministry of Community Safety and Correctional Services. (2016a). About death investigations in Ontario. Retrieved from https://www.mcscs.jus.gov.on.ca/english/DeathInvestigations/DI_intro.html

Ontario Ministry of Community Safety and Correctional Services. (2016b). Centre of Forensic Sciences. Retrieved from http://www.mcscs.jus.gov.on.ca/english/centre_forensic/CFS_intro.html

Ontario Ministry of Community Safety and Correctional Services. (2016c). Office of the Fire Marshal and fire departments: Common goals, different roles. Retrieved from http://www.mcscs.jus.gov.on.ca/english/FireMarshal/aboutofm/OFMandFD/About_GoalsRoles.html

Ontario Ministry of Community Safety and Correctional Services. (2016d). Ontario Sex Offender Registry. Retrieved from http://www.mcscs.jus.gov.on.ca/english/police_serv/sor/sor.html

Ontario Ministry of Community Safety and Correctional Services. (2017a). About the Ontario Police College. Retrieved from https://www.mcscs.jus.gov.on.ca/english/police_serv/OPC/OPC_about.html

Ontario Ministry of Community Safety and Correctional Services. (2017b). Private security and investigative services. Retrieved from http://www.mcscs.jus.gov.on.ca/english/PSIS/PSIS_main.html

Ontario Provincial Police. (2016a). Corporate services. What we do. Retrieved from http://www.opp.ca/index.php?id=115&entryid=56b78c8b8f94ace65c28d174

Ontario Provincial Police. (2016b). Field operations. Retrieved from http://www.opp.ca/index.php?id=115&entryid=56b78e138f94ac9f5828d173

Ontario Provincial Police. (2017a). Indigenous policing. Retrieved from http://www.opp.ca/index.php?id=115&entryid=56b7838d8f94ace85c28d172#sec0

Ontario Provincial Police. (2017b). Investigations and organized crime. What we do. Retrieved from http://www.opp.ca/index.php?id=115&entryid=56b78f7f8f94ace65c28d175

Ontario Provincial Police. (2017c). Traffic safety and operational support. What we do. Retrieved from http://www.opp.ca/index.php?id=115&entryid=56b790418f94ac9f5828d174

Ontario Provincial Police. (n.d.a). *2016 annual report*. Retrieved from https://www.opp.ca/index.php?id=115&entryid=595648f18f94ac6f26f3b475

Ontario Provincial Police. (n.d.b). Who we are. Retrieved from http://www.opp.ca/index.php?id=123

Ontario Special Education Tribunals. (n.d.). What we do. Social Justice Tribunals Ontario. Retrieved from http://www.sjto.gov.on.ca/oset/what-we-do/

Ontario Works Act, 1997, SO 1997, c 25, Schedule A.

OPAC. (2015). Our role. Retrieved from http://policearbitration.on.ca/

Parole Board of Canada. (2016). Roles and responsibilities of a board member. Retrieved from https://www.canada.ca/en/parole-board/services/board-members/roles-and-responsibilities-of-a-member

Police Services Act, RSO 1990, c P.15.

Public Safety Act, SNL 1996, c P-41.01.

Public Safety Canada. (2015a). Border strategies. Retrieved from https://www.publicsafety.gc.ca/cnt/brdr-strtgs/index-en.aspx

Public Safety Canada. (2015b). National security. Retrieved from https://www.publicsafety.gc.ca/cnt/ntnl-scrt/index-en.aspx

Public Safety Canada. (2016). Emergency management. Retrieved from https://www.publicsafety.gc.ca/cnt/mrgnc-mngmnt/index-en.aspx

Public Safety Canada. (2017a). Connecting with Canadian communities. Retrieved from https://www.publicsafety.gc.ca/cnt/ntnl-scrt/crss-cltrl-rndtbl/index-en.aspx

Public Safety Canada. (2017b). Countering crime. Retrieved from https://www.publicsafety.gc.ca/cnt/cntrng-crm/index-en.aspx

Public Safety Canada. (2017c). Public Safety Canada quarterly financial report for the quarter ended June 30, 2017. Retrieved from https://www.publicsafety.gc.ca/cnt/rsrcs/pblctns/qrtrl-fnncl-rprt-20170630/index-en.aspx

RCMP External Review Committee. (2016). Mandate of the RCMP External Review Committe (ERC). Retrieved from http://www.erc-cee.gc.ca/cnt/bt/mndt-en.aspx

Residential Tenancies Act, RSNS 1989, c 401.

Royal Canadian Mounted Police. (2007). Federal and international operations. Retrieved from http://www.rcmp-grc.gc.ca/fio-ofi/index-eng.htm

Royal Canadian Mounted Police. (2013). Online child sexual exploitation. Retrieved from http://www.rcmp-grc.gc.ca/ncecc-cncee/index-accueil-eng.htm

Royal Canadian Mounted Police. (2016a). About the RCMP. Retrieved from http://www.rcmp-grc.gc.ca/about-ausujet/index-eng.htm

Royal Canadian Mounted Police. (2016b). National security criminal investigation program. Retrieved from http://www.rcmp-grc.gc.ca/nsci-ecsn/index-eng.htm

Royal Canadian Mounted Police. (2016c). National Sex Offender Registry. Retrieved from http://www.rcmp-grc.gc.ca/to-ot/cpcmec-ccpede/bs-sc/nsor-rnds/index-eng.htm

Royal Canadian Mounted Police. (2017a). Forensic Science and Identification Services. Retrieved from http://www.rcmp-grc.gc.ca/fsis-ssji/index-eng.htm

Royal Canadian Mounted Police. (2017b). Organizational structure. Retrieved from http://www.rcmp-grc.gc.ca/about-ausujet/organi-eng.htm

Royal Canadian Mounted Police. (2017c). *Quarterly financial report for the quarter ended June 30, 2017.* Retrieved from http://www.rcmp-grc.gc.ca/en/quarterly-financial-report-the-period-ending-june-30-2017

Royal Canadian Mounted Police. (2017d). Royal Canadian Mounted Police 2017–18 departmental plan. Retrieved from http://www.rcmp-grc.gc.ca/en/royal-canadian-mounted-police-2017-18-departmental-plan#A10

Safety, Licensing Appeals and Standards Tribunals Ontario. (n.d.). Ontario Civilian Police Commission. Role of the commission. Retrieved from http://www.slasto.gov.on.ca/en/ocpc/Pages/default.aspx

Security of Information Act, RSC 1985, c O-5.

Social Benefits Tribunal. (n.d.). What we do. Social Justice Tribunals Ontario. Retrieved from http://www.sjto.gov.on.ca/sbt/what-we-do/

Somalia affair: The paper chase. (1996, April 9). *CBC Digital Archives.* Retrieved from http://www.cbc.ca/archives/entry/somalia-affair-the-paper-chase

Somalia debacle a high-level cover-up. (1997, July 2). *CBC Digital Archives.* Retrieved from http://www.cbc.ca/archives/entry/somalia-debacle-a-high-level-cover-up

Special Investigations Unit. (2016). What we do. Retrieved from http://www.siu.on.ca/en/what_we_do.php

Special Investigations Unit. (2016–2017). *Annual Report 2016–2017.* Retrieved from https://www.siu.on.ca/pdfs/siu_ar_2016-17_eng_online_f.pdf

EXERCISES
True or False?

_____ 1. The Department of Justice Canada performs both the attorney general and the minister of justice functions.

_____ 2. It is not unusual for justice ministers to find that their political advice contradicts their legal advice.

_____ 3. The attorney general is responsible for deciding whether to prosecute criminal offences.

_____ 4. Government attempts to influence the professional actions of judges contravene the principle of judicial independence.

_____ 5. The existence of the Office of the Commissioner for Federal Judicial Affairs is one way of guaranteeing judicial independence.

Multiple Choice

1. The Department of Justice Canada

   a. monitors the quality and relevance of Canadian law and legal institutions

   b. watches over the administration of justice in areas of federal jurisdiction

   c. advises the federal government on legal matters

   d. a and b

   e. b and c

2. At the federal level, the minister of justice function involves

    a. considering issues of fairness in the justice system

    b. monitoring federal legislation

    c. commenting on issues that are before the courts

    d. a and b

    e. b and c

3. The rationale for the subjudicial rule is that

    a. some cases before the courts are hot political issues

    b. politicians need a convenient way to avoid controversy

    c. public faith in the justice system may be undermined by politicians' comments

    d. officials' opinions might be perceived as influencing the judicial process

    e. b and c

4. Civilian agencies monitor police activity

    a. to give objectivity to investigations of alleged police misconduct

    b. to ensure the integrity of policing

    c. to report to the solicitor general on the adequacy of police services

    d. to report to the solicitor general on the effectiveness of police services

    e. all of the above

5. The Ontario Ministry of Community Safety and Correctional Services is similar to its federal counterpart in all respects except

    a. it operates prisons

    b. it is responsible for inmates serving sentences of two years or more

    c. it forms part of a larger ministry

    d. its mandate is provincial in scope

    e. none of the above

Short Answer

1. Outline the broad mandate of the Department of Justice Canada. How does the department protect the federal justice system from political interference?

2. Compare and contrast the roles of the public safety minister and the justice minister at the federal level. Who is considered the chief law officer, and why?

3. Drawing on fundamental principles of democracy discussed in Chapter 1, explain why it is critical that justice agencies establish and maintain clear channels of communication while in pursuit of their respective mandates.

4. What is the justification for civilians to oversee the police? Do you agree with this justification? Explain.

5. Under what circumstances do you think governments are justified in actively influencing the justice system? What risks do they take in this regard?

6. Outline some of the ways that governments attempt to protect the independence of the judiciary. Why is this independence so important?

PART IV

Bringing It Home

Don't Just Sit There— Do Something!

11

LEARNING OUTCOMES

After completing this chapter, you should be able to

■ understand how a grasp of politics and public administration can enhance your personal and professional life;

■ list some activities in which you can participate as a citizen in order to better understand and appreciate the political process; and

■ assemble an intellectual "tool box" to help you analyze and understand a variety of political issues.

Introduction

No one pretends that democracy is perfect or all-wise. Indeed, it has been said that democracy is the worst form of Government except all those other forms that have been tried from time to time.

—Winston Churchill (1992, p. 202)

With all the negative news stories that we are exposed to on a daily basis, it is tempting to dismiss politicians and the political process as irretrievably corrupt and hopelessly inefficient. One reason for this may be that so many of our political opinions are based on sensational media reports that tend to simplify complex political issues and emphasize particular types of stories, such as personal scandal and fiscal mismanagement. While the media no doubt play a critical role in keeping governments accountable to their constituents, it can be argued that the power they have to manipulate the political process presents an equal danger.[1] If we as citizens are to hold our elected representatives accountable for their actions, we need to familiarize ourselves with the process, procedures, and constraints under which they operate.

As a constituent, you may believe that your role in the political process is simply to vote when there's an election. In a democratic country such as Canada, voting is indeed one of the fundamental privileges of being a Canadian citizen. However, leaving it at that misses the point of this book, which is to acquaint you with politics and help you to make informed decisions about the people, parties, and processes that characterize the Canadian political system. We hope that, having come this far, you feel more attuned to the world of politics. However, like many people, you may also feel powerless to do anything about what is going on in the world of government and politics. This chapter suggests some ways you can begin to make a difference while honing your political acumen.

Common Excuses for Avoiding Politics

When first confronted with politics, many students admit that they are confused, intimidated, or disgusted by the subject, or a combination of the three. This is not surprising, given popular stereotypes and the mass media's obsession with scandal. Hopefully, with the knowledge you have gained from this book and the course it represents, you will be able to critically analyze political events in a way that informs both your personal and professional life. Below are a few of the most common excuses given for avoiding politics, and some counterarguments.

The Political System Is Corrupt

This is a throwaway generalization that not only irks most politicians and public servants but also is unfair and untrue. The vast majority of government officials are honest, hard-working individuals who dedicate themselves to public life in order to benefit their constituents. In addition, it is wise to remember that even when our representatives fail to meet the high standard expected of those in public office, the institutions they

---

1   One of the most prominent scholars to explore this phenomenon is Noam Chomsky. See Herman & Chomsky (1988) and Chomsky (1991). For related subject matter, see Chomsky (1994).

represent—Parliament, provincial legislatures, and municipal councils, along with the bureaucracies that support them—remain as untainted symbols of democracy, integrity, and accountability. It is to their credit that they continue to serve in spite of the negative stereotypes reinforced by the popular media. Politics turns the popular adage "No news is good news" into "Good news is no news at all," for we rarely learn from the media that politicians are doing a good job. This rebuttal is not intended to be an indictment of all media, for they, too, serve a purpose as watchdogs over public affairs. But the industry's tendency to simplify and shorten news stories may mask the complexity of some issues and thus misstate the issues. In any case, it's important not to approach the subject of politics from a cynical perspective. Keep an open mind and realize that, ultimately, politics is the art of compromise.

It Doesn't Affect Me

Nothing could be further from the truth. When it comes to politics, ignorance is *not* bliss. Law enforcement students sometimes believe that political issues not directly related to policing are of no concern to them. The reality is that it is virtually impossible to isolate the impact of political decisions. Government spending in one area may mean cutbacks in other areas or an increase in taxes to cover the extra cost. For example, spending more on health care may mean cutbacks to environmental programs monitoring water quality. The end result may be that contaminated water sources end up increasing health costs more than the amount of the cutbacks. These connections extend through municipal, provincial, and federal levels of government. Having a sound knowledge of the relationships among these many political actors allows you, as a citizen, to form opinions in a context that then informs the decision you ultimately make come election time. As well, this knowledge can help you understand the decisions made by others that affect your day-to-day work life. And being aware of "the greater good"—that is, that we as citizens need to watch out for one another—is a responsibility we should all take seriously. In a democracy, it is important to take an interest in politics and public life. Just because something does not affect you directly does not mean you should sit by and let it affect other people. Staying involved is not just about looking out for yourself.

Politicians Break Election Promises

Economist John Kenneth Galbraith once described politics as the art of "choosing between the disastrous and the unpalatable" (1999, p. 328). Admittedly, politicians as a group are not known for keeping promises, but they should not be blamed exclusively for this shortcoming. As you have learned in the second half of this text, actually fulfilling pledges made during political campaigns poses significant challenges in the world of public policy. In addition, the contemporary game of politics requires that issues be simplified so that they appeal to as many voters as possible. This approach can backfire, however, when it comes to actually implementing the promised solution to a problem. When governments change direction on given issues, rather than berate them, perhaps it is better to ask ourselves: Do we want a government that ignores the current reality, adhering doggedly to a campaign promise, or do we want a government to react to the situation as it changes, to make the right decision in the best interests of all Canadians?

Let Someone Else Do It

Although this statement suggests laziness, it may also stem from the reality that even those of us who choose not to participate in the political realm reap the benefits it bestows on Canadian society. For example, most of us assume that, regardless of whether or not we are involved, fundamental services such as hospitals and schools will continue to be provided by our governments. Law enforcement will protect us and our property, and social problems, when they occur, will be dealt with accordingly. This may be true, but as the old saying goes, "The devil is in the details." If you disagree with a government's policy direction or want to have a say regarding an issue that affects you directly, you have to be knowledgeable about *how* the system responsible for the decision has arrived at that decision. Remember, bureaucracies run on formal rules and procedures; they are not equipped to respond to emotional outbursts and rants. Getting angry and calling the local news media may be a useful first step; however, it may grant you only a brief public audience. Knowing such things as the individuals or departments in government who are responsible, the nature of the timeline for approval, and the avenues of appeal empowers you to challenge and possibly change government decisions. At the very least, officials must respond to your concerns. Think about it—saying nothing means you won't have a voice at all.[2]

Dazed and Confused?

Politics is by no means an easy science to grasp. Changing events, players, and circumstances render useless any hard and fast rules and formulas. Understandably, this can intimidate some people. However, you can take some steps toward overcoming this feeling.

1. Keep up on political events. Warnings aside, tuning into ongoing media coverage of current events will help to familiarize you with the people, policies, and priorities of the day. Reading one or two news sources with journalistic integrity each day is a great way to do this.

2. Discuss current political issues with friends. Talking over coffee or while walking home tests your understanding of events and exposes you to perspectives that differ from your own. And don't be afraid to *engage* your friends who are not involved. Remember, when you do, the point is to listen and share information and your enthusiasm for being involved, not only to argue for your view or team.

3. Make it a point to inform yourself at election time. Attend all-candidates' meetings, ask questions on subjects that concern you, and base your vote on the information and impressions you have gathered. Yes, some effort is involved, but it will have been well worth it when you finally cast your ballot as an informed citizen.

Sometimes the most difficult part of becoming politically aware is the overwhelming feeling that there are just too many things to which you could turn your attention and effort. This, in turn, can easily slide into cynicism and cause you to retreat from the process. However, a smarter way to approach this challenge is to select an area of interest and become involved, if not professionally as a career choice, then personally as a volunteer.

---

2   As a group, college students may already have overcome one of the great barriers to participation, in that they are educated. Poverty also has a significant impact on political participation, particularly in pressure groups. "One of the great weaknesses of the poor in the political system is that they are generally disorganized and collectively inarticulate. They lack the skills to organize effectively as pressure groups, primarily because they are without the education, time and money to develop such skills" (Dyck, 2002, p. 37).

Getting Involved

By volunteering, you accomplish several purposes. First, you gain valuable experience that contributes to your resumé and hence future job prospects. Second, you learn how to work in cooperation with others to achieve a common goal. Finally, you open yourself to different viewpoints and career options through the contacts and experience you acquire. As a result, you will broaden your political horizons and develop a much better sense of your community and the many others who are a part of it.

Volunteering to contribute to your community can be done several ways. Here, Georgian College justice program students participate in the annual Ruck Walk to honour first responders and their families, and to raise funds for student scholarships.

Volunteer opportunities abound. You should decide first what your interests are and then pursue opportunities in those areas. If you are not sure where to start, contact a community volunteer placement centre or try running terms such as "volunteer" and "social service organizations" through a search engine such as Google. For best results, ensure that you have enabled location-sensitive protocols. Many coaching positions are also available in local youth sports leagues. These are valuable references for anyone considering a career working with young offenders.

To be directly involved in politics, you might consider becoming a candidate for municipal government, but many other avenues of participation are open to you if you are interested in formal politics. Survey the various political parties in your area to find out whether your political views tend to complement one particular party's platform (but be careful not to look for the "perfect" party—remember, politics is the art of compromise). You can join a party, help at the constituency office, and/or assist in party-sponsored events. Elections provide excellent opportunities to volunteer and make contacts in your community that may be of help to you later.

If you are concerned about a specific issue, you may wish to join a related interest group. There are many active groups in Canada supporting a huge variety of causes. Neighbourhood Watch, Road Watch, and local police auxiliary services are just a few examples of organizations interested in civil peace and respect for the law. There are a host of socially-oriented causes in the areas of environmentalism, poverty reduction, and social justice. The Council of Canadians, the National Anti-Poverty Organization, and the Centre for Social Justice are just three examples. You can also attend local council meetings and forums that focus on particular issues of local concern. Again, elections provide many opportunities of this nature, including all-candidates' meetings and party rallies.

As you can see, there are a wide variety of opportunities out there in which you can participate, at whatever level you find comfortable. Make your choice according to the amount of time and energy you have available. Volunteering demands some commitment if you and the organization are to derive any benefit from it, but remember that the rewards to yourself and your community are directly related to the amount of time you invest.

An Informed Student's Intellectual Tool Box

A recurring theme of this text has been the importance of your responsibility as a citizen in the political process. Below are some tips to help you enhance your own intellectual tool box. You'll also find a Quick Reference Checklist at the end of this chapter.

Tune In, Turn On, Talk It Out

Media scrums are a common occurrence on Parliament Hill. In her role as minister of foreign affairs, Chrystia Freeland briefs reporters.

Earlier, you were cautioned to be wary of the popular media because of the way they package news items. Still, there are ways to overcome this obstacle. First, when sizing up an issue, consider a variety of media (print, radio, television, digital). Within each medium, individual providers reflect specific areas of the political spectrum in their news coverage and general viewpoints. For example, newspapers such as *The Globe and Mail*, the *National Post*, and the *Toronto Sun* represent a spectrum of right-of-centre conservative positions, while the *Toronto Star* reflects a left-of-centre liberal approach to current events. Each also markets itself to a different target audience to attract a certain niche of advertisers. The *Toronto Sun*, for example, is aimed more at moderately educated working-class readers, while *The Globe and Mail* and the *National Post* are targeted at well-educated, wealthier, middle- to upper-class readers. These distinctions can be a little more subtle in other mainstream media, but by observing how and what each presents, you should be able to figure out where that media provider fits on the political spectrum and what audience it is trying to appeal to.

Assess a Source's Credibility

A good rule of thumb when listening to political messages is not to trust anyone who is wordy or unable to deviate from talking points. Don't allow yourself to be conned by slick presentations or sources that play to your emotions alone. Mentally step back to examine the argument being presented and the evidence being given to support it. Is the source quoting specific, credible data or making sweeping general statements without backing them up? Thinking about research in this way will help you to base your own opinions on solid evidence rather than on emotion alone. You can add the latter to your viewpoint once you have made up your mind on an issue.

In this regard, online sources can pose a more daunting challenge because they often contain little evidence of tested empirical data and are often accompanied by graphics and other distracting media. Remember, too, that the Internet has become an attractive vehicle for selling virtually everything, including values and viewpoints. It is your responsibility to distinguish academically credible sources from those that simply "spout off" about a particular topic. In each case, ask yourself:[3]

- Is it "personal"? Web pages are cheap and relatively easy to design, and there is no parent organization or domain to vouch for what's there. Personal web pages are not bad per se, but they necessitate further research into the credibility of the information being presented.

- What is the domain? That is, is it government (.gc.ca for federal, .gov.on.ca for Ontario), education (.edu), or non-profit (.org)? Is the content appropriate for the domain? This helps "weed out" irrelevant and superfluous material.

- Who is the "publisher"? This refers to the parent organization responsible for page content. Can you link directly with that organization? If unsure about content credibility, contact the parent from its website to verify what has been stated.

Keep an Open Mind

Try to keep an open mind when considering political issues. You may initially favour one side over another, but don't let these prejudgments turn into prejudices. Allow yourself some time to gather the facts and determine whether they counter your initial reaction. Open-mindedness in politics is not about having any opinion; rather, it is about listening to opposing viewpoints, weighing and challenging their credibility, and then drawing conclusions. Employing this strategy helps you to avoid being pigeonholed into one or another position before you have had a chance to explore the details of an issue. And finally, remain mindful that sometimes even news sources you have come to trust can get it wrong. Checking a number of sources can help in this regard and give you a better perspective on the issues at hand.

---

3 These questions are based on guidelines developed by the University of California at Santa Cruz (2017) on its library website.

Get Real!

Thinking Globally, Acting Locally—Making a Difference Where You Live

Now that you've made it this far through the text, you should be familiar with Canada's system of government: how it was formed, how it functions, and how each level of government contributes to the overall political process. As important as the government is, we haven't touched on one of the most crucial figures in our democratic system—you! Besides voting, there are many ways to become involved. Did you know, for example, that in Canada you can join a political party at the age of 14? Belonging to a party also means you can vote for the party's leader. It is interesting to think you could play a role in selecting the next prime minister of the country at such a young age.

On a less formal but equally important level, there are other ways to contribute to the political well-being of your community. What do you like or dislike about the community you live in? Could you help improve or change something?

Many municipalities have volunteer boards that assist council in making decisions. People who want a position on a particular board can apply to their municipality to be considered and, if accepted, appointed by council. These volunteer boards can cover a wide range of topics, for example, heritage conservation. In Kingston, Ontario the Heritage Kingston Committee reviews proposals to designate or de-designate properties as heritage and reviews applications for new construction on designated properties, alterations to properties, etc. (City of Kingston, 2017). Then the committee makes recommendations to council on whether to proceed and, if so, how. Since these recommendations are taken seriously, board members have an important impact on the history, development, and visual aesthetic of the municipality.

Or consider an organization such as the non-profit Georgian Bay Biosphere Reserve Inc., which oversees Georgian Bay Biosphere Reserve in the province of Ontario. The United Nations Educational, Scientific and Cultural Organization (UNESCO) designated this area as a biosphere reserve.[4] In Canada, designation as a biosphere reserve—an area where economic growth is to be balanced with conservation—is a 10-year process; there are 18 reserves in the country. The Georgian Bay Biosphere Reserve, which encompasses about 347,000 hectares stretching along the eastern coast from Port Severn to the French River, is home to a variety of plants, mammals, birds, reptiles, and amphibians. It's made up of wetlands, open waters, sand and cobble beaches, bedrock shores, sheltered bays, and more.[5] The organization promotes conservation and sustainable development with the help of volunteers. Some of the ways the organization does this is by offering educational programs and festivals for youth. It also relies on volunteers to identify any species-at-risk sightings to assist with its efforts in protecting these species.

The individuals who are participating in these activities are just like you—typical citizens exercising their rights in a free and democratic society to support causes they believe contribute positively to their communities. We all benefit from a more involved and politically literate population. So don't just sit there—do something!

---

4 See the UNESCO website at http://unesco.ca.

5 See more about the Georgian Bay Biosphere Reserve at http://www.gbbr.ca/about-us/gbbr/.

CHAPTER SUMMARY

Many people avoid politics because they have not had the opportunity to review our political structure and reflect on their engagement through a course and text like this. Others might avoid politics because of frustration with aspects of the political process, opposition to certain issues or movements, and even galvanizing events.

Constituents have an important role to play in the political process, and getting involved means more than simply casting a vote in an election. It can mean volunteering for a political party, becoming informed about political issues and party platforms by attending all-candidates' meetings, or simply keeping up on political events through the mass media (while avoiding the kind of saturation that leads to cynicism).

No matter what your level of involvement, a greater understanding of the political process and current issues can enhance your personal and professional life, and can help you to make a more informed decision when it comes time to cast your ballot.

WEBSITES

Aljazeera (Qatar): http://www.aljazeera.com

BBC (British): http://www.bbc.com

Canada Without Poverty: http://www.cwp-csp.ca

CBC: http://www.cbc.ca

CCTV (China): http://english.cctv.com

CNN: http://www.cnn.com

The Council of Canadians: https://canadians.org

CTV: http://www.ctvnews.ca

Deutsche Welle (German): http://www.dw.com/en/top-stories/s-9097

Euronews: http://www.euronews.com

France 24 (France): http://www.france24.com/en/

Global News: http://globalnews.ca

The Globe and Mail: https://www.theglobeandmail.com/?intcmp=dwhg

The Hamilton Spectator: https://www.thespec.com

La Presse: http://www.lapresse.ca/actualites/montreal/

Maclean's: http://www.macleans.ca

National Post: http://nationalpost.com

NHK World (Japan): https://www3.nhk.or.jp/nhkworld/

OPP Auxiliary: https://www.opp.ca/index.php?id=115&entryid=56b758c48f94ac9e5828d172

Ottawa Citizen: http://ottawacitizen.com

Press TV (Iran): http://www.presstv.ir

RT (Russian): https://www.rt.com

Toronto Star: https://www.thestar.com

Toronto Sun: http://www.torontosun.com

REFERENCE LIST

Chomsky, N. (1991). *Necessary illusions: Thought control in democratic societies*. Toronto: Anansi.

Chomsky, N. (1994). *Secrets, lies and democracy*. Tucson, AZ: Odonian Press.

Churchill, W. (1992). In *Oxford Dictionary of Quotations* (4th ed., p. 202:23). Oxford: Oxford University Press.

City of Kingston. (2017). Municipal heritage. Retrieved from https://www.cityofkingston.ca/city-hall/committees-boards/inactive/municipal-heritage-committee

Dyck, R. (2002). *Canadian politics: Concise student edition*. Toronto: Thomson Nelson.

Galbraith, J.K. (1999). Quoted from a letter to US President John F. Kennedy, March 2, 1962. In *Oxford Dictionary of Quotations* (5th ed., p. 328:11). Oxford: Oxford University Press.

Herman, E.S., & Chomsky, N. (1988). *Manufacturing consent: The political economy of the mass media*. New York: Pantheon.

UNESCO. (n.d.). Retrieved from http://unesco.ca

University of California Santa Cruz. (2017). Evaluate content from the Web. Retrieved from http://library.ucsc.edu/help/research/evaluate-content-from-the-web

EXERCISES

True or False?

____ **1.** Politics necessitates compromise.

____ **2.** Politics has no effect on public law enforcement.

_____ **3.** Carrying out election promises is a significant challenge in the world of public policy.

_____ **4.** One way to prevent being confused by politics is to keep up on political events by reading news sources regularly.

_____ **5.** Casting your vote at election time is one of your basic democratic rights.

Multiple Choice

1. Media coverage of political issues can be coloured by

a. a tendency to simplify and shorten news stories

b. a focus on the negative while ignoring politicians who are doing a good job

c. the commentator's position on the political spectrum

d. a news source's attempt to appeal to a particular audience

e. all of the above

2. Becoming better informed about politics and political issues can help you

a. make better decisions as a voter

b. understand how political decisions affect your personal life

c. know more about your community

d. understand how political decisions affect your professional life

e. all of the above

3. Making an informed decision about any issue involves

a. going along with whatever your friends say

b. gathering information from credible sources

c. sticking with your first reaction to the issue

d. taking a cynical attitude toward anything you read or hear

e. tuning out anything you don't agree with

Short Answer

1. Make a short list of some possible volunteer activities that interest you. What types of questions would you want answers to before considering each of these opportunities?

2. Would you consider running as a candidate for public office? Why or why not?

3. When considering political issues, why should you consult a variety of news sources?

4. How have your views of politics and public administration changed since you began reading this text? Give at least three specific examples.

5. Fill out the chart on the following pages as a reference for future inquiries.

Quick Reference Checklist

Member of Parliament (MP)

Name: _____   Political Party: _____

Phone: _____

Email: _____

Website: _____

Mailing Address: _____

_____

Constituency Office Location: _____

Member of Provincial Parliament (MPP)

Name: _____   Political Party: _____

Phone: _____

Email: _____

Website: _____

Mailing Address: _____

_____

Constituency Office Location: _____

Mayor/Reeve

Name: _____

Phone: _____

Email: _____

Website: _____

Mailing Address: _____

_____

Constituency Office Location: _____

Local Councillor

Name: _____

Phone: _____

Email: _____

Website: _____

Mailing Address: _____

_____

Constituency Office Location: _____

Chief of Police

Name: _____

Phone: _____

Email: _____

Website: _____

Mailing Address: _____

_____

Main Police Location: _____

Chief By-Law Officer

Name: _____

Phone: _____

Email: _____

Website: _____

Mailing Address: _____

_____

By-Law Office Location: _____

Canada and the World

12

LEARNING OUTCOMES

After completing this chapter, you should be able to

- describe the origins of Canadian foreign policy, from Confederation to the present;

- explain Canada's role in the creation and maintenance of major international institutions following the Second World War;

- understand current debates regarding Canada's changing role in international relations;

- explain the role of Global Affairs Canada in overseeing and coordinating the country's interests in foreign affairs, including the areas of foreign policy, international trade, and international development; and

- consider the challenges posed by involvement in these areas, as exemplified by Canada's involvement in Somalia during the 1990s.

Introduction

Up to now, you have learned how Canada's governments and administration function internally, mostly concerning domestic matters. But government actions, policies, and decisions not only respond to or are affected by what's going on within the country. They are also influenced by the actions of other countries, be it an armed conflict halfway around the world, a new trade agreement between countries, or the election of a new president south of the border.

For example, during the first six months of Donald Trump's presidency, thousands of asylum seekers made their way across the US border into Canada, many in fear of the Trump administration's immigration rhetoric ("Canadian army," 2017). Many of those who crossed the border in remote and often dangerous locations did so to circumvent a 2004 agreement between the two countries that required refugees to apply for asylum in the first country they arrived in. One of the nationalities that sought asylum in Canada during the first half of 2017 was Haitian ("Canadian Army," 2017). The trek to Canada was spurred by a May 2017 threat by the Trump administration to rescind a humanitarian program that would ultimately put nearly 58,000 Haitians living in America at risk for deportation ("Canadian Army," 2017).

Examples such as this remind us that the political realities within which our governments operate are part of a larger international environment, requiring constant attention from both our elected leaders and civil servants to preserve our national interests and define a meaningful role for Canada among the nations of the world. What follows is a quick overview of Canada's role in international relations, from our beginning as a former British colony to our current role as an active participant beyond our borders. The journey has been—and continues to be—one of challenge and opportunity.

The Big Picture: Canada's Changing International Role

From Confederation through the turn of the century, Canada's relationship with the rest of the world was dominated by Britain, as were those of the other colonies and countries within the British Empire. Along with other territories such as Australia, New Zealand, and South Africa, the Dominion of Canada deferred to and took direction from Britain's Colonial Office as the latter coordinated foreign policy to align with that of the mother country. Canada's first tentative move away from this arrangement occurred in 1909 with the establishment of the Department of External Affairs. It was headed by a secretary of state and at the time was so small it fit above a barber shop on Sparks Street in Ottawa (Dutil, 2015, p. 241).

For most of the period between Confederation and the end of the First World War, however, Britain continued to exercise control over Canadian foreign policy, and, for all intents and purposes, Canadians seemed content with this arrangement. For example, when Britain declared war on Germany in August 1914, there was no question that Canada would play a dutiful role as member of the British Empire. As Canadian historian Donald Creighton put it, Canada's "choice—which was automatic and took no thought of possible alternatives—was in favour of instant and active participation" (1957, p. 437). This unquestioning support waned as the war dragged on and caused many Canadians to reconsider their country's relationship with Britain and the rest of the world. During the latter years of the conflict, Britain's partners increasingly insisted that they be included in military and other foreign policy decisions. Prime Minister Robert Borden made this clear at a meeting of the Imperial War Cabinet in 1917, arguing that the dominions should be granted more control over their internal and foreign affairs. This change in tone, along with significant Canadian-led military victories such as the battle at Vimy Ridge that April, helped plant the seeds of a unique Canadian identity, distinct from Britain. Although deserved, this gradual transformation came at a dear price. With a population of only 8 million, Canada had contributed nearly 625,000 soldiers to the front along with hundreds of nurses. Of these, 60,000 died while many more were seriously injured (Francis, Jones, & Smith, 2008, pp. 225–226). At home, Canada's national debt increased from $463 million in 1913 to $2.46 billion by 1918 (Francis, Jones, & Smith, 2008, p. 234). And the decision by Prime Minister Robert Borden to introduce conscription in 1917 divided the country, particularly between the English- and French-speaking parts (Francis, Jones, & Smith, 2008, p. 240).

In recognition of its new place among the nations involved in the war, Canada signed the *Treaty of Versailles* in 1919 as an independent nation, no longer content to have Britain sign on its behalf. Borden also insisted that Canada be included in the newly created League of Nations, an international body that, although doomed to fail, would ultimately lay the groundwork for the establishment of the United Nations nearly three decades later.

The United Nations was created in the aftermath of the Second World War as a way to help countries manage international relations. This photo shows member nation flags outside the UN General Assembly in New York.

As outlined in Chapter 3, Canada (often at the prompting of its former colonizer) took more steps toward nationhood through agreements such as the *Balfour Declaration* and the *Statute of Westminster*, but it would take another world war to solidify the transformation.

Canada came into the Second World War as one of Britain's allies in 1939 and once more distinguished itself as a valuable partner in the struggle. As if to signify its changing self-identity, the Canadian government waited a full week after the British decision before declaring war on Nazi Germany. Canada gave more than $3 billion to the war effort, mostly in war production: Canada built dozens of warships and hundreds of aircraft (Francis, Jones, & Smith, 2008, p. 318). Also, more than 130,000 **Commonwealth** aviators were trained by Canadians on Canadian soil. The human cost was also great: from Canada's population of 11.5 million, more than 1 million Canadians served with the military over the course of the conflict. Of those, 42,000 were killed in action while another 55,000 came home wounded (Francis, Jones, & Smith, 2008, p. 331). The war also helped strengthen ties between Canada and the United States.

Commonwealth
an international organization of nations exclusively composed of the former territories of the British Empire, including Canada, Australia, South Africa, and India among many others.

United Nations (UN)
an international diplomatic organization that coordinates action, relief, and cooperation among all nation states while underscoring human rights, freedoms, and dignity

Universal Declaration of Human Rights
an international document adopted by the United Nations that states the basic rights and fundamental freedoms to which all people are entitled

World Bank
an institution that provides loans and other financial assistance to nations in need

World Trade Organization
an intergovernmental organization that regulates trade on an international level

Cold War
a period of tension from 1945 to 1991 between the United States and the Soviet Union, which was underscored by the threat of nuclear conflict

North Atlantic Treaty Organization (NATO)
largest peace-time military alliance in the world; originally designed to protect Western countries against aggression by the Soviet Union

Warsaw Pact
a treaty signed by the Soviet Union and its client states in 1954 designed to mirror NATO

North American Aerospace Defence Command (NORAD)
a military agency headquartered in Colorado that monitors aerospace threats

As the war wound down, Canadians worked with their allies to craft a new world order, hoping to build stability back into international relations. The clearest example was the creation of the **United Nations (UN)**, founded in 1945 with the aim of promoting peace, security, and justice, and providing a venue for international problem-solving and debate. A founding pillar was the adoption in 1948 of the ***Universal Declaration of Human Rights*** to enshrine guaranteed rights for all individuals.[1] Interestingly, one of the main authors of the Declaration was Canadian John P. Humphrey, then director of the UN's Human Rights division. Humphrey is responsible for the Declaration's inclusion of a provision asserting that everyone has the right to health care, education, and employment. Since its creation, the document has served as a model for constitutions later drafted in countries around the world, including the *Canadian Charter of Rights and Freedoms*.

Canada also participated in the creation of a number of other major international organizations shortly after the Second World War, including the International Monetary Fund, which was created to avoid the economic depression that occurred after the First World War by establishing economic cooperation among member countries. And, as a member of the United Nations Relief and Rehabilitation Administration, Canada became a major contributor of aid to war-torn countries (Francis, Jones, & Smith, 2008, p. 345). Other organizations Canada helped found include the International Bank for Reconstruction and Development (which later became the **World Bank**) and the General Agreement on Tariffs and Trade (which later became the **World Trade Organization**).

The other major international issue that profoundly shaped the post-war order was the emergence of the **Cold War**. The United States, now the undisputed leader of the Western democracies, faced the Communist bloc of nations, led by the Soviet Union. Each side crafted military alliances to support its ideological ambitions—the **North Atlantic Treaty Organization (NATO)** in the West and the Communist-backed **Warsaw Pact** in the East. The battle between the two superpowers dominated the next half-century of world politics, as both sides attempted to attract other nations to their respective sphere of influence. During this period, Canadian diplomacy helped resolve major international disputes, most notably the Suez Crisis in 1956, sparked by Egypt's then-President Gamal Abdel Nasser's nationalization of the Suez Canal. The canal was an important trade route, especially for oil, which connected the Mediterranean Sea to the Red Sea. Up to that point, the canal had been under British and French control, and the matter soon developed into an international crisis involving the superpowers and neighbouring countries. In an effort to ease tensions and provide an opportunity for dialogue, Canadian Foreign Minister (and future Prime Minister) Lester Pearson proposed the establishment of a UN-sponsored peacekeeping force to act as an honest broker and peacefully enforce a ceasefire. For his efforts, Pearson was awarded the 1957 Nobel Peace Prize, and the idea of peacekeeping gained international legitimacy. The event epitomized what became known as "Pearsonian diplomacy" and highlighted Canada's unique role as a "middle power," acting as an honest broker among the competing interests of nation states both great and small for the benefit of the international community.

Canada remained closely tied to the United States from the post-war period, cooperating in the formation of the Distant Early Warning defence system (known as the "DEW Line") and the North American Air Defence Command (**NORAD**) to detect and deter any possible Soviet aggression. In 1981, NORAD changed its name to **North American Aerospace Defence Command**, keeping its acronym, to better address the scope of its operations. In trade relations, both countries signed the Auto Pact in 1965 to facilitate cross-border

---

1   See United Nations (n.d.).

production in the automobile industry. As the decade drew to a close, Canada began to expand its foreign-policy horizons beyond this bilateral focus and look for new markets to enhance its economic prospects. With the election of Prime Minister Pierre Trudeau in 1968, this approach gained momentum. Trudeau slashed Canada's contribution to NATO, instituted policies of economic nationalism, and attempted to demonstrate Canada's independence in foreign affairs (Tomlin, Hillmer, & Hampson, 2008, pp. 6–7). He extended diplomatic recognition to Communist China in 1970 in an attempt to forge a new Canadian direction and establish good trade relations with countries other than the United States (Tomlin, Hillmer, & Hampson, 2008, p. 7). These initiatives notwithstanding, Canada's foreign-policy focus remained closely linked with its neighbour to the south.

The election of Brian Mulroney in 1984 marked a renewed focus on Canada–US relations, with the signing of a Free Trade Agreement in 1988 and an expanded **North American Free Trade Agreement (NAFTA)** including Mexico in 1993. The last decade of the 20th century also witnessed the collapse of the Soviet Union, ending the Cold War as well as peacekeeping missions in the Balkans, Somalia, and Rwanda. The period also saw Canada play a major role in international efforts to implement an international treaty banning land mines and to promote the creation of the International Criminal Court (Tomlin, Hillmer, & Hampson, 2008, p. 11).

The terrorist attacks of September 11, 2001 changed the international landscape once more, with countries refocusing internal and external policies to reflect new security concerns and guard against future threats (Tomlin, Hillmer, & Hampson, 2008, p. 12). Since then, Canada has participated in US-led coalition efforts, fighting in Afghanistan, but not in Iraq, in 2003 (Tomlin, Hillmer, & Hampson, 2008, p. 12). As you will see below, Canada's overall objectives in foreign policy appear to be in a period of transition once more, as the country under Justin Trudeau's administration seeks to return to the international stage as an active and enthusiastic participant in international affairs. How this will play out remains unclear; however, a brief exploration of some key policy areas may shed some light on this new direction.

North American Free Trade Agreement (NAFTA)
a free trade agreement among Canada, the United States, and Mexico

Current Challenges to the International Order

A Tale of Two Stars: From Bono to Obama

"If I can borrow a phrase," outgoing US President Barack Obama (2016) told Canadians in his formal address to Parliament in Ottawa shortly before the end of his final term, "the world needs more Canada." The phrase was made famous by Bono, a rock star of the group U2 and a noted internationalist, in 2003 ("The world needs more Canada," 2016). While Bono was lauding Canada's long-standing role as a leading member of the international community (and its refusal to follow the US-led invasion of Iraq earlier that year), Obama, by contrast, used it over a decade later to chide Canada for consistently failing to meet the basic security commitment represented by the NATO obligation to spend at least 2 percent of GDP per year on defence ("Military spending by NATO members," 2017).

Whether Parliament, especially those in government, got the hint amid the praise—praise from the most popular US president in decades and the leader of the nation that Canadians most often compare themselves to and crave attention from—is not immediately clear. Canadian defence spending did rise significantly the following year, up 70 percent, but remained far below NATO's gross domestic product (GDP) benchmark of 2 percent. The recent surge in spending had far less to do with Obama's subtle comment—that Canada renew its capacity to engage with the world through interventionist resources—than with his successor Donald Trump's open disdain for NATO and the threat to Western collective security that this represents. All NATO members are feeling similar pressure and confusion in the era of President Trump's "America First" Doctrine ("Canada to boost military budget by 70%," 2017; "Defend me maybe," 2016).

You may find that focusing on defence spending is an odd means of examining Canada's role in the world today. And you would be right: Canada's role in the world is about far more than military engagement and deployment. Military spending, in this context, is to be taken as a symbol for the capacity and intention to act; that is, a commitment to fund and maintain broad interventionist resources (often deployed to support and protect other resources) but not necessarily to use them at every opportunity or invitation—an invitation, for example, such as the US-led invasion of Iraq in 2003. Obama's clever turn of phrase gets to the heart of an interesting contradiction about Canada that is critical when examining Canada's role in the world. Canada has a long-standing commitment to international institutions and causes, as you learned about in the previous section of this chapter. Its reputation as a model global citizen is undoubtedly deserved. The question is whether Canada has done enough since initially establishing that reputation to maintain it.

In recent years, concerns regarding Canada's status in the international community have become the focus of debate among many with an interest in this area. For example, shortly after the 9/11 terrorist attacks in the United States, Canada's then Foreign Affairs Minister John Manley ventured that Canada was "trading on [a] reputation that was built two generations and more ago" (Cohen, 2003, p. 1) and had not been properly maintained since. His comment sparked a national debate among Canadian journalists and academics, which was later neatly summed up by Carleton University Professor Andrew Cohen (2003, p. 2), who observed that

> our vision is less broad today than it was in the past, especially in the decade or so after the Second World War. We are no longer as strong a soldier, as generous a donor, and as effective as a diplomat, and it has diminished us as a people. Our decline isn't a secret, but it seems more acute in 2003, amid rumours of war, calls to arms, pleas for moderation and negotiation, threats of terrorism, and laments for the poor and victims of disease, all of which have stirred Canadians at different times in different places.

This is a challenging and understandably upsetting summary for many Canadians to read, especially those who have grown up learning about Canada's great international reputation and proud contributions, and who want to do their part to continue the tradition and change the world. The point, however, is not that Canada has betrayed its core principles. Cohen is being romantic about an earlier era—an era, he wishes, to which contemporary Canada would pay more respect. The point, then, is that no country, not even one with a popular brand and great international reputation such as Canada, should take its reputation for granted. Its reputation must be actively maintained. Both Manley and Cohen are, in fact, being incredibly hopeful about Canada and its future. What they are actually saying is that we are more than the sum total of what we have already achieved, and we can do more.

Writing in direct response to Cohen the following year, Oxford University Professor Jennifer Welsh (a Canadian living abroad) reframed the debate by taking a more constructive approach in her book *At Home in the World*. Welsh argued that Canada had not so much turned its back on the achievements of a previous era as it had stopped articulating a clear and purposeful message of values and intentions. Writing specifically of Canada's confusing response to 9/11, she charged, "Canada's leaders have lost the capacity, or desire, to explain their policy positions and the effects of those positions to allies and the wider public" (2004, pp. 19–20). Canada, in other words, sent mixed messages to its neighbours, its allies, the world in general, and, perhaps most dangerously, to itself. Accordingly, Canada's underlying challenge in the world today is not only to decide when and where it will commit itself but to communicate those decisions to the world and to one another here at home (Welsh, 2004, pp. 19–20).

How to approach this challenge is the question. To this, Welsh has an interesting answer, and it may change how you think of Canada and its approach to many of the international challenges of today and tomorrow. Think of Canada less as a Pearsonian "middle power" and more of a problem-solver not limited by geography or history. Solving a problem, after all, is the core of Pearsonian internationalism. The idea is not to abandon our internationalist tradition but, rather, to reframe how we think of Canada. The middle-power framework is ultimately limiting. It emphasizes what we cannot do rather than what we can do by making too much of the actions and capacities of other, more populous nations such as the United States. As Welsh (2004, p. 54) writes, "The challenge for countries such as Canada is to turn America's fondness for short-term fixes into new and sustained commitment to build the necessary architecture for peace and security in the twenty-first century." That is, Canada can play a significant role all over the world by focusing on long-term solutions. After all, as Cohen (2003, p. 15) notes,

> Canada is a member of virtually every other agency and organization, whatever the size, global or regional. No country belongs to more clubs. . . . If Canada isn't a paid-up member of a club, such as the Association of Southeast Asian Nations, it is often a partner.

But we can only play an important world role by clearly defining and communicating our intentions. And this brings us full circle to Obama's clever turn of phrase. America does indeed need all NATO partners to fulfill their minimum defence contribution. For Obama to underscore the point for Canadians, in their own House no less, is actually a hopeful way of reminding a close and admired friend, who is perhaps not as focused or confident lately, that it is capable of much more. Canadians regularly express such sentiments to Americans, and we should not be surprised to hear such things in return. This is, after all, what friends do.

Foreign Policy in Action—Welcome to Global Affairs Canada

Global Affairs Canada oversees Canada's role in international affairs in a number of areas. Perhaps the easiest way to understand this complicated task is by examining the specific roles assigned to the three ministers responsible for coordinating Global Affairs Canada: foreign affairs, international trade, and international development. Using these portfolio perspectives, we can survey many of the current challenges to the international order that these ministers have to navigate. This section builds upon your knowledge about the origin of our modern international institutions (and Canada's role in shaping them) from the previous section of this chapter while keeping in mind the new way of thinking about Canada as more than just a middle power. Your job here is to engage with the issues and think about how the department might use both state and private resources to solve problems that not only secure Canada's interests but also maintain the integrity of international institutions. The goal is not only to help you to see the big picture of Canada and the world, but also to help you make broader connections with what you have already learned about public administration.

As has already been noted, Global Affairs Canada has evolved out of a tradition of international participation dating back more than a century. With a budget in 2017–2018 totalling $6 billion, it plays a major policy-coordinative role in Canada's federal government today (Global Affairs Canada, 2017; "Government expenditure plan," 2017). Exploring the department's three major branches—foreign policy, trade, and development—provides a logical approach to understanding some of the current challenges facing Canada in the world today.

Global Affairs Canada the federal department that houses the ministers of foreign affairs, international trade, and international development

Foreign Affairs

WHAT IS FOREIGN POLICY?

foreign policy
a course of action
prescribing how one state
behaves toward another

The best way to think of **foreign policy** is how states behave toward one another. In essence, foreign policy facilitates a set of relationships between states and groups of states: one acts, therefore another reacts, and so on. Obviously foreign policy is a lot more complicated than this, especially since it is largely the domain of dedicated diplomatic professionals and is always affected by both history and geography. In our context here, think of foreign policy in a couple of distinct but complementary ways. First, think of foreign policy as a predetermined course of action designed to anticipate the action of another state, for example, the immediate declaration of war by one state against another in the event that one of its close allies is attacked. This foreign policy issue is referred to as "collective security." Another way to think of foreign policy is as a delivery mechanism for both trade and development initiatives. This is why modern Canadian governments have increasingly folded trade and diplomatic services into the same department. It makes coordinating governmental policy much more efficient and ensures broader national alignment of priorities. After all, can you trade with someone you are not friends with, let alone not speaking to? What about deploying aid workers to a region you know to be openly hostile to your interests? Is that safe? These are just some of the factors that inform the foreign policies of nation states as they interact with one another.

Consider, for example, Canada–US relations. As an inescapable symptom of both history and geography, Canadian foreign policy is almost always underscored by some reference to Canada–US relations. Its relationship to the United States is by far Canada's most important one, as observed earlier, originally mediated not by Canada itself but by Britain. An enduring theme in Canada–US relations on the Canadian side is for Canadians to see themselves as the "best friend" of America. Jennifer Welsh argues that this is both an "invitation to disappointment" and likely to result in the pursuit of "the wrong policy choices" (Welsh, 2004, p. 24). Canadians and Americans, she argues, are not so much friends as they are family. This is why many aspects of the relationship are taken for granted and why such implicit assumptions, on either side, are so complicated and prone to misunderstanding. In the spirit of Welsh's broader argument in favour of a clearer articulation of Canada's values and intentions, she suggests that Canadians and Americans build a more formal working relationship based on regular and explicit consultation to produce greater trust (2004, pp. 81–84).

Although Canada and the United States preside over the world's largest undefended border and enjoy a highly integrated trade relationship (e.g., in 2016, 76 percent of Canada's total exports went to and 52.2 percent of its total imports came from the United States) and an integrated continental military partnership through NORAD (where the second in command is always a Canadian), many challenges remain (Statistics Canada, 2017). Most challenges flare up during cyclical changes in governments on both sides of the border. For example, whereas Canadians generally welcomed the internationalist tone of President Obama and his administration—the continuation of long-standing policies and objectives—they remain quite apprehensive about President Donald Trump's isolationist tone and ill-defined "America First" doctrine. In fact, an unpredictable, inward-looking, and protectionist America is perhaps the single greatest challenge for Canada in the world today. Where Canada–US relations have traditionally been a natural point of departure for Canadian foreign policy prior to Trump, Canada must carefully anticipate sudden changes after years of predictability in American policy that may run counter to previously established goals and shared interests. When you cannot even take for granted what is happening in your own backyard, the world looks a lot different, doesn't it? Just ask states all around the world that deal with persistent regional challenges and threats, such as Israel or South Korea (Statistics Canada, 2017).

TERRORISM AND SECURITY

Following the September 11, 2001 terrorist attack on the United States, improving security and coordination among security agencies became a major international foreign-policy concern. The Cold War security framework, which gave rise to NATO, provided solutions for a world where two superpowers battled for ideological supremacy, but it did not provide a comprehensive framework for combatting acts of terrorism by what are essentially stateless groups or individuals. The challenge for the United States following 9/11 has been to aggressively secure its interests internationally against such attacks, while the challenge for its allies and regional partners has been to collaborate on new intelligence networks and perhaps participate in military deployments. The challenge for the rest of the world has been to try to comply with US requirements where possible or stay out of the United States' way.

Canada has had to adjust its foreign policy accordingly. That has meant supporting the US-led invasion of Afghanistan in 2001 but refusing to join the US-led invasion of Iraq in 2003. Similarly, Canada responded to pressure to upgrade its border security personnel by arming members of the Canadian Border Services Agency (CBSA) for the first time in 2006. However, despite raising military spending by 70 percent in 2017, Canada has still not met NATO's minimum contribution of 2 percent of GDP.

As if these new security challenges were not complicated enough, Canada must also work to balance its respect for human rights with its broader commitment to justice despite US pressure. So far, Canada has done a poor job of protecting its own citizens caught up by US officials in new counter-terrorism pushes. In 2007, the government formally apologized to Maher Arar (with whom it settled for $10 million), a Canadian citizen who was deported from the United States to his native Syria where he was tortured in 2002. More recently, the government formally apologized to Omar Khadr (with whom it settled for $10.5 million), a Canadian citizen and child soldier captured in Afghanistan by the United States in 2002 and detained at the infamous Guantanamo Bay detention centre in Cuba for ten years until 2012. Khadr was remanded to Canadian custody following his detention by US authorities and released in 2015 after a prolonged court battle to clear his name. Arar and Khadr have very different stories, but they are important reminders that there is no one-size-fits-all solution to combatting stateless terrorism. What's more, countries like Canada must now be prepared to actively intervene on behalf of their own citizens caught up in post-9/11 anti-terrorism efforts, regardless of their innocence or guilt ("Ottawa reaches $10M settlement with Arar," 2007; Tasker, 2017) .

ECONOMIC SANCTIONS

Historically, foreign policy has generally involved an exchange of threats of violence and shows of force. **Economic sanctions** are a relatively modern tool used to apply pressure and produce results at the state level without violence. Global Affairs Canada distinguishes between the following types of economic sanctions that it reserves the right to deploy:

- arms embargo,
- asset freeze,
- export/import restrictions,
- financial prohibitions, and
- technical assistance prohibitions.

In 2017, Global Affairs Canada had economic sanctions levelled against 19 countries, including North Korea, Russia, Lebanon, Myanmar, and Venezuela. The sanctions against Russia, which stem from Russian President Vladimir Putin's "illegal annexation

economic sanctions
a non-violent foreign policy tool designed to convey displeasure and provoke change (e.g, tariffs, arms embargoes)

of Crimea" (Global Affairs Canada, 2016) in 2014, take the form of asset freezes and financial prohibitions. Effectively, they are a means of punishing Russia financially but also limiting trade opportunities with Canadian organizations and individuals. Whether Russia, a nation of approximately 145 million people, finds itself troubled by economic sanctions from Canada, a nation of approximately 36 million people, is unlikely. However, when combined with those of other countries, these sanctions can be very effective in isolating countries in order to provoke change. And, as is evident from Global Affairs Canada data, Russia's economy has certainly felt the weight of many economic sanctions from a number of countries (Global Affairs Canada, 2016; "This is going to hurt," 2014).

MIGRATION AND BORDERS

refugees
people who have had to leave one country for another due to violence, a humanitarian crisis, or a natural disaster without preparation

The UN Refugee Agency (UNHCR) estimates that there are approximately 65.6 million forcibly displaced people around the world. Among these, 22.5 million are **refugees** "over half of whom are under the age of 18" (UN Refugee Agency, 2017). In an era where border security has been refined and countries are increasingly suspicious of individuals' ties to terrorist organizations (real or imagined), international conflict may be at a relatively low point historically, but internal conflict between groups within a single state continues. The Syrian Civil War alone, a war that began in 2011, has displaced over 6.5 million people. Turkey has taken in 3 million Syrians but is struggling to integrate them ("Turkey is taking care of refugees," 2017). Germany has taken in nearly 1 million and is thus far succeeding in integration ("How Germany is integrating its refugees," 2017). Canada, by contrast, has accepted approximately 40,000, and, a year on, these refugees are generally struggling to support themselves after resettling (#WelcomeRefugees, 2017; Kassam, 2017). The core point here is that the countries that are fortunate enough to avoid the sort of internal conflicts that result in the mass displacement of people are currently poorly equipped to support the ones that are struggling with mass displacement. Refugees have always been a humanitarian concern, but the world is struggling to come up with a solution to a growing mass displacement problem. As with economic sanctions, this is another example of where broader foreign-policy coordination among countries could produce a better outcome. If Canada and other countries jointly applied pressure to eliminate the root causes of displacement and developed a better international infrastructure to help displaced people, this would go a long way toward addressing this challenge (UN Refugee Agency, 2017; "Turkey is taking care of refugees," 2017; "How Germany is integrating its refugees," 2017; #WelcomeRefugees, 2017; Kassam, 2017).

Borders might be a lot tighter in the post-9/11 world, but that has certainly not discouraged people from moving around the world with increasing frequency in a clear effort to better their situation. As *Globe and Mail* journalist Doug Saunders chronicled in his highly regarded 2010 book, *Arrival City*, the modern era has produced a remarkable pattern of increasing urbanization from across the developed world. Canada regularly benefits from this with an influx of skilled immigrants who meet its strict points-based immigration system. As a matter of policy, Canada needs such immigrants to make up for a shortfall in domestic births in order to avert an economically disastrous decline in population. Regardless, the movement of people, of their own free will or otherwise, remains one of the critical challenges of the early part of this century (Saunders, 2010; Saunders, 2017).

HUMAN RIGHTS AND THE RESPONSIBILITY TO PROTECT

Responsibility to Protect
a doctrine charging UN member states to accept responsibility for their own citizens within internal state conflicts and acknowledge the right of the international community to intervene if any state fails to do so

At the United Nations World Summit in New York in September 2005, all member states adopted a new doctrine called the **Responsibility to Protect**, which holds the following:

Each individual State has the responsibility to protect its populations from genocide, war crimes, ethnic cleansing and crimes against humanity. This responsibility entails the prevention of such crimes, including their incitement, through appropriate and necessary means. We accept that responsibility and will act in accordance with it. The international community should, as appropriate, encourage and help States to exercise this responsibility and support the United Nations in establishing an early warning capability.

The international community, through the United Nations, also has the responsibility to use appropriate diplomatic, humanitarian and other peaceful means, in accordance with Chapters VI and VIII of the Charter, to help protect populations from genocide, war crimes, ethnic cleansing and crimes against humanity. In this context, we are prepared to take collective action, in a timely and decisive manner, through the Security Council, in accordance with the Charter, including Chapter VII, on a case-by-case basis and in cooperation with relevant regional organizations as appropriate, should peaceful means be inadequate and national authorities manifestly fail to protect their populations from genocide, war crimes, ethnic cleansing and crimes against humanity. We stress the need for the General Assembly to continue consideration of the responsibility to protect populations from genocide, war crimes, ethnic cleansing and crimes against humanity and its implications, bearing in mind the principles of the Charter and international law. We also intend to commit ourselves, as necessary and appropriate, to helping States build capacity to protect their populations from genocide, war crimes, ethnic cleansing and crimes against humanity and to assisting those which are under stress before crises and conflicts break out. (United Nations General Assembly, 2005, p. 30)

The doctrine can be understood as a deliberate response to the humanitarian crises that resulted in mass violations of human rights and genocidal bloodshed of the previous decade. Too little, too late, some might say, and that would certainly be fair. The world needs to do more to prevent atrocities, especially in light of what you just learned about displaced people. What makes the doctrine particularly remarkable for Canadians is that it came out of the Canada-led International Commission on Intervention and State Sovereignty (ICISS). And it certainly fits with Canada's broader global reputation as a concerned citizen, but does it fit with Global Affairs Canada's efforts since? That is difficult to say. And this, too, is another challenge for Canada in the world: translating well-meaning initiatives and doctrines into domestic action and global cooperation ("Responsibility to protect," 2017).

International Trade

WHAT IS INTERNATIONAL TRADE?

If the best way to think of foreign policy is how states behave toward one another, then the best way to think of **international trade** is how states exchange goods and services with one another. Of course, they do so within the framework of how they behave with one another, but once states work that out (if states work that out), they are free to trade (and even trade freely!). Unlike foreign policy, over which the state maintains a traditional monopoly (in the way it maintains a monopoly on violence), the state plays a secondary role as trade facilitator. Outside of establishing a national trade policy and applying tariffs and sanctions as needed (often for non-business reasons), the state generally leaves the exchange of goods and services to the private sector. In fact, the state is often just another client for businesses on the open market, pursuing bulk contracts for everything from mass transit infrastructure to the latest medical technology from corporations all around the world.

Trade has a basic foundation—the exchange of goods and services between parties—but can become complicated for two reasons. First, some states trade freely with others—historically referred to as "reciprocity"—while other states do not. Canada has a long and storied history of trying to establish reciprocity with the United States. When a state does not agree to trade freely with another, it imposes a tariff or an import tax on all or specific goods and services, making them more expensive. There are a few reasons why states use

international trade
the exchange of goods and services among nations facilitated by governments but maintained by private and public business enterprises

tariffs. As we looked at with foreign policy, tariffs can be a clear way of sending a message or trying to influence behaviour. Alternatively, they can be a protectionist means of trying to eliminate foreign competition and thereby protect domestic industry or labourers. Most affluent countries in the world today practise some form of free trade either broadly or with a specific group of other countries. This is, after all, how most of them became affluent. There is a correlation between trade and growth, and that is why Canada, for example, sees such a close link between foreign policy and trade.

Second, trade can become complicated even between two countries that have few formal trade barriers through an imbalance of goods and money on one side. Germany, for example, came under scrutiny in 2017 for running as much as a $300 billion trade surplus (China, for context, had only a $200 billion trade surplus). Critics argue that Germany should be reinvesting that money back into the global economy instead of accumulating it ("Why Germany's current-account surplus," 2017).

FREE TRADE VERSUS PROTECTIONISM

free trade
an agreement between states to significantly reduce or eliminate outright tariffs on goods and services exchanged between them

protectionism
a policy whereby a state takes specific economic measures to support a domestic business or industry

With the election of President Trump in 2016, the global economy was forced to confront the return of an old debate: **free trade** versus **protectionism**. Trump is the first US president to seriously advocate protectionist measures—that is, overt preferential treatment of US industry and corporations at home and abroad—in more than half a century. Free trade is popular for the obvious reciprocal effect on domestic and global growth (more trade, more growth) but also because it is widely credited for facilitating the capitalist engine that defeated Communism and ended the Cold War. Following the Cold War, trade has become an integral part of foreign policy and global discourse. For its part, Global Affairs Canada actively promotes investment and trade. The challenge, of course, is to find willing partners.

During the 2016 US presidential campaign, then-candidate Donald Trump promised to renegotiate the North American Free Trade Agreement (NAFTA), which had been in place since 1994, should he win the election. Following his surprising ascent to office, Trump followed through by invoking his country's right to renegotiate the agreement. Talks began in August 2017 and were ongoing at the time of writing. Trump's protectionism aside, the United States actually runs a substantial trade deficit with both of its NAFTA partners, Canada and Mexico. In other words, Canada and Mexico respectively export more goods and services to the United States than the United States exports to them. Whether or not punitive action against Canada and Mexico would resoundingly save American industry is in serious doubt. The outsourcing of jobs from America to other places in the world is not caused by NAFTA alone but by broader global trade patterns (Campbell, 2017).

Trade with the United States is critical to Canada's future and has been an enduring theme in Canadian history, but regardless of what happens to NAFTA, the commercial trade relationships between Canada, the United States, and Mexico that underscore it will no doubt endure, although in what particular form remains uncertain.

OTHER GLOBAL TRADE TRENDS

Apart from renegotiating NAFTA and dealing with the United States' flirtation with the trade protectionist policies of a bygone era, there are two other global trade trends that present challenges to Canada and the world more generally. The first is the return of nationalism. The rise of a specific brand of ethnic nationalism in America is partly responsible. But there is another strain that is equally concerning. Take, for example, Britain's recent referendum to withdraw from the European Union. Former British Prime Minister David Cameron, on the heels of a close victory for the union against an independence-seeking Scotland, agreed to hold another national referendum on whether the United Kingdom should leave the European Union. On June 23, 2016, the United Kingdom shocked the world by voting in favour of leaving the European Union by very nearly 2 percentage points (51.9 percent). The unexpected outcome has unnerved many investors and led several businesses to consider moving elsewhere. The global challenge to Canada is that the underlying trade assumption, that no state would seriously jeopardize its economy for any reason, including a faint rise in nationalist sentiment, cannot be taken for granted. In the space of a single year, both Canada's ancestral trading partner and its closest natural trading partner threw caution to the wind and leaped without looking. Nor are the United States and the United Kingdom alone, as other European countries are also dealing with an increase in nationalist fervour. France has thus far bucked the trend, but whether that counter-trend takes hold remains to be seen ("Businesses are preparing," 2017).

The other global trade trend is the overall volatility of the market. The provinces that became Canada were each founded as resource-exploring colonies by Europeans. Despite recent efforts to diversify Canada's economy away from the exploitation of natural resources and toward a knowledge economy fuelled by technology and innovation, the Canadian economy remains very much dependent on a market for natural resources. As such, it remains vulnerable to forces of nature or climate that threaten either the supply or market for natural resources, technological disruption that upends traditional supply chains and established businesses, and the inherent trends in global finance such as the selling of toxic assets (e.g., subprime mortgages), which nearly brought about a second Great Depression in 2008. Given these new realities, the challenge for Global Affairs Canada is not only to defend the concept of free trade amid an apparent resurgence of nationalism, but also to ensure that the framework for global trade and finance is maintained.

International Development

WHAT IS INTERNATIONAL DEVELOPMENT?

If the best way to think of foreign policy is how states behave toward one another and the best way to think of international trade is how states exchange goods and services with one another, then the best way to think of **international development** is how states that are more fortunate can help to lift up states that are less fortunate. While foreign policy proceeds directly from state policy and international trade proceeds from facilitating business networks and relationships among those in private industry, international development is about working alongside other states and international organizations on specific projects and initiatives without a profit motive or exploitive goal. International development is about doing good and being a good neighbour. If not sharing the wealth exactly, international development aims to empower others with the opportunity to become self-sufficient. Just as relationships between individuals are about giving, so, too, are those among nation states. As mentioned in the previous section of this chapter, Canada is unique among many countries as a founder of numerous international organizations. In fact, as Andrew Cohen (2003, p. 15) remarked, Canada is as much a leader as a joiner: "Canada is a member of virtually every other agency and organization, whatever the size, global or regional." This means that we have a lot of partners and a lot of global networks for affecting change in a positive way. Let's look at how Global Affairs and the minister of international development work today and some of the challenges they may face tomorrow.

The International Development wing of Global Affairs Canada does a lot of work, and none of it is as glamorous or popularly received as its interdepartmental counterparts in Foreign Affairs or International Trade. International Development has to invest in long-term planning in order to make the most of scarce resources and scant funding while also planning for unpredictable situations (e.g., hunger) and needs (e.g., medicine) in locations around the world. As if that were not complicated enough, it has to navigate complex political situations in unstable countries and regions (often where foreign-policy

international development
the recognition by wealthier states that they have a responsibility to help developing states build infrastructure, reduce poverty, and increase domestic business networks

Table 12.1   Canada's Primary Multilateral Development Partners

• African Development Bank (AfDB) • Asian Development Bank (ADB) • Caribbean Development Bank (CDB) • Commonwealth • European Bank for Reconstruction and Development (EBRD) • Gavi, the Vaccine Alliance • Global Environment Facility (GEF) • Global Fund to Fight AIDS, Tuberculosis and Malaria • Inter-American Development Bank (IDB) • International Fund for Agricultural Development (IFAD) • International Monetary Fund (IMF)	• International Red Cross and Red Crescent Movement (RCM) • La Francophonie • UNAIDS (Joint United Nations Programme on HIV/AIDS) • UNICEF (United Nations Children's Fund) • United Nations Development Programme (UNDP) • United Nations High Commissioner for Refugees (UNHCR) • United Nations Population Fund (UNFPA) • World Bank Group (WBG) • World Food Programme (WFP) • World Health Organization (WHO)

Source: Key multilateral partners (2017).

response lags or takes time to develop) and ensure that the organizations it works with are following the appropriate ethical standards for ensuring human rights and dignity: "More than one third of Canada's official development assistance is channelled through trusted multilateral organizations" ("2030 agenda," 2017; "About humanitarian assistance," 2017; "Key multilateral partners," 2017; "Canada's feminist international assistance policy," 2017). These 21 global organizations are worth listing in full (see Table 12.1). Perhaps most important, International Development also provides an underlying narrative that promotes human rights and dignity.

The International Development wing of Global Affairs Canada has built an open data resource on its website to help Canadians and international partners track the deployment aid and development projects around the world. This is a critical, if understated, resource for fostering support for international initiatives but also allows the department to make better connections between projects and initiatives ("Project Browser," 2017).

Despite International Development's best efforts, challenges remain. Perhaps the most persistent and difficult among them is indifference. Attention span remains a global challenge, especially in the digital age. Closer to home, Canada has to navigate another issue: despite Canada's best intentions to commit to as many causes in as many needy places as possible, Global Affairs Canada must ensure that it does not spread itself too thin.

The common ground linking many of these current challenges is climate change. Massive and sudden climate change has the potential to displace any group of people in any country all over the world and swell the ranks of the 65 million people who are already displaced. Three successive hurricanes in the United States in the summer of 2017 and wildfires in northern California that fall underscore the fact that no country is immune from this dramatic change. Unaddressed, climate change over a long enough timeline has the potential to exhaust even the most robust emergency aid budgets. Thus far, attempts to develop and coordinate a coherent and sustained international response have been a challenge. Canada may, indeed, have an important part to play in this discussion. However, as many critics have pointed out, regardless of which countries struggle to deal with an increasing number of extreme weather events, a solution to climate change will require a truly global response at a time when nations are increasingly tempted to turn away from international trust and cooperation in critical areas.

Get Real!

Canadian Peacekeepers Shock the World

In this chapter, you learned that Canada helped found some important international institutions following the Second World War. One of those—under the United Nations (UN)—was the first official peacekeeping force. This has come to be an important milestone for Canada and has shaped the country's identity in many ways. Since the creation in 1956 of Emergency Forces, commonly known today as "peacekeepers," Canada has served in a number of peacekeeping missions, some successful and some less so. The actions of some Canadian peacekeepers serving in Somalia in the 1990s provides a sobering example of the latter.

Canadian diplomat Lester Pearson, who later became prime minister of Canada, won the Nobel Peace Prize in 1957 for coming up with the idea to use United Nations Emergency Forces—now commonly referred to as "peacekeepers"—as a means to separate opposing sides during the Suez Crisis. Here, a contingent of Canadian peacekeepers stands in formation at a public ceremony.

When the Second World War ended, many countries that were once colonies of major European empires claimed independence. One such country, Somalia, located in the horn of Africa, had formerly been made up of a number of colonies. It became a country in 1960, and in the decades following independence, the country struggled through conflicts, uprisings, and droughts ("Canadian Armed Forces," 2017). In the 1990s, the country experienced both a civil war and severe famine. In response to the conflict, the UN stepped in with a peacekeeping mission meant to deliver aid and create some stability. Canada joined the peacekeeping efforts from 1992 into 1993, helping to deliver aid, remove landmines, and destroy thousands of weapons ("Canadian Armed Forces," 2017).

Revelations about the conduct of some troops in the Canadian Airborne Regiment shocked many Canadians, provoking outrage and leading ultimately to the disbanding of the regiment. Pictures surfaced of Canadian troops posing next to a blindfolded and bloodied 16-year-old Somali named Shidane Arone (Gerster, 2013). Arone, who had snuck into the compound, had been captured and tortured, dying hours later. News of Arone's death followed allegations that Canadian troops were also involved in an execution-style killing of another Somali intruder (Gerster, 2013). In the aftermath, two Canadian soldiers were charged. Private Kyle Brown was convicted and sentenced to five years in jail for manslaughter and torture in the Arone case. Master Corporal Clayton Matchee, who suffered brain damage from a suicide attempt in 1993, was deemed unfit to stand trial. His charges were stayed in 2008 (Gerster, 2013).

It has since come to light that a drug meant to prevent malaria could have played a role in the actions of the soldiers that fateful day. Soldiers who know the convicted, as well as Dr. Remington Nevin—a US expert on the side effects of the drug—believe the convicted soldiers were suffering psychological side effects from the drug when they killed Arone (Pratt, 2016). From 1992 to 1993, the 900 Canadian Airborne soldiers were given the drug Mefloquine as part of a clinical trial administered by the Canadian army. They were among the very first Canadians to use the drug. Side effects of the drug include aggression, paranoia, anxiety, and vivid dreams (Pratt, 2016).

However, when the images were first made public, Canadians were horrified. In 1994, the federal government launched an inquiry into the violence perpetrated against Somalis at the camp. The inquiry's report was delivered in 1997. Among the findings, the Canadian military was criticized for a lack of training and preparation of its soldiers, and senior military officials were criticized for trying to cover it up (Schneider, 1997, p. A22). As a result, changes were made to military training and standards, including stricter education requirements and the appointment of an ombudsman to prevent such atrocities from happening again (Gerster, 2013).

Despite reform, more than 20 years later the Somalia case still serves as a haunting reminder of one of Canada's most disgraceful moments in history.

CHAPTER SUMMARY

The story of Canada's role in the world has been one marked by historical attachment and growing self-awareness as an independent nation state. From its rather inauspicious beginnings as a new dominion working within the parameters of British foreign policy, the country gradually expanded its relationships beyond British influence, particularly with the United States. Following the Second World War, Canada played an integral role in helping shape and define the post-war international order, distinguishing itself in such institutions as the United Nations and the development of peacekeeping. In this capacity, its international role and foreign policy have adjusted and adapted to changing circumstances, manifested in the changes evident in its foreign affairs ministry, now referred to as Global Affairs Canada. In its current incarnation, this branch of Canada's federal government provides direction in the three critical areas of foreign policy, trade, and development. Its challenges are many, and as the international community continues to evolve, so, too, must the mandate and mission of the department.

KEY TERMS

WEBSITES

Global Affairs Canada (Federal government's website): http://www.international.gc.ca

NATO (North Atlantic Treaty Organization): https://www.nato.int

Political fight brewing over Canada's peacekeeping role: http://www.macleans.ca/politics/peacekeeping-fight-ottawa/

UNHCR (The United Nations Refugee Agency, Canada): http://www.unhcr.ca

What Canada can do if Donald Trump kills NAFTA: https://www.thestar.com/opinion/commentary/2017/10/12/what-canada-can-do-if-donald-trump-kills-nafta-walkom.html

REFERENCE LIST

2030 agenda for sustainable development. (2017, June 8). Government of Canada. Retrieved from http://international.gc.ca/world-monde/issues_development-enjeux_development/priorities-priorites/agenda-programme.aspx?lang=eng

About humanitarian assistance. (2017, June 7). Government of Canada. Retrieved from http://international.gc.ca/world-monde/issues_development-enjeux_developpement/response_conflict-reponse_conflits/about_humanitarian-a_propos_humanitaire.aspx?lang=eng

Businesses are preparing for the worst version of Brexit. (2017, August 3). *The Economist*. Retrieved from https://www.economist.com/news/britain/21725780-uncertainty-about-britains-departure-eu-deepens-bosses-are-preparing-move

Campbell, A.F. (2017, September 5). The US, Canada, and Mexico are renegotiating NAFTA—here's what each country wants. Vox Media. Retrieved from https://www.vox.com/policy-and-politics/2017/9/5/16156924/nafta-negotiations

Canada to boost military budget by 70% after pressure from US to spend more. (2017, June 17). *The Guardian*. Retrieved from https://www.theguardian.com/world/2017/jun/07/canada-increase-military-spending-nato

Canada's feminist international assistance policy. (2017, October 19). Government of Canada. Retrieved from http://international.gc.ca/world-monde/issues_development-enjeux_developpement/priorities-priorites/policy-politique.aspx?lang=eng

Canadian Armed Forces in Somalia. (2017, May 1). Veterans Affairs Canada. Government of Canada. Retrieved from http://www.veterans.gc.ca/eng/remembrance/history/canadian-armed-forces/somalia

Canadian army builds 500-person border camp as asylum-seeker numbers rise. (2017, August 9). *The Guardian*. Retrieved from https://www.theguardian.com/world/2017/aug/09/canada-military-asylum-seekers-camp-border

Cohen, A. (2003). *While Canada slept: How we lost our place in the world*. Toronto: McClelland and Stewart.

Creighton, D. (1957). *Dominion of the North: A history of Canada*. Toronto: University of Toronto Press.

Defend me maybe: Donald Trump casually undermines the world's most important alliance. (2016, July 28). *The Economist*. Retrieved from https://www.economist.com/news/europe/21702771-donald-trump-casually-undermines-worlds-most-important-alliance-defend-me-maybe

Dutil, P. (2015). The institutionalization of foreign affairs (1909–2013). In D. Bratt & C.J. Kukucha (Eds.), *Readings in Canadian foreign policy: Classic debates and new ideas* (3rd ed., p. 241). Don Mills: Oxford University Press.

Francis, R.D. Jones, R., & Smith, D.B. (2008). *Destinies: Canadian history since Confederation* (6th ed.). Toronto: Nelson Education.

Gerster, J. (2013, March 16). 20 years after Somalia affair of tortured teen. *Toronto Metro*/The Canadian Press. Retrieved from http://www.metronews.ca/news/canada/2013/03/16/saturday-marks-anniversary-of-somalia-affair.html

Global Affairs Canada. (2016, March 18). Canadian sanctions related to Russia. Retrieved from http://www.international.gc.ca/sanctions/countries-pays/russia-russie.aspx?lang=eng

Global Affairs Canada. (2017, October 13). About. Government of Canada. Retrieved from http://www.international.gc.ca/gac-amc/index.aspx?lang=eng

Government expenditure plan and main estimates (Parts I and II). (2017, February 23). Government of Canada. Retrieved from https://www.canada.ca/en/treasury-board-secretariat/services/planned-government-spending/government-expenditure-plan-main-estimates.html

How Germany is integrating its refugees. (2017, September 16). *The Economist*. Retrieved from https://www.economist.com/news/europe/21728992-it-seems-be-managing-how-germany-integrating-its-refugees

Kassam, A. (2017, December 9). Syrian refugees in Canada lose support one year on: How are we going to live? *The Guardian*. Retrieved from https://www.theguardian.com/world/2016/dec/09/syria-refugees-canada-government-stipend-justin-trudeau

Key multilateral partners. (2017, July 13). Government of Canada. Retrieved from http://international.gc.ca/world-monde/international_relations-relations_internationales/multilateral-multilateraux/index.aspx?lang=eng

Military spending by NATO members. (2017, February 2017). *The Economist*. Retrieved from https://www.economist.com/blogs/graphicdetail/2017/02/daily-chart-11

Obama: "The world needs more Canada." (2016, June 29). *CBC News*. [Video]. Retrieved from http://www.cbc.ca/news/obama-the-world-needs-more-canada-1.3659172

Ottawa reaches $10M settlement with Arar. (2007, January 25). *CBC News*. Retrieved from http://www.cbc.ca/news/canada/ottawa-reaches-10m-settlement-with-arar-1.682875

Pratt, S. (2016, November 14). Veterans urge another look at Clayton Matchee case in light of malaria drug's side effects. *Saskatoon Star Phoenix*. Retrieved from http://thestarphoenix.com/news/national/veterans-urge-another-look-at-clayton-matchee-case-in-light-of-malaria-drugs-side-effects

Project Browser. (2017, October 23). Government of Canada. Retrieved from http://w05.international.gc.ca/projectbrowser-banqueprojets/

Responsibility to protect. (2017, October 10). The United Nations Office on Genocide Prevention and the Responsibility to Protect. Retrieved from http://www.un.org/en/genocideprevention/about-responsibility-to-protect.html

Saunders, D. (2010). *Arrival city: How the latest migration in history is shaping our world*. Toronto: Knopf Canada.

Saunders, D. (2017). *Maximum Canada: Why 35 million Canadians are not enough*. Toronto: Knopf Canada.

Schneider, H. (1997, July 3). Panel blames brass for misdeeds in Somalia. *Washington Post*, p. A22. Retrieved from http://www.washingtonpost.com/wp-srv/inatl/longterm/canada/stories/somalia07397.htm

Statistics Canada. (2017, June 19). Canada's merchandise trade with the United States by state. Retrieved from http://www.statcan.gc.ca/daily-quotidien/170619/dq170619b-eng.htm

Tasker, J.P. (2017, July 7). Government formally apologizes to Omar Khadr, as Andrew Scheer condemns "disgusting" payout. *CBC News*. Retrieved from http://www.cbc.ca/news/politics/cabinet-explain-omar-khadr-settlement-1.4194467

"The world needs more Canada," Bono tells Global Fund conference. (2016, September 17). *CBC News*. [Video]. Retrieved from http://www.cbc.ca/news/the-world-needs-more-canada-bono-tells-global-fund-conference-1.3767394

This is going to hurt. (2014, August 2). *The Economist*. Retrieved from https://www.economist.com/news/europe/21610322-cost-vladimir-putins-gamble-ukraine-going-up-he-shows-no-sign-changing

Tomlin, B., Hillmer, N., & Hampson, F.O. (2008). *Canada's international policies: Agendas, alternatives, and politics.* Don Mills: Oxford University Press.

Turkey is taking care of refugees, but failing to integrate them. (2017, June 29). *The Economist*. Retrieved from https://www.economist.com/news/europe/21724413-if-syrians-become-permanent-underclass-country-headed-trouble-turkey-taking-care

UN Refugee Agency. (2017, June 19). Figures at a glance. Retrieved from http://www.unhcr.org/figures-at-a-glance.html

United Nations. (n.d.). History of the Document. Retrieved from http://www.un.org/en/sections/universal-declaration/history-document/index.html

United Nations General Assembly. (2005). 2005 World Summit outcome. Retrieved from http://www.un.org/womenwatch/ods/A-RES-60-1-E.pdf

#WelcomeRefugees: Canada resettled Syrian refugees. (2017, May 4). Immigration and Citizenship. Government of Canada. Retrieved from http://www.cic.gc.ca/english/refugees/welcome/index.asp

Welsh, J. (2004). *At home in the world: Canada's global vision for the 21st century.* Toronto: HarperCollins.

Why Germany's current-account surplus is bad for the world economy. (2017, July 8). *The Economist*. Retrieved from https://www.economist.com/news/leaders/21724810-country-saves-too-much-and-spends-too-little-why-germanys-current-account-surplus-bad

EXERCISES
True or False?

_____ 1. The creation of a Department of External Affairs was one of Canada's first moves toward foreign policy independence.

_____ 2. When Britain declared war in 1914, Canada hesitated and debated about whether or not to participate.

_____ 3. Prime Minister Robert Borden's conscription decision divided some French- and English-speaking parts of Canada.

_____ 4. A Canadian was one of the main authors of the *Universal Declaration of Human Rights*.

_____ 5. Peacekeeping was born out of a conflict during the Second World War.

Multiple Choice

1. When US President Barack Obama told Parliament in 2016 that "the world needs more Canada," he specifically meant that

   a. Canada should expand its geographical territory by any means necessary, including aggressive military action or even war

   b. Canada should increase its birth rate (and perhaps immigration quota) so there are more Canadians in the world

   c. Canada should work to influence the culture and behaviour of other nations by increasing its exports and trade outreach efforts

   d. Canada should increase its military spending and, with it, the ability to take a more active role in a variety of international operations around the world, from standard NATO military operations, to peacekeeping, to facilitating foreign-aid outreach

   e. Canada is perfect and should simply stand up as a model for others around the world

2. Jennifer Welsh suggests that Canada and the United States can improve their relationship with each other by

   a. establishing more formal diplomatic relations and conventions whereby the wants and needs of both countries are clearly identified and addressed

   b. building a physical wall along the Canada–US border

   c. negotiating a deal to become one country or to have Canada become a US state

   d. renegotiating the North American Free Trade Agreement (NAFTA)

   e. ignoring their long history in North America together

3. Where countries would have threatened each other with violence in the past, they can now use economic sanctions to influence behaviour or register their displeasure. Identify all of the economic sanctions available to Global Affairs Canada below.

   a. arms embargo

   b. asset freeze

   c. export/import restrictions

   d. financial prohibitions

   e. technical assistance prohibitions

4. Why do nations tend to prefer free trade over protectionism?

    a. Fewer trade restrictions between countries increases the volume of trade and, with it, opportunities for economic growth.

    b. Protectionism is seen as isolationist and self-serving.

    c. Free trade guarantees domestic jobs by protecting them from foreign competition.

    d. a and b

    e. Free trade generates tax revenue.

5. International development allows a wealthy country like Canada to

    a. channel state funds into foreign investment opportunities with a high probability for a significant profit, regardless of how it affects the citizens of that country

    b. help private businesses secure lucrative investment contracts in less privileged but resource-rich countries around the world

    c. channel state funds into specific international projects and partnerships aimed at, first, alleviating immediate humanitarian crises and, second, providing long-term solutions through targeted infrastructure spending (e.g., water wells, farming projects, educational initiatives)

    d. give money to another country for free without restrictions or oversight

    e. make its citizens feel less guilty about having more than others

Short Answer

1. How did Canada contribute to the international world order following the Second World War?

2. What is "Pearsonian diplomacy"?

3. Throughout the history of the federal department now known as Global Affairs Canada, the trade portfolio has grown to rival that of foreign affairs itself. Discuss how trade came to join foreign affairs in the same department and why it is on par with diplomacy today.

4. Discuss the best way to think of foreign policy, particularly with reference to trade and international development. Think of an example of how Canadian foreign policy has changed in the last decade.

5. Discuss how the United Nations' adoption of the "Responsibility to Protect" doctrine provides an international framework to avert humanitarian crises and even genocidal violence in the future.

Appendix

The Canadian Charter of Rights and Freedoms

Part I of the Constitution Act, 1982

Whereas Canada is founded upon principles that recognize the supremacy of God and the rule of law:

Guarantee of Rights and Freedoms

Rights and freedoms in Canada

1. The *Canadian Charter of Rights and Freedoms* guarantees the rights and freedoms set out in it subject only to such reasonable limits prescribed by law as can be demonstrably justified in a free and democratic society.

Fundamental Freedoms

Fundamental freedoms

2. Everyone has the following fundamental freedoms:

(a) freedom of conscience and religion;

(b) freedom of thought, belief, opinion and expression, including freedom of the press and other media of communication;

(c) freedom of peaceful assembly; and

(d) freedom of association.

Democratic Rights

Democratic rights of citizens

3. Every citizen of Canada has the right to vote in an election of members of the House of Commons or of a legislative assembly and to be qualified for membership therein.

Maximum duration of legislative bodies

4. (1) No House of Commons and no legislative assembly shall continue for longer than five years from the date fixed for the return of the writs at a general election of its members.

Continuation in special circumstances

(2) In time of real or apprehended war, invasion or insurrection, a House of Commons may be continued by Parliament and a legislative assembly may be continued by the legislature beyond five years if such continuation is not opposed by the votes of more than one-third of the members of the House of Commons or the legislative assembly, as the case may be.

Annual sitting of legislative bodies

5. There shall be a sitting of Parliament and of each legislature at least once every twelve months.

Mobility Rights

Mobility of citizens

6. (1) Every citizen of Canada has the right to enter, remain in and leave Canada.

Rights to move and gain livelihood

(2) Every citizen of Canada and every person who has the status of a permanent resident of Canada has the right

  (a) to move to and take up residence in any province; and
  (b) to pursue the gaining of a livelihood in any province.

Limitation

(3) The rights specified in subsection (2) are subject to

  (a) any laws or practices of general application in force in a province other than those that discriminate among persons primarily on the basis of province of present or previous residence; and
  (b) any laws providing for reasonable residency requirements as a qualification for the receipt of publicly provided social services.

Affirmative action programs

(4) Subsections (2) and (3) do not preclude any law, program or activity that has as its object the amelioration in a province of conditions of individuals in that province who are socially or economically disadvantaged if the rate of employment in that province is below the rate of employment in Canada.

Legal Rights

Life, liberty and security of person

7. Everyone has the right to life, liberty and security of the person and the right not to be deprived thereof except in accordance with the principles of fundamental justice.

Search or seizure

8. Everyone has the right to be secure against unreasonable search or seizure.

Detention or imprisonment

9. Everyone has the right not to be arbitrarily detained or imprisoned.

Arrest or detention

10. Everyone has the right on arrest or detention

(a) to be informed promptly of the reasons therefor;

(b) to retain and instruct counsel without delay and to be informed of that right; and

(c) to have the validity of the detention determined by way of *habeas corpus* and to be released if the detention is not lawful.

Proceedings in criminal and penal matters

11. Any person charged with an offence has the right

(a) to be informed without unreasonable delay of the specific offence;

(b) to be tried within a reasonable time;

(c) not to be compelled to be a witness in proceedings against that person in respect of the offence;

(d) to be presumed innocent until proven guilty according to law in a fair and public hearing by an independent and impartial tribunal;

(e) not to be denied reasonable bail without just cause;

(f) except in the case of an offence under military law tried before a military tribunal, to the benefit of trial by jury where the maximum punishment for the offence is imprisonment for five years or a more severe punishment;

(g) not to be found guilty on account of any act or omission unless, at the time of the act or omission, it constituted an offence under Canadian or international law or was criminal according to the general principles of law recognized by the community of nations;

(h) if finally acquitted of the offence, not to be tried for it again and, if finally found guilty and punished for the offence, not to be tried or punished for it again; and

(i) if found guilty of the offence and if the punishment for the offence has been varied between the time of commission and the time of sentencing, to the benefit of the lesser punishment.

Treatment or punishment

12. Everyone has the right not to be subjected to any cruel and unusual treatment or punishment.

Self-crimination

13. A witness who testifies in any proceedings has the right not to have any incriminating evidence so given used to incriminate that witness in any other proceedings, except in a prosecution for perjury or for the giving of contradictory evidence.

Interpreter

14. A party or witness in any proceedings who does not understand or speak the language in which the proceedings are conducted or who is deaf has the right to the assistance of an interpreter.

Equality Rights

Equality before and under law and equal protection and benefit of law

15. (1) Every individual is equal before and under the law and has the right to the equal protection and equal benefit of the law without discrimination and, in particular, without discrimination based on race, national or ethnic origin, colour, religion, sex, age or mental or physical disability.

Affirmative action programs

(2) Subsection (1) does not preclude any law, program or activity that has as its object the amelioration of conditions of disadvantaged individuals or groups including those that are disadvantaged because of race, national or ethnic origin, colour, religion, sex, age or mental or physical disability.

Official Languages of Canada

Official languages of Canada

16. (1) English and French are the official languages of Canada and have equality of status and equal rights and privileges as to their use in all institutions of the Parliament and government of Canada.

Official languages of New Brunswick

(2) English and French are the official languages of New Brunswick and have equality of status and equal rights and privileges as to their use in all institutions of the legislature and government of New Brunswick.

Advancement of status and use

(3) Nothing in the Charter limits the authority of Parliament or a legislature to advance the equality of status or use of English and French.

English and French linguistic communities in New Brunswick

16.1. (1) The English linguistic community and the French linguistic community in New Brunswick have equality of status and equal rights and privileges, including the right to distinct educational institutions and such distinct cultural institutions as are necessary for the preservation and promotion of those communities.

Role of the legislature and government of New Brunswick

(2) The role of the legislature and government of New Brunswick to preserve and promote the status, rights and privileges referred to in subsection (1) is affirmed.

Proceedings of Parliament

17. (1) Everyone has the right to use English or French in any debates and other proceedings of Parliament.

Proceedings of New Brunswick legislature

(2) Everyone has the right to use English or French in any debates and other proceedings of the legislature of New Brunswick.

Parliamentary statutes and records

18. (1) The statutes, records and journals of Parliament shall be printed and published in English and French and both language versions are equally authoritative.

New Brunswick statutes and records

(2) The statutes, records and journals of the legislature of New Brunswick shall be printed and published in English and French and both language versions are equally authoritative.

Proceedings in courts established by Parliament

19. (1) Either English or French may be used by any person in, or in any pleading in or process issuing from, any court established by Parliament.

Proceedings in New Brunswick courts

(2) Either English or French may be used by any person in, or in any pleading in or process issuing from, any court of New Brunswick.

Communications by public with federal institutions

20. (1) Any member of the public in Canada has the right to communicate with, and to receive available services from, any head or central office of an institution of the Parliament or government of Canada in English or French, and has the same right with respect to any other office of any such institution where

(a) there is a significant demand for communications with and services from that office in such language; or

(b) due to the nature of the office, it is reasonable that communications with and services from that office be available in both English and French.

Communications by public with New Brunswick institutions

(2) Any member of the public in New Brunswick has the right to communicate with, and to receive available services from, any office of an institution of the legislature or government of New Brunswick in English or French.

Continuation of existing constitutional provisions

21. Nothing in sections 16 to 20 abrogates or derogates from any right, privilege or obligation with respect to the English and French languages, or either of them, that exists or is continued by virtue of any other provision of the Constitution of Canada.

Rights and privileges preserved

22. Nothing in sections 16 to 20 abrogates or derogates from any legal or customary right or privilege acquired or enjoyed either before or after the coming into force of this Charter with respect to any language that is not English or French.

Minority Language Educational Rights

Language of instruction

23. (1) Citizens of Canada

(a) whose first language learned and still understood is that of the English or French linguistic minority population of the province in which they reside, or

(b) who have received their primary school instruction in Canada in English or French and reside in a province where the language in which they received that instruction is the language of the English or French linguistic minority population of the province,

have the right to have their children receive primary and secondary school instruction in that language in that province.

Continuity of language instruction

(2) Citizens of Canada of whom any child has received or is receiving primary or secondary school instruction in English or French in Canada, have the right to have all their children receive primary and secondary school instruction in the same language.

Application where numbers warrant

(3) The right of citizens of Canada under subsections (1) and (2) to have their children receive primary and secondary school instruction in the language of the English or French linguistic minority population of a province

(a) applies wherever in the province the number of children of citizens who have such a right is sufficient to warrant the provision to them out of public funds of minority language instruction; and

(b) includes, where the number of those children so warrants, the right to have them receive that instruction in minority language educational facilities provided out of public funds.

Enforcement

Enforcement of guaranteed rights and freedoms

24. (1) Anyone whose rights or freedoms, as guaranteed by this Charter, have been infringed or denied may apply to a court of competent jurisdiction to obtain such remedy as the court considers appropriate and just in the circumstances.

Exclusion of evidence bringing administration of justice into disrepute

(2) Where, in proceedings under subsection (1), a court concludes that evidence was obtained in a manner that infringed or denied any rights or freedoms guaranteed by this Charter, the evidence shall be excluded if it is established that, having regard to all the circumstances, the admission of it in the proceedings would bring the administration of justice into disrepute.

General

Aboriginal rights and freedoms not affected by Charter

25. The guarantee in this Charter of certain rights and freedoms shall not be construed so as to abrogate or derogate from any aboriginal, treaty or other rights or freedoms that pertain to the aboriginal peoples of Canada including

(a) any rights or freedoms that have been recognized by the Royal Proclamation of October 7, 1763; and

(b) any rights or freedoms that may be acquired by the aboriginal peoples of Canada by way of land claims settlement.

Other rights and freedoms not affected by Charter

26. The guarantee in this Charter of certain rights and freedoms shall not be construed as denying the existence of any other rights or freedoms that exist in Canada.

Multicultural heritage

27. This Charter shall be interpreted in a manner consistent with the preservation and enhancement of the multicultural heritage of Canadians.

Rights guaranteed equally to both sexes

28. Notwithstanding anything in this Charter, the rights and freedoms referred to in it are guaranteed equally to male and female persons.

Rights respecting certain schools preserved

29. Nothing in this Charter abrogates or derogates from any rights or privileges guaranteed by or under the Constitution of Canada in respect of denominational, separate or dissentient schools.

Application to territories and territorial authorities

30. A reference in this Charter to a province or to the legislative assembly or legislature of a province shall be deemed to include a reference to the Yukon Territory and the Northwest Territories, or to the appropriate legislative authority thereof, as the case may be.

Legislative powers not extended

31. Nothing in this Charter extends the legislative powers of any body or authority.

Application of Charter

Application of Charter

32. (1) This Charter applies

(a) to the Parliament and government of Canada in respect of all matters within the authority of Parliament including all matters relating to the Yukon Territory and Northwest Territories; and

(b) to the legislature and government of each province in respect of all matters within the authority of the legislature of each province.

Exception

(2) Notwithstanding subsection (1), section 15 shall not have effect until three years after this section comes into force.

Exception where express declaration

33. (1) Parliament or the legislature of a province may expressly declare in an Act of Parliament or of the legislature, as the case may be, that the Act or a provision thereof shall operate notwithstanding a provision included in section 2 or sections 7 to 15 of this Charter.

Operation of exception

(2) An Act or a provision of an Act in respect of which a declaration made under this section is in effect shall have such operation as it would have but for the provision of this Charter referred to in the declaration.

Five year limitation

(3) A declaration made under subsection (1) shall cease to have effect five years after it comes into force or on such earlier date as may be specified in the declaration.

Re-enactment

(4) Parliament or a legislature of a province may re-enact a declaration made under subsection (1).

Five year limitation

(5) Subsection (3) applies in respect of a re-enactment made under subsection (4).

Citation

Citation

34. This Part may be cited as the *Canadian Charter of Rights and Freedoms*.

Glossary

administrative-coordinative department department that facilitates the operation of government services

administrative law body of legislation that details the rules civil servants must follow in doing their jobs

amending formula a legal process for changing a constitution

attorney general function the function of the federal Department of Justice Canada to safeguard the legal interests of the federal government

authority government's ability to make decisions that are binding on its citizens

bicameral legislature a government structure that consists of two Houses of Parliament—in Canada, the House of Commons and the Senate

bill a proposed law

bureaucracy the organizational structure through which government exercises its power

bureaucrat public servant

bureaucratic entrepreneur a model of public policy in which bureaucratic experts within government come up with policy ideas and then approach elected officials to obtain the resources and public legitimacy necessary to implement their programs

by-law a local or municipal law

Cabinet the government body that consists of MPs, appointed by the prime minister, who oversee government departments and act as advisers in major policy areas

Cabinet solidarity the united front that Cabinet presents on given policy matters, although individual Cabinet ministers may privately be opposed

Canadian Charter of Rights and Freedoms part of the Canadian Constitution that guarantees certain fundamental rights and freedoms to people in Canada

capitalism an economic system based on private ownership and competition in a free market

charismatic authority authority based on the unique talents and popular appeal of an individual

civil service people who are directly tied to the administrative function of a particular level of government; see also *public administration*

classical technocratic a model of public policy in which decisions originate with politicians, who then provide bureaucrats with clear direction as to what should be done

Cold War a period of tension from 1945 to 1991 between the United States and the Soviet Union, which was underscored by the threat of nuclear conflict

common law a body of law that has grown out of past court cases and is based on precedent or custom

Commonwealth an international organization of nations exclusively composed of the former territories of the British Empire, including Canada, Australia, South Africa, and India, among many others.

community policing approach to policing based on the police and the community working together

Confederation the union of former British colonies that resulted in the formation of Canada on July 1, 1867

constituency department department that provides services directly to citizens

Constitution a document that outlines the basic principles of government of a country and the fundamental rights and freedoms enjoyed by its citizens

continuity the long-term or ongoing nature of a bureaucracy; continuity means that the people working within an organization are full-time employees who can make a career out of what they do

cost sharing funding of provincial programs that combines federal contributions with provincial funding

delegated legislation legislation handed down from a parent department that grants a regulatory agency political powers

department government division responsible for carrying out some aspect of government policy

deregulation reducing or eliminating bureaucratic processes that may hinder private enterprise and limit economic growth

discretionary power interpretive flexibility granted to some government employees to act within a given setting

division of powers jurisdiction over major policy areas, as divided between the federal and the provincial governments

economic sanctions a non-violent foreign policy tool designed to convey displeasure and provoke change (e.g, tariffs, arms embargoes)

executive branch (federal) the branch of government that includes the monarch's representative (governor general), the elected head of state (prime minister), and Cabinet

executive branch (provincial) the branch of government that includes the monarch's representative (lieutenant governor), the elected head of state (premier), and the Cabinet

expertise knowledge of or ability in a particular area or subject

federal spending power the power of the federal government to raise the greatest share of tax revenues

federal system Canada's government structure, which divides political power between the federal government and the provincial governments, with greater power resting in the federal government

foreign policy a course of action prescribing how one state behaves toward another

free trade an agreement between states to significantly reduce or eliminate outright tariffs on goods and services exchanged between them

Global Affairs Canada the federal department that houses the ministers of foreign affairs, international trade, and international development

government a formal system within which political power is exercised

government bill a bill proposed by a member of Cabinet

hierarchy an organized system of labour characterized by a superior–subordinate relationship

human relations management approach that recognizes and addresses the personal and social needs of individuals

impersonality the objective nature of jobs and routines in a bureaucracy, based on written rules and records

Indigenous self-government greater autonomy of First Nations to pursue their own political, social, cultural, and economic objectives with limited interference from the federal government

international development the recognition by wealthier states that they have a responsibility to help developing states build infrastructure, reduce poverty, and increase domestic business networks

international trade the exchange of goods and services among nations facilitated by governments but maintained by private and public business enterprises

isolationism an economic remedy characterized by a refusal to trade with other countries

judicial branch the branch of government that consists of the court system

jurisdiction sphere of influence or power

laissez-faire capitalism free-market capitalism with minimal government interference (*laissez-faire* is French for "let act")

left wing a political attitude or philosophy that favours more government intervention to help achieve social equality

legal authority authority based on the rule of law

legislative branch (federal) the law-making branch of government (House of Commons and Senate)

legislative branch (provincial) the law-making branch of government, called the National Assembly in Quebec and the Legislative Assembly in all other provinces

legislative union a structure of government in which power is concentrated in a central Parliament

legitimacy the moral obligation citizens feel to obey the laws and pronouncements issued by those in authority

majority government a government whose members make up more than half of the total MPs in the House of Commons

member of Parliament an elected representative in the House of Commons who represents a riding

minimalist state approach to government in which state resources are used in the interest of the business, or capitalist, classes, to promote individual wealth and economic growth

minister of justice function the function of the federal Department of Justice Canada to monitor federal legislation, directives, and regulations and to consider other justice-related issues

ministerial responsibility principle of parliamentary government that makes ministers responsible for the official activities of their departments

minority government a government that has the greatest number of MPs in the House of Commons but not more than half of the total MPs

multiculturalism cultural and racial diversity; in Canada, a constitutionally enshrined policy that recognizes the diversity of our population

municipal council the governing body of a municipal government

neo-conservatism a conservative political philosophy that argues that government should revert to the limited role it played at the beginning of the 20th century, particularly in social and economic areas

new public management an approach based on the belief that government has overextended itself by doing too much and becoming preoccupied with bureaucratic procedure

North American Aerospace Defence Command (NORAD) a military agency headquartered in Colorado that monitors aerospace threats

North American Free Trade Agreement (NAFTA) a free trade agreement among Canada, the United States, and Mexico

North Atlantic Treaty Organization (NATO) largest peace-time military alliance in the world; originally designed to protect Western countries against aggression by the Soviet Union

party loyalty the requirement that all members of a political party vote according to the wishes of their leader

patriation the process of removing the Canadian Constitution from British control and bringing it under Canadian control

police services board civilian board that oversees a local police service

policy-coordinative department department that coordinates policy across government

policy instrument a method employed by governments to ensure compliance with public policy and to achieve their goals

political culture the basic attitudes people have toward one another, the state, and authority

political spectrum a model that shows political philosophy on a continuum from left wing to right wing

politics the social system that decides who has power and how it is to be used in governing the society's affairs

politics–administrative dichotomy theoretical framework that views politics as the decision-making apparatus of government and administration as performing the implementation function

portfolio areas of responsibility or duties of a Cabinet minister, including those related to a department

private bill a bill proposed by a senator

private member's bill a bill proposed by a non-Cabinet MP

proportional representation a distribution of political power in direct proportion to votes cast

protectionism a policy whereby a state takes specific economic measures to support a domestic business or industry

public administration the branch of the political structure, consisting of public employees, that turns the policy decisions of elected politicians into action

public good the complex fabric of publicly funded goods and services that contribute to the collective well-being of a state

public policy what government does or does not do

public service civil service or public administration

refugees people who have had to leave one country for another due to violence, a humanitarian crisis, or a natural disaster without preparation

representative government government that is based on members elected by citizens to represent their interests

Responsibility to Protect a doctrine charging UN member states to accept responsibility for their own citizens within internal state conflicts and acknowledge the right of the international community to intervene if any state fails to do so

responsible government government that is responsible to the wishes of its citizens, as embodied in their elected representatives

right wing a political attitude or philosophy that favours more individual freedom and less government intervention

rule of law the concept that all citizens, regardless of social rank, are subject to the laws, courts, and other legal institutions of the nation

scientific management management approach based on using resources in ways that maximize productivity and minimize waste

stagflation a situation where an economy experiences high unemployment and high inflation at the same time

subjudicial rule a rule that prohibits government officials from commenting on an issue that is before the courts

theory of representativeness theory that the public service should represent a cross-section of Canadian society in order to be responsive to the needs of all Canadians

traditional authority authority on the basis of heredity, religion, or divine right

triple E Senate a Senate that is equal, elected, and effective

United Nations (UN) an international diplomatic organization that coordinates action, relief, and cooperation among all nation states while underscoring human rights, freedoms, and dignity

Universal Declaration of Human Rights an international document adopted by the United Nations that states the basic rights and fundamental freedoms to which all people are entitled

Warsaw Pact a treaty signed by the Soviet Union and its client states in 1954 designed to mirror NATO

World Bank an institution that provides loans and other financial assistance to nations in need

World Trade Organization an intergovernmental organization that regulates trade on an international level

Index

P

Credits

CHAPTER 1
Photo (Justin Trudeau): © Meunierd | Dreamstime

Photo (police services): © Photographerlondon | Dreamstime

CHAPTER 2
Photo (last spike of CPR): Images from Library and Archives Canada

CHAPTER 3
Photo (repatriation of Constitution): THE CANADIAN PRESS/ Ron Poling

Photo (Meech Lake): THE CANADIAN PRESS/Fred Chartrand

CHAPTER 4
Photo (Parliament Hill): © Aqnus Febriyant | Dreamstime

Photo (Barack and Jean): THE CANADIAN PRESS/Sean Kilpatrick

CHAPTER 5
Photo (Singh): THE CANADIAN PRESS/Chris Young

Photo (Oka): THE CANADIAN PRESS/Shaney Komulainen

Photo (Domm): Used with permission of Chief John C. Domm, M.O.M., BAA, MA, CMMIII Chief of Police Rama Police Service.

CHAPTER 6
Photo (Marx): Public Domain.

Photo (Weber): Public Domain.

Photo (Taylor): Public Domain.

Photo (Mayo): Public Domain.

CHAPTER 7
Photo (Keynes): Sueddeutsche Zeitung Photo/Alamy Stock Photo

Photo (prison farms): THE CANADIAN PRESS IMAGES/Lars Hagberg

CHAPTER 8
Photo (Trudeau Cabinet): THE CANADIAN PRESS/Justin Tang

Photo (soldier): CP PHOTO/Chuck Mitchell

CHAPTER 9
Photo (Service Ontario): THE CANADIAN PRESS IMAGES/Lars Hagberg

Photo (CBC building): © Nuvista | Dreamstime

Box (Get Real!): Used with the express permission of Howard Sapers

CHAPTER 10
Photo (CSIS): THE CANADIAN PRESS IMAGES/Lars Hagberg

Photo (SIU): THE CANADIAN PRESS/Sean Kilpatrick

Photo (Howard Sapers): Used with the express permission of Howard Sapers

Box (Get Real!): Used with the express permission of Howard Sapers

CHAPTER 11
Photo (volunteers): Courtesy of Geoffrey Booth

Photo (Chrystia Freeland): THE CANADIAN PRESS IMAGES/ Matthew Usherwood

CHAPTER 12
Photo (UN flags): © Andraž Naglič | Dreamstime

Photo (peacekeepers): THE CANADIAN PRESS/Patrick Doyle